Dear John,

Thank you for l

podcast.

Sincerely,

Michael [illegible]

PRAISE FOR
THE FOUR-MINUTE RETIREMENT PLAN

"You likely can't run a four-minute mile, but Michael's new book parses all you need to know to win the workaday retirement race. Readable, authoritative, and thorough, you'll want to spend a lot more than four minutes with it."

Ken Fisher
Founder, Executive Chairman and Co-CIO, Fisher Investments; *New York Times* bestselling author and global columnist

"The sooner you embark on *The Four-Minute Retirement Plan*, the sooner you'll start heading in the right direction. This fun, practical, and thoughtful book is packed with investment wisdom; investors of all ages should read it now."

Joel Greenblatt
Managing Principal, Gotham Asset Management; *New York Times* bestselling author, *The Little Book That Beats the Market*

"In order to preserve and protect your pile of hard-earned capital, you need to be coached by pros like Michael. He has both the experience and performance in The Game to prove it. This is a great Full Cycle Investing #process book!"

Keith McCullough
Chief Executive Officer, Hedgeye Risk Management; author, *Diary of a Hedge Fund Manager*

"*The Four-Minute Retirement Plan* masterfully distills the wisdom and experience Michael acquired through years of highly successful wealth management into a concise and actionable plan that can be implemented by everyone. With its clear guidance, hands-on approach, and empowering message, this book is essential reading for anyone who wants to take control of their finances and secure a prosperous future."

Vincent Deluard

Director of Global Macro Strategy, StoneX

THE FOUR-MINUTE RETIREMENT PLAN

MICHAEL CANNIVET

04:00

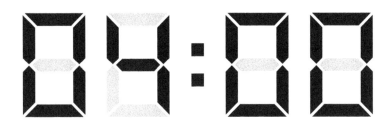

THE FOUR-MINUTE RETIREMENT PLAN

PRESERVE YOUR PAST, SECURE YOUR FUTURE, LIVE FOR TODAY

Forbes | Books

Published by Forbes Books, Charleston, South Carolina.
An imprint of Advantage Media Group.

Printed in the United States of America.

10 9 8 7 6 5 4 3 2 1

ISBN: 978-1-95588-494-5 (Hardcover)
ISBN: 978-1-95588-495-2 (eBook)

Library of Congress Control Number: 2023922934

Book design by Megan Elger.

To my sons, Nicholas and Zachary,

If you read this book and apply its lessons, the project was worth it.

And to my wife, Jennifer,

Thank you for running this race with me. You are the light of my life.

CONTENTS

SECTION III: THE SAVINGS LAP

SECTION IV: THE INVESTING LAP

SECTION V: THE LIFESTYLE LAP

SECTION VI: THE LEGACY LAP

SECTION VII: CONCLUSION

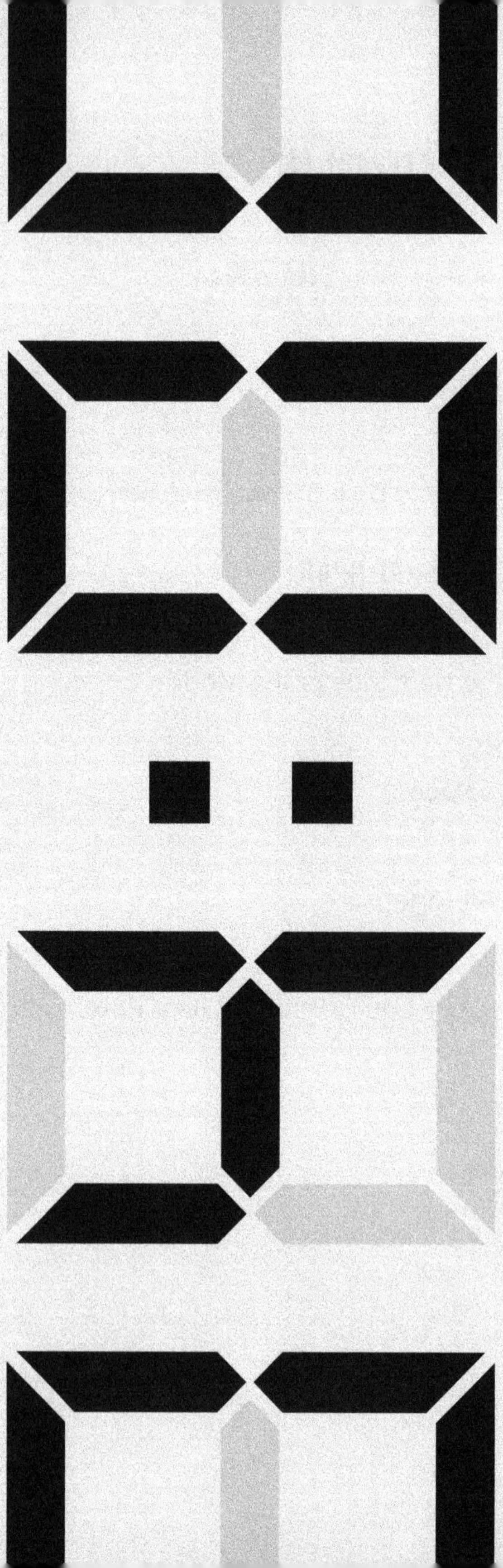

ACKNOWLEDGMENTS

I wrote this book to help average people conquer their biggest financial challenge: planning for retirement. I'm proud of the finished product and sincerely hope you enjoy it. It would not have been possible to write this book without the contributions of many important individuals.

First, I want to thank my wife, Jennifer. She was my first reader and was instrumental in helping me develop the organizational structure.

Second, I would like to thank Ed Flores. He was my second reader and always gives constructive feedback and advice.

Next, I would like to thank the Forbes Books team. Suzanna de Boer was my book coach, and I very much appreciated her patient and positive coaching style. Stephen Larkin and Heath Ellison were my editors. Stephen provided valuable feedback early in the process, and Heath was the quarterback for the project to its conclusion. The book writing process can be grueling at times. Evan Schnittman gets that and was a great problem solver behind the scenes of this book. I also appreciate the contributions of Megan Elger, who played a vital role in the visual design.

I would also like to thank a number of my professional mentors. Early in my career as an equity analyst, Ken Fisher taught me how to be independent minded, ask the right questions, and never stop innovating. John Tamny is my editor at RealClearMarkets. When I started writing a blog, John was the first to recognize my work and publish it for a bigger audience. His encouragement and professionalism meant a lot to me then and still does to this day. Halah Touryalai was my first editor at Forbes, and I appreciate that she gave me a shot at writing for a publication I've always deeply admired. And I would like to thank Bob Gorman—my first writing coach, who taught me how to write clearly with confidence.

Finally, I want to thank Roger Bannister. When I read his obituary in 2018, I was inspired by his story of grit and resilience. *The Four-Minute Retirement Plan* is an extension of his four-minute mile.

SECTION I

THE RETIREMENT RACE

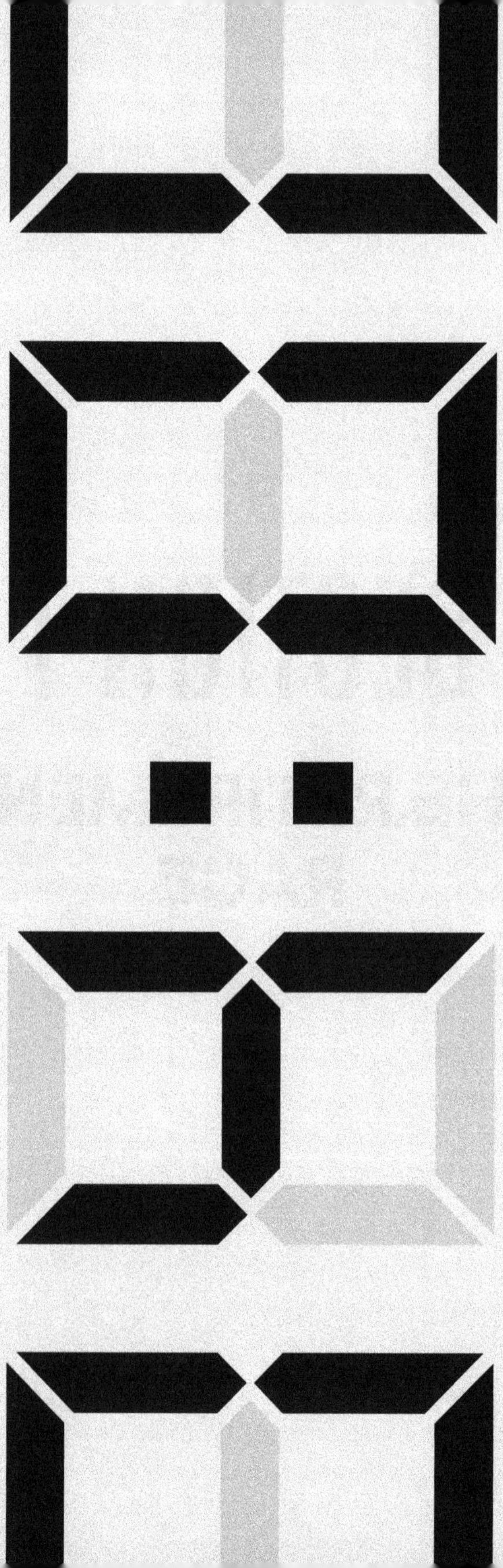

CHAPTER 1
WINNING THE RETIREMENT RACE

I trained for less than three-quarters of an hour, maybe five days a week—I didn't have time to do more. But it was all about quality, not quantity—so I didn't waste time jogging, ever.

—ROGER BANNISTER

Fewer people have run a four-minute mile than have scaled Mount Everest. The first runner to do it was Roger Bannister.

On May 6, 1954, Bannister won a race on his home track in Oxford, England. His finishing time was three minutes, 59.4 seconds.

The previous record for running a mile in competition was 4:01. After nine years of no one beating the time, many thought it was impenetrable.

As runner after runner failed to eclipse the record, a negative mystique grew around the four-minute mile. People came up with strange theories—such as that the human body was simply not designed to ever run that fast. There was even speculation that trying to do so could be lethal.[1]

Roger Bannister saw the problem differently; he saw an opportunity to end his running career on a high note.

On paper, he wasn't the most logical choice to run the first four-minute mile. After a disappointing showing at the 1952 Olympics, Bannister was in the twilight of his track career. By 1954, he was a twenty-five-year-old medical student at Oxford, which limited his capacity to train. Since he wasn't the most physically gifted runner to begin with, he could have easily just retired.

Instead, Bannister managed to successfully conquer the four-minute mile. He did so by leveraging a series of mental models that differentiated him from his peers.

A mental model is a framework for how we see the world. They guide how we interpret information and subconsciously influence our decisions.

Mental Model #1: Positive Story

At a time when most runners saw the four-minute mile as an impossible challenge, Bannister was optimistic about the task at hand.

He told the Associated Press in 2012, "There was no logic in my mind that if you can run a mile in 4 minutes ... you can't run it in 3:59. I knew enough medicine and physiology to know it wasn't a physical barrier, but I think it had become a psychological barrier."

Optimism is essential for any major achievement. We must believe a goal is possible, or it won't be. Therefore the first and most important step in many endeavors is to simply convince ourselves that it is possible, and that our efforts will be rewarded.

Bannister, who would later become a prominent neurologist, was well attuned to the power of the mind. He knew it was important to be inspired, and he operated from a state of positive expectancy.

As part of his training, he visualized every step of the race. He saw himself crossing the finish line. He heard the roar of the crowd. He felt the pride of victory. He even put a piece of paper in his shoe while he ran that read "3:58."

Bannister broke through by telling himself a positive story.

Mental Model #2: Effective Strategies

Bannister didn't have as much time to train as his competitors. Sometimes all he could spare was thirty minutes during his lunch hour. So he had to be very productive with only a short amount of time.

Bannister's advantage was being a gifted "systems thinker." Most people are biased toward activity. Yet the most important activity is deciding *where* to direct our attention. That's what Einstein meant when he said that if he had an hour to solve a problem, he'd spend fifty-five minutes to define it properly, and five minutes thinking about solutions.

As a medical student, Bannister naturally blended the scientific method into his training regimen. Everything about his approach was evidence based. "Each new race is an experiment," he wrote.[2]

After studying an array of performance factors related to running, Bannister devised an innovative training plan. Here's how the *New Yorker* described it:

> "Bannister took a cerebral approach to the four-minute barrier. He studied running's physiological demands, measured his own oxygen-consumption levels, and produced papers with titles like 'The Carbon Dioxide Stimulus to Breathing in Severe Exercise.'
>
> "Bannister discovered that running consistent lap times demanded less oxygen than varying the pace. So he focused on his quarter-mile splits. During lunch breaks, he would run ten of them, stopwatch in hand, punctuated by two-minute breaks. In five months, he brought down the average time he could run these intervals from sixty-three seconds to fifty-nine."[3]

Bannister broke through with an effective strategy.

Mental Model #3: Straightforward Plan

Bannister simplified his approach to the four-minute mile using a tactic called "chunking."

Chunking is deconstructing a big goal into smaller goals that are easier to execute. This helps build momentum.

Bannister understood that **every long run is a series of short runs**. So, he decided to run a consistent pace over all four laps. He trained by running sixty-second laps, taking short breaks in between.

Running a lap in one minute doesn't require going incredibly fast. It's about fifteen miles per hour. Bannister's marvel was maintaining that pace over four consecutive laps. Consistency was what separated him from everyone else.

Bannister broke through with a straightforward plan that he followed without fail.

■ ■

On the day of the race, Bannister stuck to his game plan. For most of the race, he flirted with the lead but ran at a similar pace as the pack.

About halfway through lap four is when the race became historic. As the other runners began to tire and slow, Bannister unleashed his finishing kick—the "Bannister Burst." He pulled away from the pack, completing the final lap in just under fifty-nine seconds.

Shortly after, a writer for *Sports Illustrated* observed, "There is no fuss and fanfare about Bannister. When he was asked to explain that first four-minute mile—and the art of record breaking—he answered with original directness: 'It's the ability to take more out of yourself than you've got.'"[4]

Roger Bannister may not have been blessed with abundant resources when he set out to run his "Miracle Mile," but he had something even more important going for him—he was *resourceful.*

After Bannister succeeded, the mystique surrounding the four-minute mile receded. Two months later, in Finland, an Australian runner named John Landy recorded a time of three minutes fifty-eight seconds. Within a year, three more runners accomplished the feat. Today, even top high schoolers can run a four-minute mile.

When our beliefs change, we change.

The Retirement Race

Nobel Laureate William Sharpe calls retirement the "nastiest, hardest problem in finance."

The problem begins with poor framing. Who thought up the word "retire" anyway?

Dictionary.com defines the word retire as: *to withdraw or go away.*

Do images of *withdrawing* inspire you? Probably not. You may be reminded of death, which most people try to avoid thinking about. People don't typically enjoy weighty thoughts about getting older.

That's why this book is more about *renewal* than retirement.

We're going to pivot to a new set of mental models you can use to get where you want to go. When Roger Bannister retired from running track at the age of twenty-five, he began a new phase of life where he eventually became a world-renowned physician. Even though Bannister is most remembered for the four-minute mile, he said later that being a physician was more personally rewarding.

We should approach retirement with a similar mindset—it's not the end of our story; it's the beginning of a fresh new chapter. If we plan it right, retirement can be the time of our lives. A time when we have maximum resources. A time of maximum freedom to do whatever we want, wherever we want, with whoever we want. The only limit is the boundary of our imagination.

Sounds amazing, right? Yet somehow the whole retirement undertaking is still daunting.

A year after Bannister's historic race, in 1955, a *New York Times* columnist wrote, "To rephrase an old saying: everyone talks about retirement, but apparently very few do anything about it."[5]

The world has changed a lot since the 1950s. But the core retirement riddle remains the same: *complexity causes people to procrastinate.*

Today in America, almost half of adult citizens have nothing saved in a 401(k) plan. Zilch. Nada. Nothing. And this is the wealthiest country on earth?

The US Government Accountability Office (GAO) authored a comprehensive report on retirement savings and found the median household between the ages of sixty-five to seventy-four had only about $148,000 put away. For perspective, that's equivalent to an inflation-protected annuity of $649 a month. Probably not enough for most to get by on.

Many folks rely on social security to pay their bills. "Social security provides most of the income for about half of households age 65 and older," according to GAO's report.

Social security provides a vital lifeline for a lot of households. That's why many are concerned about its insolvency.

Social security is a system based on demographic trends from the 1930s. The numbers don't work anymore because the population pyramid that previously supported it is inverting. Those who occupy the halls of government understand this, but no one is doing anything to fix it.*

Since 1978, 401(k) programs have become the primary savings vehicle most Americans use to fund their retirement. The modern 401(k) system puts individuals more in the driver's seat, including being responsible for allocating a portion of earnings to retirement savings and choosing investments.

The programs have become easier for people to navigate over time, but there are always questions most folks don't know the answers to.

First, there are budgeting riddles. Questions like, *What's an appropriate level of monthly savings?* And *Should a retiree carry a mortgage?*

Second, there's an impossible tug of war between risk and return. Everyone wants high returns with low risk. But if these are framed as mutually exclusive goals, what's a reasonable risk profile for you?

Third, there's an investing puzzle with scattered pieces that don't easily fit together. With thousands of ETFs, mutual funds, target date funds, stocks, and bonds to sort through, how do you pick the right vehicles for you?

This book will help you devise a method for choosing investments while also teaching you how to write an empowering story that connects your most important financial goals to your most important life goals. Your story will clarify your personal values and happiness triggers so you are inspired to follow through on your financial plan.

Then, we'll use smart shortcuts to build an effective financial plan that's easy for you to personally implement.

Here's an example of what that looks like.

---

* To his credit, former Presidential candidate Al Gore did enthusiastically recommend a social security "Lock Box" idea in his 2000 Presidential Debate against George W. Bush. There is a great *Saturday Night Live* parody you can look up on YouTube.

How a Blue-Collar Worker Retired with $70 Million

Theodore Johnson spent a career at UPS never earning more than $14,000 in a single year. Yet, by following a simple formula consistently, Johnson amassed a fortune exceeding $70 million.

So how did he do it?

Johnson grew up middle-class. When he retired from UPS in 1952 as a vice president of industrial relations, his annual salary was $14,000.

Before retiring, Johnson was a diligent saver. But he didn't start out that way.

During the early years of his UPS tenure, Johnson lamented to a friend that he wasn't earning enough income to save anything extra.

The friend responded with a question that changed Johnson's life.

"What if you pretend to tax yourself?"

The friend pointed out that when Johnson's regular earnings were taxed, that money was automatically taken out of his paycheck. Since he never saw it, he never spent it. He encouraged Johnson to adopt the same approach. "Why put Uncle Sam ahead of yourself?" his friend asked.

That was an *Aha* moment for Johnson. Something simultaneously clicked in both the logical and emotional parts of his brain.

From that day forward, Johnson committed to putting 20 percent of his income straight into an investment account. That's all he did and all he had to do. Consistent saving, investing, and the power of compounding took care of the rest.

By the time he retired, Johnson had amassed about $700,000. From there, he continued to live below his means, and his money continued to grow.

Decades later, the value of Johnson's estate was $70 million. This allowed him to leave a meaningful legacy through educational grants.

So, let's recap how Mr. Johnson achieved his amazing financial breakthrough.

First, he was stuck in procrastination mode with a negative *story* he was telling himself about why he couldn't get ahead. Then, he received *effective* advice, which he was able to *easily* implement.

How long did it take for everything to change?

We weren't there to know precisely how long the conversation was. But you know what? It could have taken four minutes.

The Four Retirement Laps

1. Savings Lap 2. Investing Lap 3. Lifestyle Lap 4. Legacy Lap

The Retirement Race consists of four laps that are equally important.

- Savings Lap
- Investing Lap
- Lifestyle Lap
- Legacy Lap

This book will help you create your own customized financial plan with two key parts.

The first part is the story behind your financial plan. *Your* story. In the "Preparing for Your Retirement Race" section, I will provide examples and prompts to help you write an authentic story that underpins your Four-Minute Retirement Plan. We will spell out your top three financial goals and directly link them to your core values.

The second part is your Four-Minute Retirement Plan. Think of this as the "How We Get There" part of your plan. In sections III through VI, (i.e., "The Retirement Laps") each chapter finishes by outlining four solutions. You should be able to pick one in twenty seconds or fewer. By doing this, you'll build your very own Four-Minute Retirement Plan.

> We really can build a plan in this amount of time, and here's why: Four minutes equals 240 seconds. Twelve chapter-ending solutions multiplied by twenty seconds apiece equals 240 seconds, or four minutes.

Just as Roger Bannister once inspired a legion of runners to do something they thought was impossible, I want to inspire older and younger generations alike to think bigger and broader in how they approach the retirement race.

This is a race you can win. It doesn't matter what your starting point is. What matters is how you're going to finish the race.

Winning the retirement race involves knowing the right things to do and consistently doing those things. That's it. All anyone needs to retire well is a smart training regimen, properly customized for them.

In these pages, you're going to learn simple shortcuts to make giant leaps in how you save, manage, and think about money. Your reward for completing this book will be your own personalized retirement plan that dovetails your overall life plan.

This is not just another book about retirement. This is about the never-ending quest to be a better version of you—at any age.

We can't stop time. We can only invest it.

So, let's get started.

CHAPTER SUMMARY

- Mental models guide how we interpret things and subconsciously influence our decisions.
- The first and most important step in many endeavors is to simply convince ourselves that our efforts will be rewarded.
- Most people are biased toward activity, but the most important activity is deciding where to direct our attention.
- Every long run is a series of short runs.
- The complexity of retirement causes people to procrastinate figuring out a plan.
- The Retirement Race can be simplified into four laps that are equally important: a Savings Lap, Investing Lap, Lifestyle Lap, and a Legacy Lap.

CHAPTER 2

BALANCING YOUR PAST, PRESENT, AND FUTURE PRIORITIES

It's always Day 1 at Amazon.

—JEFF BEZOS

If you visit www.relentless.com, you're automatically linked to amazon.com. That tells you a lot about the personal philosophy of Amazon's founder, Jeff Bezos.

When Bezos penned his first amazon.com shareholder letter in 1997, he outlined the company's core values. Those included relentlessly focusing on customers, creating long-term value over maximizing short-term profit, and making many bold bets.

For Bezos and company, these principles have remained consistent for decades, and they are at the heart of Amazon's "Day 1" mentality.

According to Daniel Slater, an innovation leader at Amazon, "Day 1 is about being constantly curious, nimble, and experimental."

When asked "What does Day 2 look like?" Bezos responded, "Day 2 is stasis. Followed by irrelevance. Followed by excruciating, painful decline. Followed by death. And that is why it is always Day 1."

As a corporation, Amazon has thrived by constantly reinventing itself, while also staying true to its original core values.

At Amazon, embodying the company's core values is a daily effort. In fact, Bezos is so obsessed with reminding folks that it's always Day 1 at Amazon that top executives in the company work in a building on the Amazon campus that is literally called "Day 1."

In the 1997 letter, Bezos told a story about the kind of company he wanted to build. Then, he went out and built that company. He followed his own screenplay, essentially.

That's the purpose of creating a financial plan too: writing a screenplay for the future *you* wish to create.

Retirement is a blank canvas, the unwritten and final scenes in the movie of your life.

The right questions to ask when sitting down to write your screenplay are:

- What type of scenery inspires you?
- Where do you want to shoot the next scenes in your movie?
- What type of day-to-day engagement with your surroundings and community is going to bring out the best in the story's protagonist (i.e., *you*!)?
- What do you want your supporting cast to look like?
- How can you achieve all these things and stay within the film's budget?

And, most importantly, how will you adapt when things *don't* go according to plan?

Taking Ownership of Your Narrative

There was a time in my life when I suddenly went from feeling financially solid to financially fragile, and it happened on the morning of December 1, 2016.

I was scheduled to meet my partner in our office conference room to discuss the succession plan we had been working on for months. The lawyer we were paying to paper our deal was also supposed to be there.

I entered the room in good spirits. But when I sat down and looked across the table, I knew immediately something was off. My partner was staring at the table with a facial expression people wear at funerals. After the door closed, it didn't take long for him to cut to the chase.

"Michael, this is a very difficult day in the history of our firm," he said (still staring at the table).

That's when I realized there wasn't going to be a succession plan.

He proceeded to tell me he was terminating my employment, effective immediately.

"Why?" I asked.

Still looking at the table, he seemed to struggle for words.

The attorney chimed in, "Because you were unable to agree on a succession plan."

I thought we had a long-standing agreement that I was his successor. However, as the handoff period approached, my partner's attitude toward me became progressively colder, and he kept wanting to change the terms of the deal.

I looked from the attorney back toward my partner, who was stone-faced. My heart sank as I realized that moment would mark a significant U-turn in my career. Then, I thought about how I would have to share the disappointing news with my wife, who is the last person in the world I ever wanted to disappoint.

If you've ever been fired from a job, you know it hurts. Obviously. If you're not expecting it—like in my case—there's an extra shock factor to contend with.

I was surprised to be fired, mainly because I knew my numbers were outstanding. In the hyper-competitive money management industry, numbers matter—a *lot.*

At the time I received a pink slip, the Core Equity Strategy I was managing on behalf of the firm had outperformed the S&P 500 index and 99 percent of peers over the preceding four years.* So how on earth could something like this happen?

Based on the numbers, the firm was also thriving. When I joined in 2009, assets under management were $40 million. By the end of 2016, that number had ballooned 463 percent to $225 million. Didn't that say that we were doing something right as a team?

After seven years of dedicated service, I was not only a partner, but also the co-chief investment officer directly responsible for managing over half of the firm's assets. I thought those numbers provided me job security, but I thought wrong.

The founder was in his late fifties and operating out of his residence when I first joined. I set up shop in a spare bedroom. He originally said he planned to work full time for "a few more years." I saw an opportunity to scratch my entrepreneurial itch as his successor and believed our age gap would be a benefit to both of us.

---

* From January 2013 – December 2016, the Core Equity Strategy that Michael Cannivet managed generated an average annual gross return of 17.0% (15.6% net) compared to a 14.3% annual return for the S&P 500. During this time, Mr. Cannivet's strategy outperformed 99% of the 3,752 US equity strategies in eVestment's institutional database on a Sortino Ratio basis. Source: eVestment.

As the firm grew, so did my compensation. My personal financial plan was well on track. By the age of forty, I was projected to earn a seven-figure income and have a multi-million-dollar net worth, according to the investment banker we also hired to structure our succession plan.

Then, I had to learn the hard way that success on paper doesn't always translate to reality. In the blink of an eye, my financial plan disintegrated.

Six days after being fired, I formed an LLC and started my current firm, Silverlight Asset Management. After clients began following me to my new firm, my former partner filed a lawsuit and I countersued for equity I was owed.

Starting a new business was scary. Facing a lawsuit on top of it brought a bone chilling amount of uncertainty into my life.

Based on the numbers alone, it made little sense to continue running my business after litigation ensued. According to the Bureau of Labor Statistics, about half of new businesses fail in the first five years. Roughly 70 percent fail within a decade. Adding hundreds of thousands of dollars in litigation expenses to those daunting statistics made the likelihood of being a successful business owner almost an impossibility.

Yet, the decision of whether to fold my business wasn't just about numbers. There was something else inside me that didn't want to accept surrendering as my new narrative.

My heart and mind were at odds with one another. But deep down, I knew that I could succeed. I'd had so much success with my clients, why wouldn't I be able to do exactly the same thing with my own business?

Finding a New Narrative

For as long as I can remember, I've wanted to be an entrepreneur. I think that's because my dad is an entrepreneur. He probably became an entrepreneur because his mother was also an entrepreneur. It was psychologically hard to abandon a dream I perceived to be linked to my DNA and destiny.

I'd lay in bed at night, worrying about what my life would be like if I labeled myself a quitter in my own mind. What would the long-term repercussions be if I allowed that to become part of my story, and define the narrative of my life?

A central premise of this book is that financial planning isn't just about numbers but also finding the right narrative.

The modern financial services industry is littered with cookie-cutter solutions predicated on numbers and automation. The only problem with that is people are not cookies—they're complicated!

Everyone has a unique story. This is why two people can look at the same exact data and draw very different conclusions. There are nuances to numbers, which vary based on our backgrounds and biases.

Over the last two decades, I've worked with hundreds of families on a range of planning issues. The only common denominator is that most people want to know if they are "on track" with their finances. To which I always ask the same question: *On track to what?*

Getting on track starts with addressing three key aspects of retirement planning: **What** do you want to achieve? By **When**? And most importantly … **Why**?

One reason why I decided to write a book about retirement planning is because I know it's a financial topic that impacts nearly everyone. Retirement typically polls as the number one financial concern in surveys.

Demographic trends also make retirement a timely subject. Over the next decade, there will be about ten thousand Americans who turn sixty-five *every day*. If you're among that group, time may run out to find sustainable income solutions you can count on.

If you hail from a younger generation, you probably have more pressing concerns. Sure, you want to retire someday. But you may first need to figure out how to pay off student debt, save for a down payment on a home, and fund your unborn children's college tuition. Along the way, maybe a few guilt-free vacations would be nice.

Whatever your personal goals are at this moment, there's something important you should know: **Most people have too many goals**.

Look, I'm in favor of goal setting—generally speaking. But I also know that it's easy to feel overwhelmed if your financial plan consists of a bunch of loosely defined goals.

Sometimes we just need to slow down and narrow our focus. Without a clear definition of success, it's normal to feel like you're drifting aimlessly, no matter how well you may actually be doing financially. In many ways, achieving financial success is a quest to meet or exceed our own expectations.

What's Your Narrative Going to Be?

In this book, I will help you clarify your top financial goals over three different time horizons. This will allow you to define what being on track actually looks like for you.

Then, we'll sprinkle in another key ingredient most financial plans lack—emotional engagement. In these pages, we want to create a positive emotional feedback loop around your most important dreams. Your financial plan should function like a magnet—steadily pulling you forward.

If you want to learn about every nook, cranny, and crevasse there is in the world of retirement planning, there are plenty of books out there that delve into the minutiae. Not this one.

We won't cover every single detail of retirement accounts, tax treatment, withdrawal strategies, and so forth. That's by design. The focus of this book is to fast-forward your understanding of what I consider the "first principles" of finance.

"First principles thinking" is a method for unraveling complicated problems and generating original solutions. Many consider it an optimal way for learning how to think for yourself.

The first principles approach was employed by the ancient philosopher, Aristotle, and has been more recently cited by modern entrepreneurs such as Elon Musk.

In 2002, Musk began his quest to send the first rocket to Mars–starting the aerospace company SpaceX. "I tend to approach things from a physics framework," Musk disclosed in an interview. "Physics teaches you to reason from first principles rather than by analogy. So I said, okay, let's look at the first principles. What is a rocket made of? Aerospace-grade aluminum alloys, plus some titanium, copper, and carbon fiber. Then I asked, what is the value of those materials on the commodity market? It turned out that the materials cost of a rocket was around two percent of the typical price." Given that a finished rocket sells for tens of millions of dollars, Musk realized he could create his own company, purchase the raw materials for cheap, and build the rockets himself. That is how SpaceX was born.

I want to help you *personalize* and *simplify* the retirement planning process. First, I'll teach you how to write your own personal story that connects the dots between your top financial goals and your most important life goals. Then, I'll show you intelligent shortcuts you can use to build your own, one-of-a-kind financial plan.

Picture your narrative as a short story about who you are, who you are committed to becoming, and why managing money well is going to help you build a bridge to a better future. This part of the book alone can literally transform your life. I know that's possible because I experienced it firsthand.

In my own story, there came a point when my perspective suddenly changed. I pictured myself many years older, looking back at my life, wondering "what might have been." In that moment, I recognized that I would always be haunted by that unexpected chapter of my life if I allowed someone to bully me into giving up on my dream.

That reflection was powerful, and I realized that retirement planning is about more than just managing money.

Our inability to agree on a succession plan had, in my opinion, more to do with my former partner's emotional response to the idea of retirement than anything else. Work was a major part of his self-identity. And the last time I checked, he's still working—in his seventies.

Retirement is just another phase of life, but it can bring about big changes. If someone is too anchored to one component of their identity, they may fear the thought of an open schedule that allows them to become someone else. Change is constant, but that doesn't make everyone automatically ready for it. And when someone is afraid to change, they won't typically find comfort in numbers because what they really need help with is their narrative.

As a professional financial advisor and Chartered Financial Analyst who knows what it feels like to have their own financial plan suddenly flipped upside down, I empathize with anyone out there who has struggled to get on track financially.

No matter how well you do financially, not everything will go according to plan. Real life is full of surprises, so we must learn how to be resilient. My mission is to provide a flexible framework. I want this to be the last retirement planning book you ever need to read.

When I was mentally stuck between a rock and a hard place, I found nothing in the standard financial curriculum that provided a remedy. So, I created one for myself. And I did that by venturing beyond the traditional boundaries of finance. I spent several years building up knowledge in areas such as psychology, mindfulness, neuroscience, and classical storytelling. This book is a blend of the best of what I learned from my own voyage of self-discovery.

The most important thing I learned was that financial freedom isn't really a number—it's more of a feeling. People want to feel whole. People want to feel safe. People want to feel OK.

That's what abundance is about. Because abundance is about more than what's in the bank account. It's about life.

In many ways, wealth management is a personal quest to improve your feelings of well-being. Making and saving more money certainly helps. But there's another layer to it that most people aren't consciously aware of. You can learn how to rebalance your emotional assets and liabilities by actively managing your story.

In my legal case, I decided to press on—determined to go down swinging. And I did that because I knew I would eventually be prouder of that version of myself than the alternative. No one wants to read, write, or live a story of victimhood.

So in November 2018, I took part in a month-long jury trial that was emotionally and financially exhausting. In the end, I won my countersuit *and* was awarded attorney fees.[6]

In retrospect, the decision to fight for my business worked out well, but I recognize that the reason I made the decision wasn't based on any numbers or probability analysis. It was about hedging my future feelings. It was about protecting my narrative.

Even though this was the hardest period of my life, I'm thankful for valuable lessons I learned along the way. One key lesson was that it's easy to fall off track if we fail to communicate clearly with ourselves and others about what we truly want.

Reality is: Sometimes we're up, sometimes we're down. To me, that's what silver linings are about. Finding light in the darkness. Turning adversity into opportunity. Making the most of our time, by writing our best authentic story.

If you want to become your own financial best friend, start crafting a healthy narrative around your station in life—whatever that happens to be. This book will teach you how to do that.

Bending the Happiness Curve

Evolution genetically trained us to believe that achieving goals will make us happy. However, most people overestimate how long happiness lasts.

Economists call it the "hedonic treadmill." The theory posits that every achievement begets a new target, yielding little in the way of lasting satisfaction.

Everyone knows life consists of ups and downs. But not everyone knows they're wired to a baseline level of happiness that's consistent. People expect their life to evolve in a linear fashion. Yet, the life we experience is a series of twists and turns.

By the time many people make it into their forties, they start to notice a growing disconnect between their prior expectations and present realities. For many, this is the classic precondition for a midlife crisis.

The Happiness Curve: Why Life Gets Better after 50, is a book by Jonathan Rauch focused on an interesting body of research about a U-shaped happiness curve. Counterintuitively, happiness tends to bottom out for most people around mid-life, between the ages of forty-five to fifty. Then happiness gradually increases into our sixties and seventies. Researchers have found evidence to support the hypothesis across many cultures, countries, and even different primates.

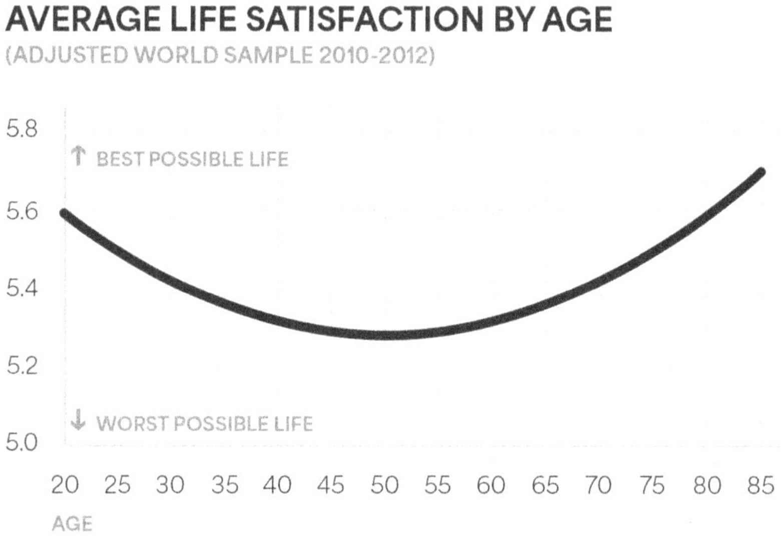

Source: The Happiness Curve: Why Life Gets Better after 50*;*
Gallup World Poll; Brookings Institution

The perfectly smooth curvature in the graph doesn't mean *everyone* is happier after age fifty. This is the kind of curve you get when a statistician takes sample data and adjusts for control variables such as age, marriage, children, health, employment, etc.

That said, there is a clear and uplifting takeaway—after the age of fifty, most people experience biological changes that help them react more positively to external events and less negatively to bad events. This makes it easier to feel at peace.

So, there is something to look forward to about getting older!

When Rauch was thirty, a writer he admired named Donald Richie told him, "Midlife crisis begins sometime in your forties, when you look at your life and think: *Is this all?* And it ends about ten years later, when you look at your life again and think: *Actually, this is pretty good.*"

Here's another piece of good news: You can proactively bend the happiness curve upward now. You can do that by consistently rehearsing an empowering narrative about your life, while steadily improving your financial resources. This produces the warm and fuzzy feeling of progress.

■ ■

Everyone faces unexpected challenges on the road to retirement. Do you have a personal central document that guides you? Would you like one?

Many important movements throughout history were guided by central documents that organized a series of core values, principles, and visions for the future.

For Amazon, the central document is Bezos's original shareholder letter.

For America, the central document is the Constitution.

For Christians, the central document is the Bible.

At different points, all of the above-mentioned movements were in jeopardy of stalling.

In the Tech Bubble, Amazon's stock lost 90 percent of its value. But the company stuck to its core values, adapted, and rebounded.

During the American Revolution and Civil War, America was tested. But the country stuck to its core values, adapted, and rebounded.

For thousands of years, Christianity has overcome adversity by sticking to its core values, adapting, and rebounding.

Your Four-Minute Retirement Plan should be a custom-tailored document to help you stay on track, relentlessly moving forward toward your goals. A document that connects your past, present, and future. A document that helps you be the best version of you.

In chapter four, we'll start building your central document. Before we get there, though, the next chapter will review some retirement planning basics everyone should be aware of.

CHAPTER SUMMARY

- Strive to constantly reinvent yourself, while honoring your core values.
- Financial planning isn't just about numbers but also finding the right narrative.
- Treat retirement as a blank canvas and design your future by setting clear goals and envisioning the life you want to lead.
- Look beyond numbers and connect emotionally to your financial goals, aligning them with your unique life aspirations.
- You can make yourself happier by consistently rehearsing an empowering narrative about your life while steadily improving your financial resources.
- Your financial plan can be a central document that keeps you on track toward your goals.

CHAPTER 3
RETIREMENT 101

What we've got here ... is failure to communicate.

—CAPTAIN FROM THE 1967 FILM *COOL HAND LUKE*

After World War II, many Americans participated in defined benefit plans where employers assumed all the planning and investment risk to fund their employees' retirements. This was my grandfather's generation.

My grandfather—a man I knew as "Papa Bill"—served in World War II, returned home, and went to work for Western Electric in the Chicago suburbs.

Several decades later, he was able to retire with a cushy pension at the age of fifty-five. He and my grandmother relocated to sunny Florida, where they enjoyed an easygoing country club lifestyle until Papa Bill passed at the age of seventy-six.

More than a quarter of my grandfather's life was a life of leisure. Not bad!

He didn't face a lot of complicated decisions before retiring either. It was all pretty much laid out for him. The government promised social security, his company promised a pension, and all Papa Bill had to do to receive those benefits was show up for work on time.

Unfortunately, that kind of straightforward deal is rare today.

Since the 1980s, the percentage of US workers with pensions has shrunk from 62 percent to 17 percent. Meanwhile, defined benefit pensions have been mostly replaced by Defined Contribution Plans (DCPs) such as 401(k)s. Compared to traditional pensions, DCPs put more responsibility on individuals' shoulders to save and invest prudently.

The percentage of workers with a 401(k) today is around 71 percent. Yet, many folks still operate in the dark when it comes to understanding key financial concepts. The US scores only slightly higher than Botswana in adult financial literacy.[7]

I was lucky because I had strong role models who introduced me to the principles of personal finance.

My grandfather taught me to be wary of debt and to avoid paying interest. Two of Papa Bill's distinctive traits were that he loved the Chicago Cubs and loathed paying interest. Speaking of the Cubbies, here's a look at my first major league baseball game back in 1980-something. My grandfather took me. That's me on the left.

Papa Bill was not a fan of credit cards or mortgages. He and my grandmother splurged occasionally; they traveled, dined out, and would park a new Cadillac in the driveway every few years. But overall, they lived below their means.

When I turned sixteen and wanted to buy a car, my grandfather volunteered to front the cost and have me pay him back, so I could avoid paying interest.

When I was accepted to Georgetown University, Papa Bill stepped up again, supplementing my tuition so I could afford to go.

I never thought of my grandparents as wealthy because they were the classic "millionaires next door." Their road to financial freedom was paved by diligently saving money they steadily invested into blue-chip dividend-paying stocks. They weren't any kind of financial geniuses. They were just normal, hardworking people who understood the most important aspects of managing money, and they were intentional about passing along that knowledge to their grandchildren.

To successfully manage money, you don't need a degree in rocket science or advanced robotics. But you do need to become familiar with a new language—a dialect called "basic financial accounting."

Growing up, my grandmother and I played a game that started with me saying, "I want to increase my vocabulary so that I may speak more intelligently." Then, she would teach me a new word—often related to personal finance—and challenge me to construct a sentence around it. Thanks to her, I could explain the basics of stocks and bonds by the time I was seven years old.

Those lessons stuck with me, too. Looking back, I now understand how building a financial vocabulary at a young age paid important dividends for me over the years. It sparked my interest in finance and planted the early seeds for this book.

The following pages will invest in building *your* financial vocabulary. Sprinkled throughout this chapter are a series of Financial Literacy Checkpoints, which offer simple explanations of key financial concepts. Let's review the first one now.

Financial Literacy Checkpoint #1: Capital

"Capital" is anything you own that pays you.

The key to building wealth is maximizing your returns on capital.

For example, let's pretend someone signs up for a credit card that charges a 15 percent interest rate, and they invest funds derived from that card to earn a 20 percent return. They win in this scenario because their return on capital exceeds the cost of capital. Trades like that make you wealthier.

How about a real-life example?

In 1995, a twenty-four-year-old named Kevin Plank was playing football at the University of Maryland when he had an idea for a new type of sports apparel company. The following year, Plank used $20,000 of his personal savings and $40,000 of credit card debt to launch a company called Under Armour.[8]

In hindsight, this was a risky move that paid off very well. Plank was able to invest those funds to build a business that generated much higher returns on capital than his starting cost of capital, and according to *Forbes* his net worth is $1.9 billion.[9]

COMPOUNDING

Those who build the biggest fortunes play the compounding game best.

Some folks are able to get rich quickly, but it's more common to get rich slowly. The key to the latter approach is learning how to properly harness time as a tailwind.

With a long enough time horizon, even mediocre returns can produce marvelous results. For example, if Christopher Columbus had invested $1 in 1492 at a 5 percent interest rate, that investment would have compounded to be worth over $50 billion today![10]

The reason financial pundits constantly advise to start saving and investing as early as possible is because time is such a critical variable in compounding.

One thing I've learned by studying successful investors and business leaders over the years is how they are usually adept at thinking beyond the short term. This allows them to recognize and take advantage of exponential opportunities.

Most people view life through a short-term, linear lens. Consequently, people overestimate what can be achieved in a day or week, and dramatically underestimate what can be achieved over months or years of dedicated effort.

In the world of money management, two plus two can equal eight thanks to a powerful thing called exponential growth.

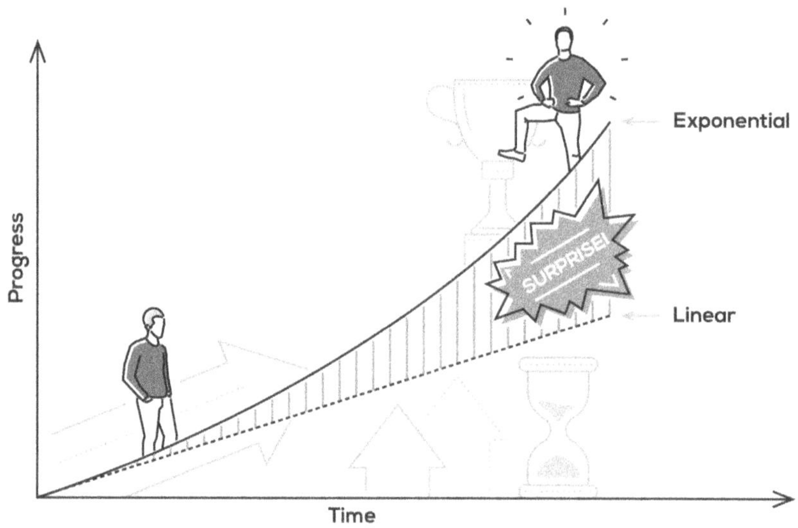

"Money makes money," my grandmother used to say.

This is how I was introduced to the concept of compounding. And if I had to pick the single most important financial principle—this would be it!

Here's how compounding works. If you invest $100 today and get a 10 percent return during the year, you start off next year with $110 to invest. So, there's a bigger pool of money available to earn interest on. That small edge, consistently magnified over time, keeps growing bigger and bigger. And there's no extra work to any of this.

That is why for a well-constructed portfolio, time is one of your strongest tailwinds.

Compounding is a crucial principle in long-term financial and retirement planning, but it can also extend beyond just money. You can enhance other areas of your life with the very same principle.

James Clear explores this idea in his book *Atomic Habits*. Clear's research demonstrates that if we get just 1 percent better every day in our habits and choices, we will end up with results that are *thirty-seven times* better after just one year.

In theory and in practice, if you want to become a better saver, a healthier person, or a better worker/manager/business owner, you don't need to make dramatic changes or completely reinvent yourself overnight. All you need are steady micro-improvements to your habits and choices, little by little, consistently over time.

The results may feel small and insignificant at first, similar to how a new diet program won't typically produce a major weight loss in the first week. But as Clear writes, "If you want to predict where you'll end up in life, all you have to do is follow the curve of tiny gains or tiny losses, and see how your daily choices will compound ten or twenty years down the line."[11]

In Japan, there's a word that embodies this principle: "kaizen." The business philosophy behind kaizen is about continuously improving systems, processes, and efficiencies, with a focus on making very small changes every day in order to achieve big gains over time. It's compound interest applied to life and business, essentially.

The company most famous for using kaizen to achieve extraordinary gains over time is Toyota Motor Corporation. Seventy years ago, Toyota was a small textile loom maker. The company focused simply on "modifying and improving our looms every day" according to Kiichiro Toyoda, the second president of Toyota Motor. Today, Toyota is the world's largest automaker.

So if you want to become wealthier, start compounding healthy habits! This will make you more productive. And as you become more useful to more people, you'll be able to accumulate more money, which you can reinvest into financial assets.

Financial Literacy Checkpoint #2: Assets versus Liabilities

Assets put money ***into*** *your pocket. Liabilities take money* ***out*** *of your pocket.*

Balance sheets—for a company or individual—are always divided into three categories: assets, liabilities, and equity. Assets add to our wealth, liabilities subtract from it, and equity is the difference between the two.

Equity is the most important part of a balance sheet because it determines net worth.

Financial Literacy Checkpoint #3: Net Worth

Net worth is what you ***own*** *minus what you* ***owe****.*

Many people know the number on their last paycheck, but not their net worth. This is something everyone should know. To successfully fund your retirement, net worth is the single most important metric to focus on.

As net worth expands, so does financial freedom. That's because the higher your net worth, the more passive income opportunities you have available. And the more passive income you can generate, the less you need to rely on a paycheck or government assistance.

Hopefully this emphasis on net worth doesn't seem intimidating to you. It shouldn't be because the good news about growing your net worth is there's a secret ingredient everyone has access to. It's called time.

Throughout life, we all operate under the common currency of time. Everything requires time. It's the only universal condition.

The billionaire and beggar both have 86,400 seconds in a day. They just use them differently.

Time is also precious. The Federal Reserve can't print more time. We can't store it anywhere. And with each passing day, our existing supply grows ever scarcer—making time that remains ever more valuable.

If you really boil it down, wealth management is a race against time. That is, we have a limited amount of time to convert our human capital into the financial capital we need to retire comfortably.

Whether you are in the "accumulation phase" of your wealth management lifecycle (i.e., in the first half of your life) or the "distribution phase"—where you will need to rely on the money you've saved to support yourself (i.e., the second half of your life), the important thing is *you still have time*. You can start building a better financial future today.

The main objective of retirement planning is to convert income we earn into wealth we can manage. We want to build assets and create passive income streams that fund our future lifestyle and legacy goals.

Financial Literacy Checkpoint #4: Passive Income

Passive income is money you can earn while sleeping–you don't have to work for it.

Passive income is wonderful because you don't have to trade your time for it.

For example, let's say an athlete signs a big contract to play ball somewhere. Their income initially jumps a lot higher than their expenses. Since all athletes have a shelf life in terms of their pro career, a wise move for them to lock in future financial freedom would be converting some of that excess cash into long-term passive income streams.

Passive income can be thought of as receiving checks in the mail. You don't have to do anything—it just shows up and lands in your pocket. That's what financial freedom looks and feels like—a beautiful thing!

For example, retired basketball star Shaquille O'Neal owns 155 Five Guys burger restaurants, seventeen Auntie Anne's Pretzels franchises, and 150 car washes. His net worth is $400 million.[12]

Shaq may not be able to play in the NBA anymore, but that's OK because unless folks stop eating burgers and pretzels, and washing their cars, Shaq is going to keep receiving checks in the mail.

You can take steps to do the same.

Financial Literacy Checkpoint #5: Liquid Assets

Assets that can be easily bought and sold.

Once we start saving money, there are myriad ways we can generate passive income. Here's a summary of the main types of assets most people have access to.

Bonds. Bonds are equivalent to loans you give to companies or the government. They pay you interest and are lower volatility instruments than stocks.

Papa Bill was OK owning bonds because *he* was the one being paid interest. Bondholders take the opposite side of those who incur debt.

Real estate. Rental properties are another form of passive income. To succeed as an investment, the rent collected must exceed the total costs of owning and maintaining a property.

Total returns from owning real estate usually come from two sources: rental yields and a property's price appreciation.*

Equities. Common equity involves owning small pieces of companies.

A big difference between stocks and bonds is that stocks pay dividends that *grow*, whereas bonds only pay static coupons.

Since bonds normally pay a fixed amount of income, if you buy a bond and hold it to maturity, you receive the yield you agreed to up front.

Stock dividends, on the other hand, represent an income stream that usually rises over time as earnings grow—so you get paid more than just your starting yield. The growth of reinvested dividends creates a compounding machine, which dramatically enhances "total returns" (price appreciation + dividends).

High-quality dividend stocks were Papa Bill's preferred investment vehicle. He patiently held stocks like Johnson & Johnson, Walmart, and Procter & Gamble for decades.

A dividend growth stock that I own, as of this writing, is biotech behemoth, Amgen. The company pays a 3.1 percent dividend yield,

---

* Andrew Demers and Andrea Eisfeldt, authors of the February 2021 paper, "Total Returns to Single Family Rentals," constructed a data set looking at rental yields and price appreciation for single family rentals from 1986–2014 across a broad cross-section of US zip codes. They found rental income (4.2 percent) and capital appreciation (4.3 percent) generated a total return of 8.5 percent. Rental yields were historically less volatile than house price appreciation.

which I expect to grow about 8 percent annually. Amgen also has debt maturing in 2053 that pays investors a fixed coupon of 2.8 percent.

The table below compares two hypothetical income streams, assuming Amgen maintains the same rate of expected dividend growth over the next ten years. Note: By year ten, the projected dividend yield on the original equity investment is more than *double* the level of the bond payout. This helps illustrate why equities tend to outperform bonds over the long term.

YEAR	BOND YIELD ON ORIGINAL INVESTMENT	DIVIDEND YIELD ON ORIGINAL INVESTMENT
1	2.77%	3.10%
2	2.77%	3.35%
3	2.77%	3.62%
4	2.77%	3.91%
5	2.77%	4.22%
6	2.77%	4.55%
7	2.77%	4.92%
8	2.77%	5.31%
9	2.77%	5.74%
10	2.77%	6.20%

Amgen hypothetical dividend yield assuming 8% CAGR over ten years.
Data source: Bloomberg.

Another income strategy is to create "Homegrown Dividends." We can do that by selling securities and converting the after-tax proceeds to income.

A key benefit of this approach is that it dramatically expands the universe of equities you can include in your portfolio. This strategy focuses on maximizing the total return of your portfolio, independent of whether your individual securities pay dividends or not.

Depending on your tax status, pursuing a higher total return strategy may be advantageous.

■ ■

When the idea of a prolonged retirement first started becoming a mainstream goal, people were lucky if they had more than five years of retirement. Nowadays, retirements are stretching longer as people are living longer. In the future, some people will be retired for as long as three or four decades.

As retirement time horizons keep expanding, we need to finance those extra nonworking years. The only reliable way to do that is by generating extra savings during our working years and investing in prudent ways that generate enough growth.

Unfortunately, the average American isn't saving nearly enough. JPMorgan estimates the average personal savings rate from 1960 to 2020 was 7.8 percent, which is well below the 10–15 percent estimated savings rate required to fund a sustainable retirement.[13]

Planning for retirement is challenging, but never out of reach. One of the first steps is developing our financial vocabulary. As you begin to understand more key concepts and connect the appropriate dots—like we've already started doing in this chapter—it will become easier to achieve whatever financial goals you have.

CHAPTER SUMMARY

- If you want to become wealthy, start expanding your financial vocabulary.
- Play the long game and try to avoid being charmed by the innate human desire to get rich quick.
- Money makes money via compounding.
- The main goal of retirement planning is to convert income we earn into wealth we can manage.
- Assets put money into your pocket. Liabilities take money out of your pocket.
- Net worth is what you own minus what you owe.
- Passive income is money you can earn while sleeping.
- You can create passive income streams from many different types of assets, including bonds, stocks, real estate, and privately owned businesses.

SECTION II

PREPARING FOR YOUR RETIREMENT RACE

CHAPTER 4

WHAT'S YOUR STORY?

I know what I'm gonna do tomorrow, and the next day and the next year, and the year after that.

—GEORGE BAILEY

There is something incredibly enduring about the story of George Bailey.

Every year, *It's a Wonderful Life* plays on major television networks. The film's protagonist, George, struggles with how to value his life. As events unfold, George makes a series of personal sacrifices to help others. He considers the rewards life is yielding back to him and grows increasingly dissatisfied. The film resonates across generations because we can all relate to the mental gymnastics George is going through. Life isn't always fair.

One thing that influences how we feel about life, however, is how we frame it.

In his book, *52 Little Lessons from It's a Wonderful Life*, Bob Welch explains why trying to keep up with the Joneses is for saps. It's because we all make a difference in our own way. "We are the proverbial pebbles in the water, our ripples going so much farther than we think," he writes.

When George Bailey was struggling with how to define his personal intrinsic value, he was emotionally fragile. In one scene, his son tells him about the neighbors' new car. George snaps back, "Well, what's the matter with our car? Isn't it good enough for you?"

George becomes bitter after life throws him a series of curveballs. Things beyond his control keep happening, which stop him from pursuing his dreams. He begins to feel restless, resentful, and unhappy.

George's predicament is common. Especially in the age of social media, envy is easy. Gratitude takes effort.

In the iconic final scene, George finds redemption by rediscovering his purpose. He remembered his family and friends were more important than his bank account or personal conquests, and that shift in focus—his new narrative—changed everything.

This chapter is about why every retirement plan should start with an authentic story.

Why Storytelling Works

Storytelling is not something we do. Storytelling is who we are.

—CARMINE GALLO

Everyone has a story about money that is best told in their own words. If you want to build a rich life, it's important to understand *your* story.

Therefore, the first step to build your Four-Minute Retirement Plan is to write a clear story about who you are now, who you are committed to becoming in the future, and why your financial goals matter to you.

Thousands of years ago, our ancestors didn't spend evenings watching ESPN, TikTok, or YouTube. They huddled around campfires and told stories.

Storytelling works because it's a communication device that parallels how we think. Leo Widrich explains how we are biologically wired for storytelling in his essay, "The Science of Storytelling: Why Telling a Story Is the Most Powerful Way to Activate Our Brains."[14] Here's an excerpt:

> We think in narratives all day long, no matter if it is about buying groceries, whether we think about work or our spouse at home. We make up (short) stories in our heads for every action and conversation ... Whenever we hear a story, we want to relate it to one of our existing experiences. That's why metaphors work so well with us. We link up metaphors and literal happenings automatically. Everything in our brain is looking for the cause-and-effect relationship of something we've previously experienced.

The London School of Business found that if people are given statistics alone, they only retain 5 to 10 percent of the information. If numbers are combined with a picture, retention rises to 25 percent. But when a *story* is used to deliver the exact same information, retention surges to 65 percent.

Storytelling is a communication superpower, and it's not being harnessed nearly enough in today's world of wealth management. That's something I want to change. I want to make wealth management fun and empowering.

Most of the greatest stories you've ever encountered consist of three acts. The best stories from books, Hollywood films, and winning sales pitches all follow the same basic formula.

There is one particular type of three-act story that especially resonates. In Joseph Campbell's 1949 book, *The Hero with a Thousand Faces*, he describes an idea known as the "Hero's Journey."

In Campbell's view, nearly every epic story consists of three stages:

1. A hero is called upon to go on a journey.
2. The hero faces trials and tribulations.
3. The hero emerges better off than before and is transformed.

Like any classic tale, your story begins with a Setup. This is the part that introduces you as the lead character. In the next chapter, we'll design the Setup for your story by exploring your personal values and happiness triggers.

Then, in Act II of your story, we'll turn our attention to what I call the "Challenge." This is when you will choose your top three goals over different time horizons.

Finally, in Act III, we'll focus on designing an easy plan to get where you want to go. This is the "Resolution" part of your story.

You can think of the story behind your financial plan as follows:

ACT I	ACT II	ACT III
The Setup	The Challenge	The Resolution
Present state of your world	Three inspiring goals	How you live happily ever after

Why do stories stick? The main reason is because storytelling engages both sides of the human brain.[15] The logical part of a story appeals to the left side, while the emotional part of a story appeals to the right side.

TIME PERSPECTIVE

I believe the next frontier in wealth management will be developing tools people can use to simultaneously improve their financial and emotional well-being.

Psychologist Philip Zimbardo believes a key factor that influences happiness and success is how people orient themselves to the past, present, and future.

In 1999, Zimbardo published a groundbreaking book titled *The Time Paradox*. In it, he introduced the concept of "Time Perspective," which is an insight showing that individuals divide the flow of human experience into different time zones. You do this automatically and unconsciously, and mounting evidence suggests your time biases explain a lot about you.

Zimbardo writes, "Time matters because we are finite, because time is the medium in which we live our lives, and because there are costs (lost opportunities) associated with not investing time wisely."[16]

There are five distinct time zones that guide our decisions and behavior.

- Past Positive
- Past Negative
- Present Hedonistic
- Future Positive
- Future Fatalistic

Zimbardo and his research partner, John Boyd, describe the optimal temporal mix as follows:

- Past positive associations provide solid roots that ground us; they connect to our identity and family.

- Future positive time perspective "gives us wings to soar to new destinations and challenges."
- Present hedonism is healthy in moderation; it's an energy spark and makes the journey fun. Sometimes it's good to just live for the moment and seek pleasurable experiences.

Time perspective influences how people manage finances. For instance, future-oriented folks have an easier time saving money compared to those with a high present hedonism bias. For the latter group, saving money is more difficult, because they value the present moment more than their future well-being.

In fact, brain scans have even shown many people think of their future self as a separate person—almost like a stranger. "One of the reasons people fail to make good choices and don't act in ways that are positive in the long term is because they feel a sense of emotional disconnect from their future selves," says Hal Hershfield, a social psychologist at UCLA Anderson.[17]

Past negative and future fatalism are the two forms of time perspective that weigh on our psyche the most. Fear and stress live in these time zones. When someone is highly geared to either time zone, they tend to be less happy and successful.

When you're dealing with someone who is caught in a negative time perspective loop, it's like they are lost in time. One telltale sign is if logic and reason don't resonate at all. As a financial advisor, I've learned through trial and error that it's very hard for someone to make rational decisions about the future if they're mentally chained to the past. Financial projections or future plans carry little weight.

When someone is stuck in a past negative state, it's often a double whammy—because they're also more likely to be future fatalistic. It's like a recession of the mind—folks mentally and emotionally contract.

They don't believe their actions today can help produce a better tomorrow. They often feel vulnerable and nervous.

To make matters worse, when someone is lost in a negative time perspective fog, they're rarely conscious of it.

The good news is that time perspective is *malleable*. You can learn how to understand your biases and take persistent steps to improve your mindset. This means you can rebalance your lens for interpreting the world much like you rebalance your investment portfolio. And you can do this by consciously and consistently editing your internal narrative. This book will show you how.

A well-balanced time perspective is like having a stronger soil to plant and sprout healthy emotions from. It's a simple trade-off decision, really. So, in the interest of nurturing a healthier time perspective for you over time, we're going to purposefully write your three-act story using that lens.

The Grass Really Is Greener

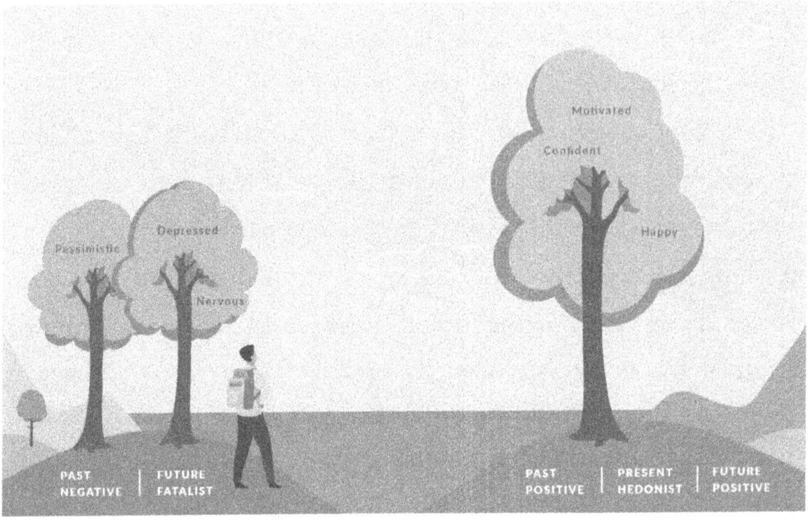

PAST NEGATIVE

Replays negative memories more than positive ones. Consequences include high anxitey and chronic depression.

FUTURE FATALIST

A persistent belief that nothing will work out, no matter the effort. Consequences include low self-esteem and self-destructive behavior.

PAST POSITIVE

Replays positive memories more than negative ones. Consequences include higher rates of happiness and self-esteem.

PRESENT HEDONIST

A mindset geared toward living each day to the fullest. Consequences include higher energy, creativity and fun.

FUTURE POSITIVE

Excited about the future. Consequences include higher motivation, confidence and enthusiasm about the journey ahead.

Life Is a Story, and Time Represents the Pages

A whole [story] is what has a beginning and middle and end.

—ARISTOTLE, *POETICS*

(WRITTEN IN THE FOURTH CENTURY BCE)

Financial planning is about more than just accumulating money and protecting it. We want the satisfaction that comes from improving our finances steadily over time, while also living a life we find rewarding and fulfilling. That's why it's important for your financial plan to be based on a multi-staged time horizon.

Time plays an important role in every story. Your three-act story is the foundation for your retirement plan, and we can build it by leveraging three distinct time perspective pillars.

Act I: Preserve Your Past. "Preserving your past" is about being past positive in your time perspective. This means honoring the good in your life. The people you love, the priceless memories, and your most sacred values are all assets you can build upon.

Most people do financial planning backward. They focus right away on strategies and tactics, when the first step should be a more thorough assessment of which goals are truly worth pursuing. Reflecting on your past is an excellent way to start planning the next chapter of your life, and we'll do that in Act I of your story ("The Setup").

Act II: Secure Your Future. "Securing your future" is about being future positive in your time perspective.

Everyone needs inspiring goals to reach for. You can literally train yourself to fall in love with your future by mentally rehearsing a focused story about what you aim to achieve and why, and we'll include that in Act II of your story ("The Challenge").

Act III: Live for Today. "Living for today" is about being present hedonistic in your time perspective.

Here's a secret: if wealth management isn't fun, you're not doing it right!

You can enjoy this period of your life while planting new seeds to bloom in the future. We'll address the secret for how to do that in Act III of your story ("The Resolution").

CHAPTER SUMMARY

- Every retirement plan should start with a story.
- The first step to build your Four-Minute Retirement Plan is to write a clear story about who you are now, who you are committed to becoming in the future, and why your financial goals matter to you.
- A key factor that influences happiness and success is how people orient themselves to the past, present, and future.
- There are five time zones that guide human behavior and decisions: past positive, past negative, future positive, future fatalistic, and present hedonistic.
- "Preserving your past" through your story will help you be more past positive in your perspective about your life.
- "Securing your future" through your story will help you become more future positive in your perspective about your life.
- "Living for today" through your story will help you be more present hedonistic in your perspective about your life.

CHAPTER 5
PRESERVE YOUR PAST

The world breaks everyone and afterward many are strong at the broken places.

—ERNEST HEMINGWAY

Don Draper was the main character in AMC's hit television show, *Mad Men*.

Above the surface, life is good for the New York City advertising executive. Don is financially secure. He has a beautiful wife and two healthy children, and he lives in a comfortable home in the suburbs. Comparing his adult life to his childhood (which he often does), he is a *raging* success.

But Don is unhappy because he knows he's living a lie.

Mad Men is a series about a man whose real name is Dick Whitman, who tries to escape a past that haunts him by assuming the identity of a fallen soldier named Don Draper.

Dick pretending to be Don is a paradox. Don can ooze charisma and light up a boardroom, but he overindulges in cigarettes and booze and has trouble connecting to his wife and children.

Don's past and present rarely overlap, especially in the office. But there's a poignant scene in season one when Don allows his true feelings to seep into his work. Here is Don speaking to the executives of Kodak about a new product that allows people to record home movies:

> Technology is a glittering lure. But there is the rare occasion when the public can be engaged on a level beyond flash, if they have a sentimental bond with the product.
>
> My first job, I was in house at a fur company with this old pro copywriter, Greek, named Teddy. And Teddy told me the most important idea in advertising was "new." Creates an itch. You simply put your product in there as a kind of calamine lotion.
>
> But he also talked about a deeper bond with the product: nostalgia. It's delicate, but potent.
>
> Teddy told me that in Greek nostalgia literally means "the pain from an old wound." It's a twinge in your heart, far more powerful than memory alone.
>
> This device isn't a spaceship. It's a time machine. It goes backwards, forwards. Takes us to a place where we ache to go again.
>
> It's not called "the Wheel." It's called "the Carousel."
>
> It lets us travel the way a child travels. Around and around and back home again to a place where we know we are loved.

As the pitch ends and the lights come on, a teary-eyed colleague excuses himself from the room. Then another colleague turns to the Kodak execs and says with a smirk, "Good luck at your next meeting."

Don excels at marketing because he understands human emotion. Yet, he is unable to reconcile his own broken places.

■ ■

Prior to becoming one of the most venerated authors of the twentieth century, Ernest Hemingway served as an ambulance driver in World War I.

One day while tending to a group of soldiers, Hemingway was wounded by Austrian mortar fire. "Then there was a flash, as when a blast-furnace door is swung open, and a roar that started white and went red," he recalled in a letter.

Ironically, getting shot turned out to be a lucky development for Hemingway. While recuperating, he fell in love with the Red Cross nurse who became his muse for writing *A Farewell to Arms*, an all-time classic war novel.[18]

In a piece titled, "Hemingway on War and Its Aftermath," Thomas Putnam writes:[19]

> Hemingway kept the piece of shrapnel, along with a small handful of other "charms" including a ring set with a bullet fragment, in a small leather change purse. Similarly, he held his war experience close to his heart and demonstrated throughout his life a keen interest in war and its effects on those who live through it.
>
> No American writer is more associated with writing about war in the early twentieth century than Ernest Hemingway. He experienced it firsthand, wrote dispatches from innumer-

able frontlines, and used war as a backdrop for many of his most memorable works.

Ernest Hemingway preserved his past. He didn't try to suppress who he was or what he had seen. Rather, he channeled his full range of experiences to become a more powerful writer.

Hemingway found strength in his broken places, and so can we.

Past Positive Perspective

Preserving your past is about honoring who you are and where you are in life.

In a study by the University of East London titled, "Time Perspective and Wellbeing," researchers defined a person with a "healthy time perspective" as someone who scores above average on three specific time perspectives—past positive, future positive, and present hedonistic. They would also score below average on their bias toward past negative and present fatalistic associations.[20]

The people in the study with a healthy time perspective also scored highly on other key measures of well-being. For instance, they were happier, more successful in their careers, and had stronger relationships with family and friends.

Ways to condition a past positive mindset include the following:

- Start a scrapbook
- Explore your family history using a service like Ancestry.com
- Record your own oral history or try a service such as Storyworth.com
- Make an appointment to call at least one old friend a week
- Plan a family reunion or a getaway trip with college friends

- Hang up more happy pictures around your home to remind you of special memories

You can also boost your past positive perspective by mentally rehearsing the story behind your Four-Minute Retirement Plan.

There is a ton of value in your past if you embrace it. When you revisit special memories, you notice patterns. The scenes vary, but certain emotions play a recurring role.

You want to always **build upon your past**. If a shark stops swimming forward, it stops breathing. Human psychology functions similarly—progress equals happiness.

Think about how Roger Bannister must have felt after losing at the 1952 Olympics in Helsinki, Finland. After all that training and buildup, he came away with a "nothing burger." At the Olympics, he finished in fourth place—just outside of a medal.

Over the following two months, Bannister considered retiring from the sport of competitive running. Instead, he dusted himself off and kept moving forward.

Your past provides clues for how to design a compelling future. Through your experiences, you've learned things you like and don't like. Now you can leverage these insights to enrich future chapters of your life.

CORE VALUES

Core values are formed during childhood.

Your formative years span from when you are born until about eight years old. During this time, your brain is the most impressionable to your surrounding environment.

Staying true to our core values helps facilitate success and happiness, whereas violating our core values has the opposite effect.

Take George Bailey's relationship with his father in *It's a Wonderful Life*. Peter Bailey raised George to be a man of integrity. This is why George was so heartbroken after he discovered Uncle Billy's accounting error. He imagined everyone in Bedford Falls viewing him as a crook. This created an identity crisis that nearly pushed George over the edge because that vision of himself represented the antithesis of what his father raised him to be.

Eventually George had an epiphany. Even though his life wasn't turning out like he originally planned—he was still on track because he was abiding by his core values.

It's easy to feel off track if the definition for being on track is overly rigid, so pay attention to how you frame things in your own mind. I learned this lesson in a roundabout way.

A few years ago, I decided to make a film for my wife, Jennifer. As an anniversary present, I wanted to chronicle the first decade of our relationship. It was quite the project.

First, I learned how to use Apple's iMovie software—a modern equivalent to Kodak's "Carousel." Then, I rummaged through pictures, videos, emails, and journal entries from over the years. As I began to assemble and edit the reel, I noticed how the story of our life together has been a series of short stories. Chapters, if you will.

Like any couple, we've had our share of ups and downs. Thrilling victories and crushing defeats. The passing of loved ones, and the amazing gift of bringing children into the world.

I chose music to weave into various parts. For example, our original wedding video was fine as is. But I prefer the version I created of my beautiful girl walking down the aisle, with Guns 'N' Roses' "Knocking on Heaven's Door" playing in the background. I get goosebumps every time I watch it.

I get teary eyed every time I hear Death Cab for Cutie's song, "I Will Follow You into the Dark." For us, that song personifies 2008—our first emotionally challenging year together.

Making the film also helped me understand my core values better.

Toward the end of *It's a Wonderful Life*, a clear message emerges. George reads a note his guardian angel has written, which says, "Dear George, remember no man is a failure who has friends. Thanks for the wings. Love, Clarence."

I used that clip at the end of my film to capture the key lesson I derived from the project. True wealth isn't measured by how much we have in our bank account. It's about the human connections we forge. The memories we share. Really, it's about finding an abundance of love.

If you were to watch a movie about your life, what do you think would stand out as most important to you?

Think of a time in the past when you felt in a peak state. A magical memory. A time when you were thriving, happy and fulfilled.

- Where were you?
- What were you doing?
- Who were you with?
- Why was that moment so valuable to you?

List three ages when you felt excited about your life.

Age #1:

Age #2:

Age #3:

List three things at each age that made you feel that way.

Age #1:

a)

b)

c)

Age #2:

a)

b)

c)

Age #3:

a)

b)

c)

Values play a starring role in everyone's story. Understanding *what* you value and *why* is key to generating positive momentum in life.

In my case, one of the core values I learned from my father was "results count." Growing up, my father didn't give a lot of advice. But he did repeat one phrase over and over to me. "Results count; everything else is BS."

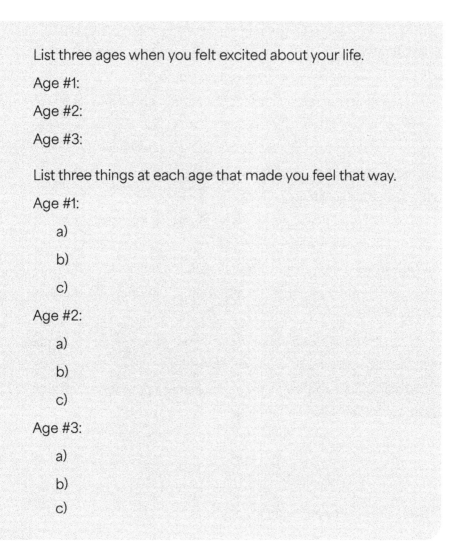

When your father says that kind of statement over and over again to you, it becomes imprinted in your mind and in your soul. It becomes part of your philosophical core.

This is why being fired after I had produced solid results was emotionally devastating. It was like the world no longer functioned as I previously thought. I was overcome by a tsunami of sadness and felt future fatalistic for the first time in my life—like it didn't matter how hard I worked going forward. Life seemed unfair and hopeless.

Then I woke up.

I dropped those negative feelings like a bad habit once I realized *they were a bad habit.*

Emotional liabilities are like financial liabilities—they only subtract from our wealth and well-being.

It makes a lot more sense to look for *good* things from our past and shine a spotlight there. These are emotional assets we can build upon.

What core values are you most proud of? Which core values do you want to carry with you into the future?

Like George, I eventually realized I stayed true to my core values all along. I produced results. That was what I was taught to value and all I controlled in the matter.

Today, I'm thankful for the silver lining that came from the experience. It took getting fired for me to learn why core values are so important and why the story behind a financial plan is so valuable.

After parsing data from over a half-million surveys in 152 languages, a consumer marketing consultant called Valuegraphics identified the top values that drive human decisions and behavior. On the next page is a summary of key values that many people share.[21]

1. Family
2. Relationships
3. Financial Security
4. Belonging
5. Community
6. Personal Growth
7. Loyalty
8. Religion / Spirituality
9. Employment Security
10. Personal Responsibility
11. Basic Needs
12. Harmony
13. Health & Well-Being
14. Experiences
15. Respect
16. Compassion
17. Social Standing
18. Creativity & Imagination
19. Trustworthiness / Honesty
20. Education

After thinking about your own formative years, write down three of the most important values you learned growing up that you want to carry into the future.

Value #1: ______________________________

Who taught you value #1, and why were they a special person in your life?

____

____

Value #2: ______________________________

Who taught you value #2, and why were they a special person in your life?

____

____

Value #3: ______________________________

Who taught you value #3, and why were they a special person in your life?

____

____

Next, let's wrap up by reviewing how core values can be used to write a setup for a story.

Client Case Study: Meet Chris

My first memory of Chris is when he was a ten-year-old boy who lived across the street from my parents. Whenever I would visit, I'd often spot him and his father playing catch in the front yard.

Eight years later, I was pleasantly surprised to learn from my mother that he had decided to attend Georgetown University. She apparently told his mother about the generous financial aid package I received, and that got the ball rolling.

Today, Chris is a man in his late twenties who lives in Austin, Texas. He's building a career in technology sales, while also dedicating time to a side hustle—his growing YouTube channel. On YouTube, Chris gives career advice for those who want to follow in his footsteps.

The opportunity to help Chris design a financial plan that maps to his life plan is a classic example of why I find my job as a financial advisor gratifying. I get to ride shotgun while people develop, mature, and grow through different stages of life.

Like any classic tale, the story behind a four-minute retirement plan begins with a setup. This is the part that introduces the lead character—in this case, Chris.

We begin this exercise with an "authenticity statement." It can be any sentence that says something uniquely positive about you, which you know is true. Imagine you're going around a room as everyone takes turns introducing themselves. Each person states their name along with a fun fact or anecdote about themselves. When it's your turn, what would you say?

Here is the setup for Chris's story, including his authenticity statement and core values:

ACT I: THE SETUP

- **Chris was nicknamed "Miracle Baby."** Before he arrived, his parents struggled for years to conceive a child. Chris was the answer to a longstanding prayer.

- **Chris values family**. He grew up in a tight-knit family with his father, mother, and younger adopted sister. One of his fondest memories from childhood is playing make-believe games with his mother and sister. Nowadays, he still enjoys playing family board games and catch with his dad whenever he is home.

- **Chris values faith**. In Chris's family, faith has always been a foundational pillar. "It's in me," he says.
- **Chris values creativity**. His mother is an artist, musician, and someone who always encourages him to explore new avenues of creative expression.
- **Chris values a strong work ethic**. He appreciates that his father spent many years putting in long hours at work, which enabled his mother to spend more quality time at home raising him and his sister. In 2019, Chris felt he was in one of the best flow states of his life. This was right after he secured his dream job at Google, moved to Austin, started attending personal development seminars, and launched his own YouTube channel.
- **Chris values courage**. He was deeply inspired by his mother's courage when she successfully battled cancer into remission, while maintaining a relentlessly positive attitude.

In the next chapter, you will see how the setup from Chris's story connects to his three most important financial goals.

Traveling back in time to reflect on what we value is a natural and logical way to brainstorm future goals. That's what I'd strongly encourage readers to do now. Take a break from reading, look back at your answers and reflect on them, and then start writing the setup of your story. Begin with your authenticity statement, then focus on describing your core values.

Act I: The Setup

CHAPTER SUMMARY

- Your story begins with identifying your core values.
- Introspection of your past helps connect the dots to a compelling future.
- Your story provides a "Why" behind your financial goals.
- Preserving your past is about honoring who you are and where you are in life.
- If a shark stops swimming forward, it stops breathing. Human psychology functions similarly–progress equals happiness.

- You must have a clear understanding of what you want to achieve and why you want to frame a positive story around a goal.
- To identify happiness triggers, think of times in the past when you felt in a peak state, and ask yourself why you felt that way.
- Staying true to our core values helps facilitate success, whereas violating core values has the opposite effect.

CHAPTER 6

SECURE YOUR FUTURE

You can't connect the dots looking forward; you can only connect them looking backwards. So you have to trust that the dots will somehow connect in your future.

—STEVE JOBS

Nerves in his face were accidentally damaged when he was pulled from the womb by forceps. As an adult this gave him a droopy look and slurred speech. Nevertheless, his dream was to make it in Hollywood as an actor.

At auditions, casting directors didn't just reject him—they told him to quit trying. "You don't look right for the business ... you don't sound right ... go do something else," they said.

On a cold and wintery day, the actor visited the New York Public Library. There, he stumbled across a book that changed his life—the stories of Edgar Allan Poe. Poe's words leaped off the page—inspiring him to try his hand at writing.

The early screenplays showed promise but failed to pay the bills. Mounting financial stress complicated his marriage. Eventually, he hocked his wife's jewelry, which basically ended their relationship.

Before long, the actor had just one thing left to his name—his dog. On the lowest day of his life, he stood outside of a store offering to sell the dog to strangers passing by. He tearfully accepted $25.

A few weeks later, the actor was watching a boxing match on television. In one corner stood Muhammad Ali, "The Greatest." In the other corner: a longshot fighter by the name of Chuck Wepner.

As soon as the match started, it became obvious Wepner was outmatched. Yet Wepner ended up shocking the boxing world that evening. Not by *winning* the bout, but by going the distance. People were impressed he lasted all fifteen rounds without being knocked out.

The actor was mesmerized because he related to the fighter's story. After the fight ended, he began writing a script. Three and a half days later, he finished the first draft, and he knew right away it was a winner.

It wasn't long before someone offered to buy the script for $100,000. For the penniless actor, this was a life-changing sum. But he had one other stipulation: he wanted to play the lead role.

Major studios balked at this request. They considered it too risky to cast an unknown as the star.

Then another offer came in at $200,000—if the actor would give up the lead.

"No deal."

Another offer—this time for $265,000, same condition.

"No deal."

The actor later agreed to sell the script for $25,000 *plus the starring role.*[22]

The script was for a film called *Rocky*, which made over $200 million at the box office. The film won three Oscars (including Best Picture) and launched Sylvester Stallone's acting career into the stratosphere.

Sylvester Stallone made some unconventional choices in his life, but no one can doubt that his perseverance paid off. The once-destitute actor earned himself a spot on the Hollywood Walk of Fame and a net worth of $425 million.[23]

It ain't about how hard you hit. It's about how hard you can get hit and keep moving forward.

—ROCKY BALBOA

Most financial advisors would have told Stallone he was crazy to reject a $265,000 offer when he was broke at the time. And yet it turned out to be a wise decision!

This shows why linking goals to our core values is so important. Not everything in life always boils down to just dollars and cents. Stallone had a distinct vision for his life, and he earned outsized rewards by sticking to the original script. You can't put a price tag on passion.

Maintaining faith in the future—even when things appear bleak—is a choice. Sometimes it's a hard choice. But for Sylvester Stallone, it was the *only* choice.

Like Stallone, you can secure your future by keeping a future positive attitude and continually pursuing goals that you're passionate about.

Embracing a Future Positive Perspective

It's much easier to stick to a goal you're excited about if you believe you can achieve it. That's part of the psychological edge that comes from keeping a future positive perspective.

With a future perspective, you can envision a future filled with hope, optimism, and power. The future gives you wings that enable you to soar to new destinations and to be confident in your ability to deal with the unexpected challenges that you might encounter on the way. It equips you to escape the status quo, the fear inherent in straying from the safe, known ways, the well-traveled roads to your destination.

—DR. PHILIP ZIMBARDO

Dr. Zimbardo recommends the following tips to become more future positive:

- Schedule regular medical, dental and vision checkups
- Regularly review a list of your goals
- Chart progress toward your goals
- Practice delayed gratification*

You can also improve your future positive perspective through your story.

Your financial plan should inspire focus and emotional engagement. This is where Act II comes into play. In this part of your story, you clarify your top three financial goals.

Step 1: Visualize "The What"

The first step in Act II is visualizing *what* you aim to achieve.

What are your most important goals now and in the future?

---

* For example, you could put out a bowl of treats and whenever tempted, just think: "Later." Then, mentally pat yourself on the back! Even if it seems silly at first, simple exercises like this improve your willpower.

In *The Time Paradox*, Dr. Zimbardo recommends an exercise to help visualize a successful future. Simply ask: *Who will I be?*

Take a few minutes to think about your life and financial goals for different points in the future. To help you brainstorm, here is a list of common types of goals:

- Retiring
- Achieving Financial Freedom
- Home purchase
- Emergency savings fund
- Paying off debt
- College savings
- Long-term health care coverage
- Donation or other estate planning goals
- Other large purchases (boat, second home, etc.)

Step 2: Figure Out "The When"

Dreams without deadlines aren't worth much. So, after you formulate your initial list of goals, group them into three distinct time zones.

1. Short-term goal (1–5 years)
2. Medium-term goal (5–10 years)
3. Long-term goal (10+ years)

Everyone has different goals over different time horizons. Act II is about clarifying where you want to go in your personal journey.

Step 3: Dig into "The Why"

Planning your dream retirement and other key goals you want to achieve starts with digging into the *Why*.

Michael Norton is a Harvard Business School professor who studies the connections between happiness and wealth. In a 2018 paper, Norton and his colleagues polled over two thousand people with a net worth exceeding $1 million. They asked the subjects two questions:

- How happy are you on a scale of 1–10?
- How much more money would you need to rate yourself at a 10?

"'All the way up the income-wealth spectrum, basically everyone says [they'd need] two or three times as much' to be perfectly happy," Norton said in an interview with *The Atlantic*.[24]

So, even millionaires want more.

That doesn't make them greedy—it makes them human.

It's natural to feel like having a lot more will automatically make you happy, but once you get there, that's not the end of the road. This is why you need to have continuous, specific goals that inspire you.

What are your favorite things to do? What makes you excited to get up in the morning?

Pick Your Three Most Meaningful Goals

I want you to compare your initial list of goals to the setup of your story. Then, using your values as guideposts, pick your top goal for each time horizon.

So, if you have two medium-term goals that you're strongly considering, pick whichever one you think *best* reflects your core values. Directly linking a goal to one of your core values will help build a powerful emotional asset. It's called motivation.

SHORT-TERM GOALS (1-5 YEARS)

WHAT	WHY (CORE VALUE)

MEDIUM-TERM GOALS (5-10 YEARS)

WHAT	WHY (CORE VALUE)

LONG-TERM GOALS (10+ YEARS)

WHAT	**WHY (CORE VALUE)**

Why only three goals? Because focus matters!

People always feel an itch to add more things to their life, but sometimes *less is more.*[*]

Knowing what you want and why you want it naturally empowers you to push forward. It inspires the grit you need to make those things you're working on happen.

For example, there was a clear reason why Katniss Everdeen volunteered for the Hunger Games. She wanted to protect her little sister because one of her core values was family.

Act II of your story can be whatever you want it to be. Just don't be afraid to challenge yourself! Keep dreaming, keep growing, and keep writing new chapters.

---

* In a 2021 study titled, "People Systematically Overlook Subtractive Changes," researchers from the University of Virginia conducted eight different problem-solving experiments. The subjects they studied consistently overlooked opportunities to improve things by subtracting. "The tendency to overlook subtraction may be implicated in a variety of costly modern trends, including overburdened minds and schedules, increasing red tape in institutions and humanity's encroachment on the safe operating conditions for life on Earth," the researchers wrote.

Effective goal setting is about connecting the dots between your key goals and core values.

Client Case Study

Remember our friend Chris from the last chapter? Below is an example of how he used the above template to outline the goals he will pursue to secure his future.

Act II: The Challenge

1. Chris wants to (what) create an emergency savings account worth nine months of his fixed living expenses (when) within two years. He wants to do this (why) because having a financial cushion will create more financial flexibility. Chris is excited about achieving this goal because it will make him feel more responsible. He will feel like he is embodying the strong work ethic he learned from his father.
2. Chris wants to (what) buy a home (when) within five years. He wants to do this (why) because he values family and owning a home will provide him a home base to organize the next chapter of his life. Chris is excited about completing this goal as he envisions celebrating holidays at his future home. He imagines being surrounded by his loved ones, and loves thinking about his children being able to play make believe games with his mother and sister and catch with his father.
3. Chris wants to (what) achieve Financial Freedom (when) within twenty years. He wants to create enough passive income (why) to alleviate having to "work" for a living. This will allow Chris to indulge his creative side, inspired by his

mother. Chris is excited about this goal because it will enable him to be more entrepreneurial and philanthropic in how he allocates his time. And it will afford him extra time to spend with his family and friends.

The future will always be uncertain, but that's nothing to fear.

Staying excited about your future is the best way to secure it. The purpose of Act II in your story is to help with that.

Knowing your three most important goals and the Why behind them provides a solid foundation for your financial plan. And by linking each goal to one of your core values, you're already on track to a degree—because you know you're chasing the *right* goals.

Take a moment now to write the Challenge part of your story. Describe three goals you are committed to pursuing that reflect your core values. Focus on what you want to achieve, when you want to achieve it, and why each goal is important to you.

Act II: The Challenge

CHAPTER SUMMARY

- You can secure your future by keeping a future positive perspective and pursuing goals that you're passionate about.
- A financial plan should inspire focus and emotional engagement.
- In Act II of your story, you clarify your top three financial goals.
- The first step is to visualize things you want to achieve.
- The second step is to group your goals into three distinct time zones: short-term goals (1-5 years), medium-term goals (5-10 years), and long-term goals (10+ years).
- The third step is to dig into the Why behind your goals.
- Effective goal setting is about connecting the dots between your key goals and core values.
- Using your values as guideposts, pick your top goal for each time horizon.

CHAPTER 7
LIVE FOR TODAY

I take it not only a day at a time, but a moment at a time, and keep it at that pace. If you can be happy right now, then you'll always be happy, because it's always in the now.

—WILLIE NELSON

Roger Bannister didn't run a four-minute mile by blasting off the line and sprinting as hard as he could for four laps. He ran each lap at a specific target pace, careful never to go too fast or too slow. Success meant sticking to the plan.

Since there are four laps in a mile, Bannister knew he needed to average just under one minute per lap. That's why he wrote fifty-nine seconds on the piece of paper he stuffed into his shoe, and why he practiced running fifty-nine-second splits.

For Bannister to execute his plan and make history, he needed help. He called in his teammates Chris Brasher and Chris Chataway to serve as pacesetters. They were like guardrails to ensure he did not deviate from the plan. Here's how Bannister recounted his thoughts during the race:[25]

As the gun fired, Chris Brasher went into the lead and I slipped in effortlessly behind him—feeling tremendously full of running. My legs seemed to meet no resistance at all. Almost as if impelled by an unknown force.

We seemed to be going so slowly. Impatiently, I shouted faster. But Brasher kept his head and didn't change the pace.

I went on worrying about the pace until I heard the first lap time; 57.5 seconds. In the excitement, my knowledge of pace had deserted me. Brasher could have run the first quarter in fifty-five seconds without my realizing it, because I felt so full of running. But I should have had to pay for it later. Instead, he had made success possible.

At one and a half laps, I was still worrying about the pace. A voice shouting "relax" penetrated to me above the noise of the crowd … unconsciously I obeyed. If the speed was wrong, it was too late to do anything about it—so why worry?

I barely noticed the half mile passed in 1:58. I was relaxing so much that my mind seemed almost detached from my body. It was incredible that we could run at this speed without strain.

I was barely aware of the fact that Chris Chataway was now going into the lead.

At three quarters of a mile the effort was still barely perceptible. The time was 2:57 seconds and by now the crowd was roaring. A four-minute mile was possible. Somehow, to do it, I had to run the last lap in fifty-nine seconds.

> Chataway led around the next bend, and then I pounced past him in the beginning of the back straight, three hundred yards from the finish. And in a moment of mixed joy and anguish, when my mind took over, it raced well ahead of my body and drew me compellingly forward. I felt the moment of a lifetime had come.

Brasher and Chataway are the unsung heroes of the first four-minute mile. When Bannister's instincts told him to run faster, his pace runners helped him stick to the game plan, ensuring he preserved enough stamina to finish the final lap on time.

As Bannister showed, the key is finding an effective strategy you can *stick to*.

Balancing Present Hedonism with a Future Positive Perspective

"Explain to me again why enjoying life when I retire is more important than enjoying life now."

Financial planning isn't just about making short-term sacrifices to achieve long-term goals. You should be able to enjoy the here and now while also having peace of mind about the future. The key is ensuring that your resources are allocated to the present and future in a balanced way.

Most retirement plans focus almost exclusively on a person's long-term goals, which means short-term wants and needs are often overlooked or cast aside. I don't agree with this approach.

When Roger Bannister described what it felt like to run the first four-minute mile, notice how he didn't strain too much? He ran "effortlessly" for most of the race. Thanks to the pace runners, he didn't have to worry or overthink things. Bannister was able to enjoy the experience of the race, as he kept steadily moving forward to his goal.

Stamina is what we need to win our retirement race, and we can gain more stamina by developing a short-term reward system that keeps us motivated as we pursue our long-term goals.

WeightWatchers applies this concept to dieting. One reason why the program works so well is because it encourages members to track their points. Points are a combination of calories and other factors. Tracking points daily takes people from eating on autopilot to eating with awareness. Even though WeightWatchers encourages disciplined eating, people can still eat anything they want as long as they stay within their overall points budget. So, pizza, chocolate, or an occasional piece of birthday cake aren't off-limits. Cheat meals can be considered part of the plan.

When someone plans a cheat meal, they create a predictable structure that protects them from the whims of their willpower, and this protects them from unintentionally falling off track.

Dwayne "The Rock" Johnson embraces cheat meals. The Hollywood and fitness icon is seriously ripped. But he's also become legendary on Instagram for posts about the *insane* cheat meals he consumes every Sunday night. On one epic cheat day, the Rock consumed twelve pancakes, four double dough pizzas, and twenty-one brownies!

A healthy dose of present hedonism is a beautiful thing.

Present hedonism is living for the moment by indulging in activities you find novel, stimulating, and fun.

When a hedonist makes a lot of money, they're typically the best at spending it. They know how to throw a great party, maximize a vacation, and are always on the lookout for new toys to buy. Hedonists embrace spontaneity, pursue hobbies, and make friends easily because they're fun to be around.

Indulging yourself is good because it energizes you. It's part of the payoff for being alive. We all need short-term rewards to keep us happy during the long, sometimes bumpy, journey to retirement.

The key is disciplined moderation.

If your personal reality is creating your personality, you are a victim. But if your personality is creating your personal reality, then you are a creator.

—DR. JOE DISPENZA

I have a client named Jim, in his late fifties, who is one of the best people I know at balancing present hedonism with a healthy future perspective.

Jim plans to retire in about five years. The last time I asked him what his main goal for retirement was, he enthusiastically replied, "I just want to keep living this life!"

Jim is one of those people who will be forever young. He lives an active lifestyle. He takes regular golf trips to Pebble Beach, hiking trips to Yosemite, skiing trips in the Alps, and he and his wife attend the Coachella Music Festival almost every year.

Jim is also a "foodie" whose monthly food and wine budget probably exceeds many people's mortgage payments.

Even though Jim knows how to have a good time, he also knows how to take care of business.

For over a decade, Jim has kept a monthly budget. He has a simple financial plan that defines the boundary of what he can and cannot afford. So, Jim is free to live it up in a stress-free manner.

Isn't this what everybody wants, ideally?

Life isn't just about achieving things in the future. It's also about enjoying things today. Budgeting "fun money" as a short-term reward system is just as important as planning how to achieve your long-term goals, because it provides the emotional fuel to help you stay on track.

Remember: No single time perspective is perfect. To experience consistent happiness and fulfillment, aim to spend more time living in a past positive, future positive, and present hedonistic state. All three of these time zones count for something good in your life.

Use Happiness Triggers to Create a "Fun Money" Budget

Everyone has happiness triggers. What do you love to do?

Some of the things I enjoy in my off time include coaching basketball, riding my bike, playing the guitar, and hanging out with my kids. I also love the escapism of going to the movies with my wife.

Do you enjoy traveling? Are you a foodie, like Jim? Do you like playing video games? Whatever you like to do—I advise doing more of it.

Being too future focused can easily morph into a never-ending grind. If you find yourself constantly thinking about future goals, try pushing pause on that. Practice indulging more in the moment. It's important to budget money and time for activities you find novel, stimulating, and fun.

Here are steps you can follow to create your own Fun Money Budget.

1. BRAINSTORM AT LEAST FIVE ACTIVITIES YOU ENJOY DOING.

Write down five things that make you happy and describe why.

WHAT	WHY (HAPPINESS TRIGGER)

2. BUDGET UP TO 30 PERCENT OF YOUR INCOME AS FUN MONEY.

Developing the habit of tracking your consumption will move you from consuming on autopilot to consuming with awareness. As long as you budget properly, you can have fun now while staying on track toward your long-term financial goals.

Aim to budget around 30 percent of after-tax income to your fun money account. Think of this as an operating account that pays for all those fun things you want to do like shopping, dining out, and traveling.

The 50/30/20 Budgeting Rule

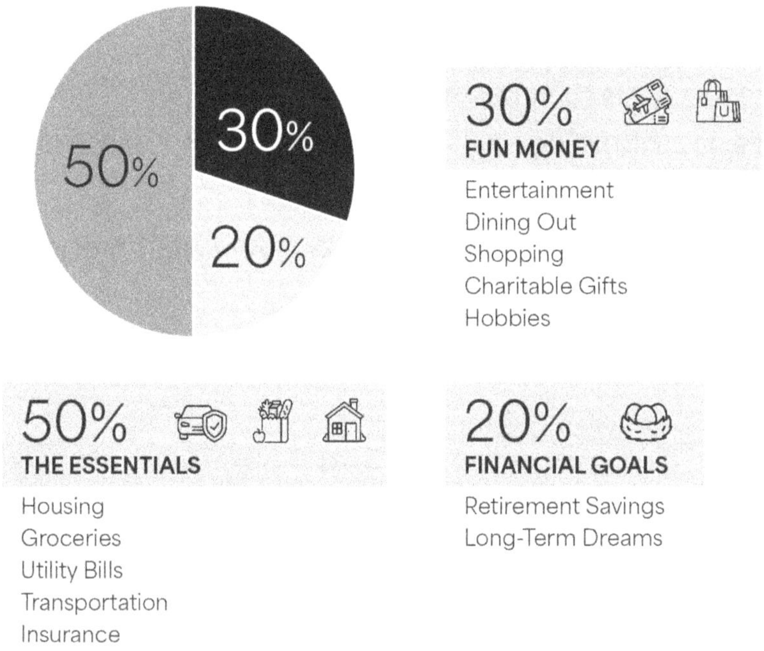

Many of the activities you enjoy likely cost some money. List each fun activity below, the estimated cost, and the portion of your after-tax income you plan to devote to it.

WHAT	COST	INCOME %

3. SCHEDULE MORE PRESENT HEDONISM INTO YOUR LIFE.

One way I actively manage my time perspective is by making a list every morning.

First, I write down three things I'm grateful for that happened the previous day. This helps me have a past positive perspective.

Second, I write down one important thing I'm dedicated to doing that day to advance toward one of my future goals. This helps me have a future positive perspective.

Third, I schedule time for present hedonism. I might book a tennis match at my club, schedule an afternoon bike ride, or pick up my kids from school and do a surprise activity.

Whatever activity you enjoy is fine. The only key is to schedule and honor the activity as an appointment that's just as important as any other on your calendar.

For example, my wife Jennifer enjoys reading, so she makes time to read every day during her lunch break.

Did You Know?

Here are the top six activities that make parents and children happy, according to a survey by *FamilyFun* magazine.[26]

TOP 6 ACTIVITIES THAT MAKE **PARENTS** HAPPY

37%	Vacations
37%	Outings (zoo, playground, museum)
27%	Time with other families or relatives
23%	Playing board or video games
22%	Eating meals together
22%	Celebrating special occasions

TOP 6 ACTIVITIES THAT MAKE **KIDS** HAPPY

42%	Vacations
35%	Celebrating special occasions
31%	Playing board or video games
26%	Outings (zoo, playground, museum)
25%	Watching movies, TV, or videos together
21%	Time with other families or relatives

4. FINISH YOUR STORY.

You can transform your life by actively managing your time perspective, and a great way to do that is through your story.

Act III of a classic story is "The Resolution." This is the part where the main character (you) makes their way off into the sunset, determined to live happily ever after.

For this part of your story, the focus is finding a healthy balance of present hedonism.

- Examples of things that qualify as present hedonism but are not future positive for you would include substance abuse, overspending your budget, or doing things that temporarily feel good but create longer-term feelings of guilt.
- Examples of things that could check both the present hedonism and future positive boxes include adopting a pet, spa days, attending church, spending time around positive people, meditating, the arts, volunteering, personal development workshops, etc.

Putting this into story form will help crystalize it in your mind. Describe what you intend to do, when you will do it, and why you know you can afford it. Spelling out the details will help solidify the commitment to yourself.

Here's what this part of Jim's story might look like:

Act III: The Resolution

Jim will play golf every week and eat out at great restaurants (wine included, please).

Jim enjoys playing golf because it relaxes him. Eating out at nice restaurants is valuable time with his wife, and he's always in admiration of what the best chefs are doing—it inspires him.

Jim knows he can afford these activities, because the "fun money" portion of his monthly budget includes the average cost of four dinners out and the green fees at his favorite

> courses, and his overall fun money budget is under 30 percent of his income.

As another example, here's what Act III of Chris's story could look like:

> Chris will get a puppy, take two vacations a year, and periodically attend personal development workshops.
>
> Chris wants a puppy to provide him companionship. He enjoys traveling because visiting new places feeds his adventurous spirit. He values personal development workshops because he recognizes that he's happiest when he feels like he's improving in his life.
>
> Chris knows he can afford these activities, because the fun money portion of his monthly budget includes the estimated cost of caring for a dog, the average cost of two vacations per year, the average cost of three seminars per year, and his overall fun money budget including these things is about 30 percent of his income.

■ ■

Take some time now to write the Resolution part of your story. This is where you'll describe how you want to allocate the fun money part of your budget. Focus on the following questions to help get started.

- What fun activity are you going to commit to doing as part of a short-term reward in your long-term plan?
- When are you going to make time for your fun activity?
- Why is this a valuable activity for you?
- How do you know you can afford to do this activity?

Act III: The Resolution

Simplify Your Affairs with a Four-Minute Retirement Plan

A four-minute retirement plan is an excellent way to simplify your financial affairs and help you stay on track toward your goals.

WHY CREATE A FOUR-MINUTE RETIREMENT PLAN?

It's important to make your financial plan easy to understand because complexity is the enemy of execution.

The main benefit of a simple, short financial plan is that you're more likely to stick to it. If a financial plan has too many pages, tables, and statistics, it's hard to ever feel on track because you can't get your arms around it. This reduces motivation and allows your plan to fall by the wayside.

Remember Theodore Johnson's story from earlier in the book? His financial plan was super simple, to the point where it felt manageable for him. He consistently saved a portion of his earnings, which he steadily invested in a company he worked for and believed in. For Johnson, following his financial plan became almost as automatic as brushing his teeth.

Figuring out what to do, for any task, is easier than it's ever been. Nowadays, we have an information superhighway at our fingertips. We can "Ask Siri." However, knowing what to do is only half the battle. We still must *do* these things. Failure to follow through is where most people come up short. Changing anything we do is hard, which is why I think most people need a financial plan that's easy to follow.

WHAT DOES A FOUR-MINUTE RETIREMENT PLAN LOOK LIKE?

In the upcoming lap section chapters, I'll discuss a variety of key issues associated with retirement planning. Then, at the end of each chapter, I'll outline four solutions you can trust to handle each issue, and you can implement whichever solution(s) you prefer.

This part of the book is structured to help you build a customized retirement plan that you can summarize succinctly. Here is an example of what the Four-Minute Retirement Plan summary page looks like:

THE SAVINGS LAP

Four strategies to start saving money:

- ☐ #1: Automate Contributions to a 401(k)
- ☐ #2: Automate Contributions to Multiple Tax-deferred Vehicles
- ☐ #3: Maximize Retirement Contributions and Start an Emergency Savings Fund
- ☐ #4: Maximize Retirement Contributions and Start a Scarcity Fund

Four strategies to manage debt wisely:

- ☐ #1: Pay Off High Interest Rate Debt First
- ☐ #2: Dave Ramsey's Snowball Method
- ☐ #3: Consolidate Your Debts
- ☐ #4: Payoff Bad Debt and Add Good Debt

Four strategies for choosing a financial advisor:

- ☐ #1: Be Your Own Financial Advisor
- ☐ #2: Hire a Robo-Advisor
- ☐ #3: Choose a Fiduciary Advisor
- ☐ #4: Choose a Fiduciary Advisor with Advanced Credentials

THE INVESTING LAP

Four safety-first investing strategies:

- ☐ #1: Invest in a Low-Volatility Index Strategy
- ☐ #2: Invest in a Low-Volatility Sector Strategy
- ☐ #3: Dollar-Cost Average
- ☐ #4: Employ an Active Defensive Strategy

Four strategies to choose a benchmark:

- ☐ #1: Focus on Maximizing Long-Term Returns
- ☐ #2: Focus on Absolute Returns
- ☐ #3: Focus on a Volatility Threshold
- ☐ #4: Focus on Finding an Advisor

Four strategies to avoid the passive bubble:

- ☐ #1: Diversify with Equal-Weighted Portfolios
- ☐ #2: Blend Passive and Active Strategies
- ☐ #3: Self-Manage
- ☐ #4: Direct Indexing

THE LIFESTYLE LAP

Four choices for where to live in retirement:

- ☐ #1: Age in Place
- ☐ #2: Home Sharing or Multigenerational Living
- ☐ #3: Retire to a Retirement Mecca
- ☐ #4: Relocate to a New State or Country

Four distinct stages of life:

- ☐ #1: Early Adulthood (twenties to early thirties)
- ☐ #2: Pre-retirement (mid-thirties to fifties)
- ☐ #3: Early Retirement (late fifties to mid-sixties)
- ☐ #4: Late Retirement (mid-sixties and beyond)

Four withdrawal strategies:

- ☐ #1: The 4 Percent Rule
- ☐ #2: The Dynamic 5 Percent Rule
- ☐ #3: The Guyton-Klinger Rule
- ☐ #4: The Yale Endowment Spending Rule

THE LEGACY LAP

Four estate planning solutions:

- ☐ #1: Engage a Low-Cost Legal Service
- ☐ #2: Engage a Full-Service Legal Professional
- ☐ #3: Create a Trust Agreement
- ☐ #4: Give with Warm Hands

Four strategies to maximize philanthropy:

- ☐ #1: Select High-Impact Charities
- ☐ #2: Use Tax-Efficient Giving Methods
- ☐ #3: Establish a Giving Plan
- ☐ #4: Make Philanthropy a Family Affair

Four ways to positively shape your legacy:

- ☐ #1: Start a Traditional Foundation
- ☐ #2: Become a Teacher
- ☐ #3: Actively Contribute to a Club
- ☐ #4: Write a Memoir or Record an Oral History

Importantly, each of the solutions proposed in this book has produced successful outcomes in the past. While the past isn't always prologue, there's a good chance these strategies will continue to work in the future. After reading each chapter, all you have to do is pick whichever strategy feels most right to you in twenty seconds or fewer and move on.

Some readers may wonder: Why the "twenty second" rule? Is that really enough time to make an important financial decision?

My answer to that question would be a resounding "Yes."

I want you to practice converting knowledge into action because that's where almost everyone falls short. By committing to a decision in twenty seconds or less, you'll eliminate the hesitation habit that stops most people from making their dreams a reality.

Truth is, there isn't just one correct way to build wealth or manage an estate plan. There are *many* correct ways. Don't fall into the trap of overthinking things. Paralysis by analysis is what stops most people from moving forward.

By choosing at least one of the end-of-chapter solutions, you're going to build a comprehensive plan that checks the most critical retirement planning boxes. There are no bad choices. You could check any of the boxes and be OK. To alleviate the potential for any anxiety, I made this process foolproof.

In total, I'm about to share with you *forty-eight proven strategies* you can use to create your dream retirement plan. You can select whatever you like from that menu and build a retirement plan that's your own unique combination of best practices!

At the end of the book in the Appendix, you be able to find a "Putting It All Together" section. This includes templates to help you prepare for your retirement race by writing your best story, and a Four-Minute Retirement Plan summary that you can fill out and personalize however you want.

CHAPTER SUMMARY

- Most retirement plans focus almost exclusively on a person's long-term goals, which means short-term wants and needs are often overlooked or cast aside.
- Present hedonism is living for the moment by indulging in activities you find novel, stimulating, and fun.
- Budgeting fun money as a short-term reward system is just as important as planning how to achieve your long-term goals because it provides the emotional fuel to help you stay on track.
- Allocate a portion of your income for activities you enjoy without feeling guilty and schedule time for present hedonism.
- Simplify your financial affairs by creating a concise financial plan, making it easy to understand and follow through.
- Commit to decisions quickly and avoid overthinking; the goal is to convert knowledge into action and eliminate hesitation.
- Understand that there are multiple correct ways to achieve financial success, so don't get stuck in analysis paralysis.
- Build a retirement plan that suits your unique needs and preferences, incorporating best practices and strategies that resonate with you.

SECTION III

THE SAVINGS LAP

CHAPTER 8
FOUR WAYS TO START SAVING MONEY

A penny saved is a penny earned.

—BENJAMIN FRANKLIN

A person's ability to delay gratification helps predict their future well-being.

That was the key finding of a 1972 study—"The Marshmallow Experiment"—led by a Stanford professor named Walter Mischel.

In the experiment, a child was asked to sit at a table where they were presented with a marshmallow. The researcher then told the child they were welcome to eat the marshmallow once they were alone in the room. But there was a catch—if the child could wait to eat the marshmallow until *after* the researcher returned, they would be given a second marshmallow.

Each child was then left alone in the room for fifteen minutes. During that time, the subjects' behavior varied. Some children ate the marshmallow right away. Others squirmed in their chairs for several minutes, then ate the marshmallow. Only a few children waited long enough to receive the second marshmallow.

The researchers stayed in touch with the children—tracking how they progressed in their lives over the following decades. Along the way, they noticed that their reactions to the marshmallow provided important clues about their respective futures.

The most striking finding pertained to the "second marshmallow kids," who in the experiment exhibited a unique ability to delay gratification. These kids went on to outperform their peers across a wide range of measurables, with:

- Better SAT scores
- Better physical condition
- Better handling of stress
- Better social skills

Second marshmallow kids understood that they could trade an enjoyable experience now for an even better experience later.

Delayed gratification is about trade-offs, and in the realm of financial planning, there's a name for it: **saving**. Being able to delay gratification in our financial lives means having the ability to set aside money now, knowing it will compound over time into more money we can use and enjoy in the future.

Why Saving Money Is So Important

The easiest way to make money is by saving money. That's why the first step to building wealth is learning how to save money effectively.

Let me lead with the bottom line: until you make expanding your net worth a priority, your money will always find ways to spend itself. There's a saying, "If you don't know where you are going, any road will get you there."

To put yourself on the right path to saving enough, we must first define how much is "enough." We need benchmarks. Otherwise, the simple act of saving any amount of money may feel like it's adequate, even if it almost certainly isn't.

The biggest life event people save for is their retirement. Everyone's number is different, but a good high-level benchmark for achieving financial freedom is saving between ten to twenty times your income. And since above-average inflation is common in many retirement spending categories, I think leaning closer to twenty times your income is smart. Quick napkin math: If you make $150,000 a year and enjoy your lifestyle, you'll probably need around $3 million at retirement to maintain your standard of living.

This is where we talk about budgeting. Here is an idea of how you should break down your spending:

50% Everyone needs to eat and a roof over their head. To save enough for the future, aim to keep essential expenses like these under 50 percent of take-home pay.

30% Not all gratification needs to be delayed. As I've written in previous chapters, people should reserve time and resources to be "present hedonistic." Enjoying life makes us better people and better workers. So, reserve about 30 percent of income for "wants" (e.g., travel, entertainment, etc.).

20% That leaves approximately 20 percent residual income you can apply to paying off debt and saving—in that order.

A creative way to organize this type of money flow is with a concept known as "reverse budgeting." The idea of reverse budgeting is simple and smart.

The first step of reverse budgeting is to max out a retirement plan using automated contributions. By saving for retirement automatically out of every paycheck, you're paying your future self (and tomorrow's bills) with today's income.

After that, the remaining money in your paycheck can be allocated toward anything else you need and want, and you don't have to feel bad about spending any of that money. Consider this a ticket to guilt-free consumption!

I'm a big fan of reverse budgeting as a retirement strategy because it makes saving your number one priority. Earning compound interest is absolutely the ticket to wealth accumulation over time, and the first step is building up your savings.

Tip: Depending on your age, you may want to slightly modify the 50/30/20 formula. For example, if you start saving for retirement in your twenties, you can probably allocate 10 percent of your income toward long-term savings. If you wait until your thirties, saving about 20 percent is prudent. If you wait until your forties, you'll likely need to save around 30 percent.

THE EARLIER YOU START, THE BETTER

"Saving for retirement may seem like a steep mountain to climb, but the climb doesn't have to be as steep as it looks," says Jeanne

Thompson, senior vice president of retirement insights at Fidelity. "Small steps now can turn into big strides later."

She's right.

The chart below shows how just $5,000 saved annually (or $417/month) over forty working years (ages twenty-five to sixty-five) grew into $1,137,570 (blue line in the chart below). This analysis assumes the person earns an annualized return of 7 percent.

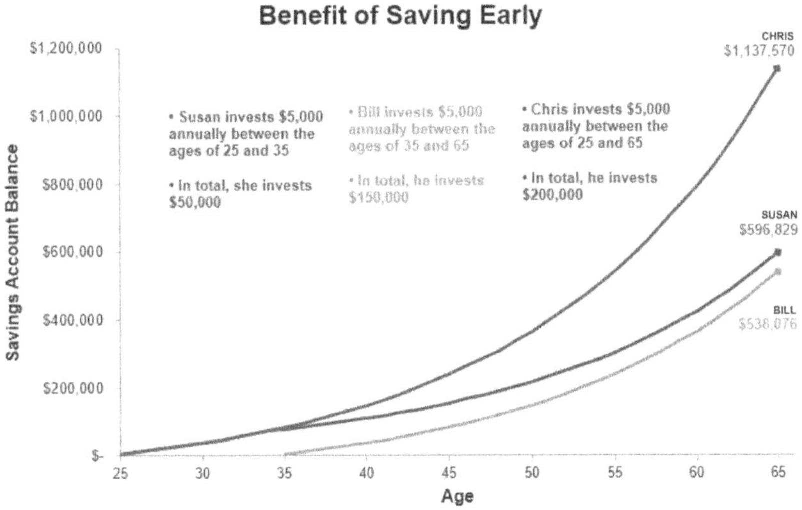

Interestingly, a person who saved $5,000/year for thirty years, from age thirty-five to sixty-five, ends up with nearly the same amount of money as a person who started ten years earlier but who only saved for ten years (ages twenty-five to thirty-five). The late bloomer saved $150,000 compared to the $50,000 saved by the early starter, but they both ended up with just under $600,000.

This example underscores the awesome power of compound interest. It also reveals that the real portfolio growth engine isn't some secret or complex strategy. It's just *time*.

AUTOMATION MAKES SAVING EASIER, AND WHERE YOU SAVE MATTERS

You can automate saving for retirement by treating it like another monthly subscription. If you pay $14.99 monthly for Netflix, Hulu, Dropbox or whatever, you're accustomed to pushing that expense to a credit card or checking account and letting the withdrawal happen without any thought.

Where you invest your savings also makes a big difference over time. Tax deferred vehicles, like IRAs and other retirement plans, are where you can achieve maximum compounding benefits.

According to the US Census Bureau, only 32 percent of Americans are currently saving for retirement via a 401(k). This number should be way higher.

If your employer offers a 401(k) program, you can contribute $18,500 annually in 2022. The numbers usually go up a little each year, so make it a point to set an annual reminder to check. After age fifty, the ceiling rises to $24,500, in what are known as "catch-up" contributions. Whatever your limit, it's wise to put aside as much as you can. Even if you don't have access to a 401(k), you can still open an IRA and enjoy similar tax benefits.

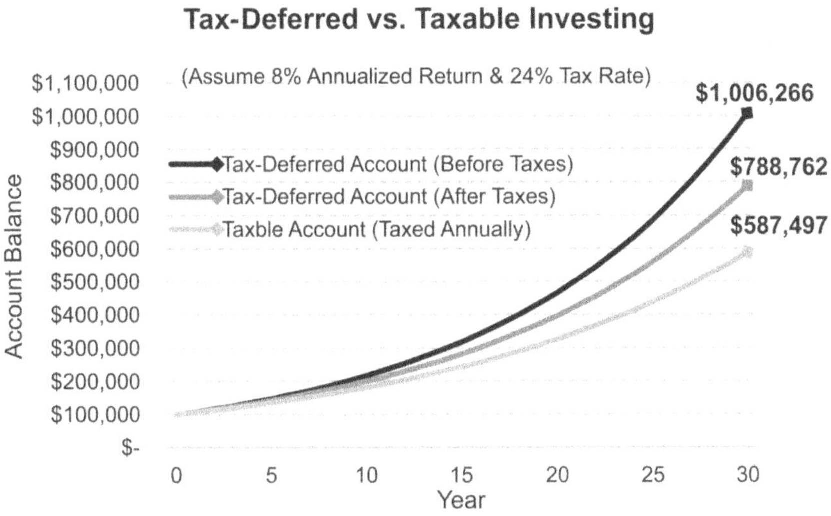

To make saving simpler, here are four effective solutions you can bank on.

#1: Automate Contributions to a 401(k)

An accidental retirement revolution began in 1978. That year, Congress passed the Revenue Act, which included a provision—Section 401(k)—providing employees a tax-free way to save money. By 1983, nearly half of large US companies offered their employees a 401(k) plan.

Today, there are trillions of dollars invested in America's 401(k) system. But only one in five people contributes enough to get a full company match, which means 80 percent of the folks in the system are turning down free money!

There's nothing complicated or intimidating about 401(k) plans. These are simply retirement accounts that employers set up to help their employees save more in a tax-efficient manner.

401(k) plans offer the following benefits:

- **Tax Advantage**. Remember when we talked earlier about how it takes money to make money? Well, the "money makes money principle" applies to 401(k)s because you can invest pretax funds. That means you can invest 25 to 40 percent more capital than you'd be able to allocate to an *after*-tax investment account. And since a 401(k) is a tax-deferred vehicle, you can invest and grow those extra funds for decades before having to pay taxes at the point of withdrawal.
- **Employer Match**. Many employers will match a portion of your 401(k) contributions. If this is available, it's equivalent to free money you don't want to ignore. Ask your human resources department what the company's matching policy is and try to maximize it. For example, your company may offer to match every dollar you invest up to 5 percent of your salary. So, if you make $75,000 a year and contribute $3,750 (5 percent), your employer will match and make your actual investment $7,500 per year.
- **Automation**. Automation makes saving money so much easier. The "out of sight, out of mind" principle applies here. If you allocate a consistent amount from your paycheck every month, you learn to live without it. Many companies are also beginning to recognize the benefit of automatically enrolling employees in 401(k) programs. Per a Vanguard study, the average participation rate in 401(k) plans with automatic enrollment is 91 percent, compared to only 28 percent in 401(k) plans with voluntary enrollment.[27] If your company only offers voluntary enrollment, don't be intimidated—it is not as hard as it seems, and you can always ask for help.

- **Flexibility**. The money you save in your 401(k) plan is portable if you switch jobs. You can convert a 401(k) to a Rollover IRA without any tax penalty. All you have to do is contact your financial advisor or brokerage firm and ask for help rolling over your 401(k).

To set up a 401(k), the first step is to contact your human resources department and ask for the paperwork to set up the account.* For now, just focus on making sure you have a tax-deferred savings account established. Later, in the Investing Lap section, we'll cover how to make appropriate investment selections.

The second step is to find out how much you're permitted to contribute each year and set that amount to be automatically deducted from your paycheck every month. Independent of whether your employer provides a match, it's worth taking advantage of the tax-deferred compounding benefits that a 401(k) plan offers.

Who Should Select This Option?

This option is appropriate for someone who wants to get started saving as easily as possible by tapping the most effective savings vehicle available.

---

* What if you are self-employed? A self-employed 401(k) is a good fit for sole proprietors and independent consultants who want to take advantage of similar benefits they'd enjoy from working at a larger company. You can usually set up a self-employed 401(k) through a major financial institution that administers 401(k) plans. Similar to self-employed 401(k)s, there are also Simple IRA and SEP IRA plans, which are tailored specifically for small business owners.

#2: Automate Contributions to Multiple Tax-Deferred Vehicles

In addition to 401(k) plans, other tax-advantaged savings vehicles include traditional and rollover IRAs, Roth IRAs, Health Savings Accounts (HSAs), and 529 plans.

A Traditional or Rollover IRA is one option. IRAs work like 401(k)s, in that contributions are made with pretax dollars and all your earnings grow tax-free. The contribution maximums are lower, however, with the maximum annual contribution of $6,000 in 2022 ($7,000 per year if you're over fifty).

Roth IRAs are another possible option. Roth IRAs are a bit different in that contributions are made with after-tax dollars and earnings grow tax-free. But unlike a Traditional IRA, you aren't taxed at the time of distribution. Saving in both IRAs and Roth IRAs can give you more control over your tax bracket in retirement, since you have pre- and post-tax dollars to choose from.[28]

Tip: A Roth IRA conversion makes sense if you anticipate being in a higher tax bracket in retirement. You pay taxes on the amount converted now, but withdrawals in retirement are tax-free. So, if you believe your tax rate will be higher when you retire, converting can save you money in the long run. It's always a good idea to consult with a financial and tax advisor before making such decisions.

There are also Health Savings Accounts (HSAs) that allow people in certain health insurance plans to save, invest, and spend money on a tax-free basis.[29] One caveat to be aware of is the money must be used for qualified healthcare expenses, so it's not as accessible as money saved in an IRA. However, with healthcare costs perennially rising, and folks in retirement spending a larger portion of income on healthcare, these accounts can shield your retirement assets from medical expenses later in life.

A final type of tax-deferred account to be aware of is called a 529 College Savings plan. These are structured like a Roth IRA but specifically meant for qualified higher education expenses. If you want to help children and grandchildren with college expenses, these vehicles are excellent. They have very high contribution limits, and all your after-tax contributions can grow and be distributed on a tax-free basis.

Tip: Money in a 529 plan can also be used to pay for elementary or high school tuition at private schools. And if a child doesn't attend college, parents can change the beneficiary to another child, a niece or nephew, a friend, or even themselves! Lots of flexibility here.

Below is a hypothetical example of two people with identical incomes. Jill steadily maximizes contributions across all the tax-deferred options available, while Jack only maximizes contributions to his 401(k). Even though they may have the same income and investment returns, Jill's $2,312,735 nest egg is 150 percent larger than Jack's aggregate savings after thirty years.

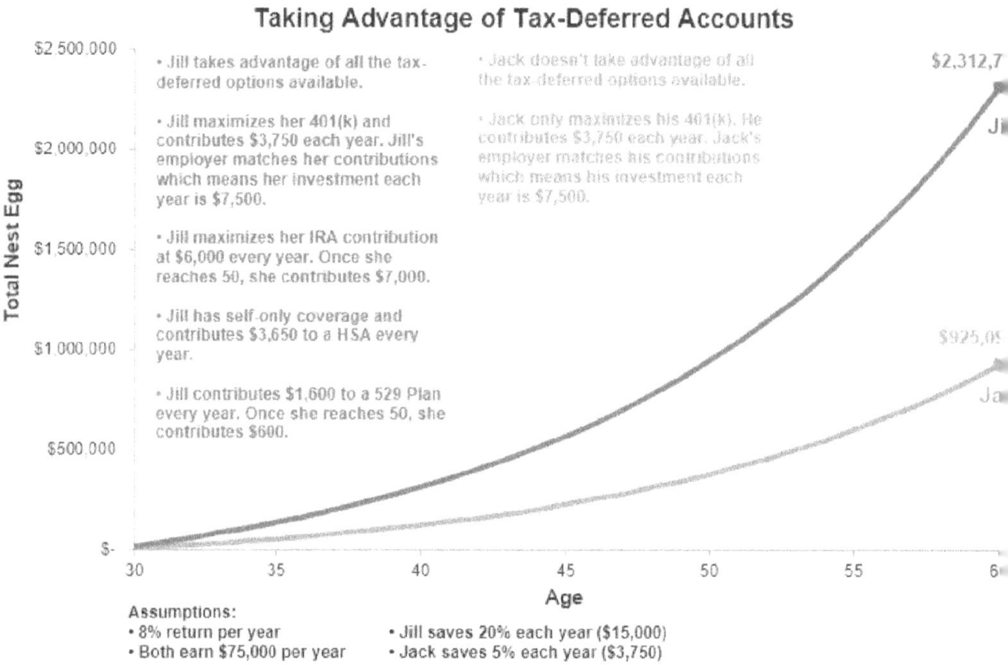

Taking Advantage of Tax-Deferred Accounts
• Jill takes advantage of all the tax-deferred options available.
• Jill maximizes her 401(k) and contributes $3,750 each year. Jill's employer matches her contributions which means her investment each year is $7,500.
• Jill maximizes her IRA contribution at $6,000 every year. Once she reaches 50, she contributes $7,000.
• Jill has self-only coverage and contributes $3,650 to a HSA every year.
• Jill contributes $1,600 to a 529 Plan every year. Once she reaches 50, she contributes $600.
• Jack doesn't take advantage of all the tax-deferred options available.
• Jack only maximizes his 401(k). He contributes $3,750 each year. Jack's employer matches his contributions which means his investment each year is $7,500.
Total Nest Egg
$2,500,000
$2,000,000
$1,500,000
$1,000,000
$500,000
$-
30
35
40
45
50
55
Age
Assumptions:
• 8% return per year
• Both earn $75,000 per year
• Jill saves 20% each year ($15,000)
• Jack saves 5% each year ($3,750)

Note: Contributions rules change over time. So, run a quick Google search to see what the current limits are.

Who Should Select This Option?

This option is appropriate for someone who wants to build their retirement nest egg more aggressively or who needs to play catch-up to their retirement goals.

#3: Maximize Retirement Contributions and Start an Emergency Savings Fund

For ambitious readers who aim to be in an even better financial position, this solution emphasizes maxing-out retirement contributions *and* creating an emergency savings fund.

An emergency savings fund is a highly liquid account where you keep between six months to twelve months' worth of living expenses. In general, the more volatile your income is, the higher your emergency savings account should be.

For example, if someone works in a commission-driven sales role, and they need $7,000 per month to cover all their expenses, then a good rule of thumb would be to save approximately $84,000 in cash or cash equivalents they can easily access. Even if they don't end up needing the money, this type of account provides peace of mind that life can go on as normal even if the unexpected happens.

An emergency savings account comes in handy when someone experiences things like an unexpected medical expense, home repair, car repair, or a sudden job loss.

The main benefit of an emergency savings account is it helps avoid the biggest financial trap out there—an unintended debt spiral. Research suggests that even minor financial shocks often turn into major shocks when people are forced to rely on credit cards or high-interest loans to cover unexpected expenses.

An emergency fund should be invested conservatively but that doesn't mean you must leave it all in cash. Other options to earn more interest over time include high-yield savings accounts, Certificates of Deposit (CDs), or short-duration US Treasury bonds. If you go any of these routes, it's important to know how quickly you can access your money and what restrictions may apply.

PRIORITIZE LONG-TERM RETIREMENT SAVINGS

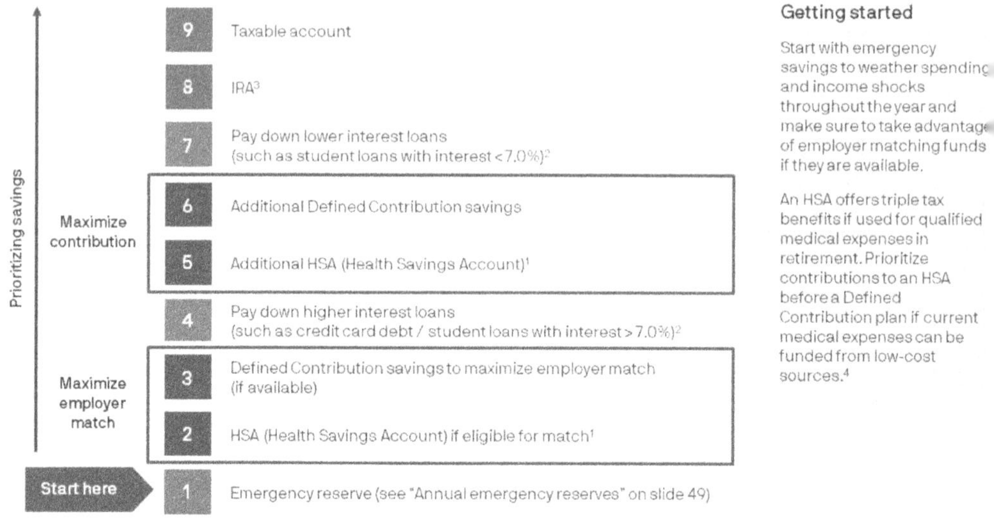

1 Must have a high-deductible health insurance plan that is eligible to be paired with an HSA. Those taking Social Security benefits age 65 or older and those who are on Medicare are inelig
Tax penalties apply for non-qualified distributions prior to age 65; consult IRS Publication 502 or your tax professional.
2 This assumes that a diversified portfolio may earn 7.0% over the long term. Actual returns may be higher or lower. Generally, consider making additional payments on loans with a higher inte
rate than your long-term expected investment return.
3 Income limits may apply for IRAs. If ineligible for these, consider a non-deductible IRA or an after-tax 401(k) contribution. Individual situations will vary; consult your tax professional.
4. Examples of low-cost funding souces include cash and current income.
Source: J.P. Morgan Asset Management analysis. Not intended to be a personal financial plan.

Source: JPMorgan's 2022 Guide to Retirement

Who Should Select This Option?

This option is appropriate for someone who wants to expand their savings beyond just tax-advantaged accounts. It's also ideal for readers with a "safety-first" mindset who see value in establishing an emergency savings account to improve their sleep-at-night factor.

#4: Maximize Retirement Contributions and Start a Scarcity Fund

This solution is the same as the previous one but adds an additional creative twist. Here you fully fund all tax-deferred vehicles available to you and create what I call a "scarcity fund."

The purpose of a scarcity fund is to sustain you through any tough period when money grows scarce. But instead of keeping all the money in cash or cash-equivalent reserves, you invest approximately half in cash and the other half in scarce assets.

The latter could be any type of collectible or "treasure asset." Examples: art, fine wine, classic cars, baseball cards, memorabilia, precious metals, jewelry, etc. There are only two requirements: (i) the asset must be in scarce or limited supply, and (ii) you must enjoy owning it.

In the event a crisis does show up on your doorstep, you can deal with it by first tapping into your most liquid cash reserves (since half of your scarcity fund is allocated to cash-like instruments). Then, if you need more than that (because it's the kind of problem that lingers), you sell your treasure assets if necessary.

Treasure assets with scarce supply features are not easy to recreate. Thus, they generally hold their value over time.

The other benefit of naming your emergency reserves a "scarcity fund" is it will serve as a reminder for the rest of your life of an important economic lesson, and that is: **scarcity creates value**. I don't care if you're investing in companies, collectibles, or your career: it always pays to favor assets with special traits that can't be easily duplicated. These are the types of investments that compound best and most reliably.

I already have a scarcity fund established for my children in the form of their comic books. Spider-Man and Batman comic books from the 1960s are valued by collectors because they can't be reproduced—so they retain value. My kids enjoy owning them, and we could sell them on eBay if we absolutely needed to.

Meanwhile, my kids enjoy tracking how their comics have increased in value over time. This is teaching them to appreciate the benefits that come from delayed gratification. They're learning how to be second marshmallow kids.

Guess what? It's never too late to become a second marshmallow kid. So, hop to it! And once you've mastered the skill, pass it on to someone you care about.

Who Should Select This Option?

Readers who want to combine the benefits of tax deferred compounding with a form of emergency savings that is more fun to own than just cash.

■ ■

Now that we've reached the end of the chapter, it's time for you to practice taking action.

In twenty seconds or less, pick whichever of the four solutions we just reviewed you think is the best fit to help you save more money. Remember: There are no bad choices!

Building your four-minute retirement plan is a mission of progress over perfection.

THE SAVINGS LAP

For each category, pick whichever of the four solutions is the best fit for you in twenty seconds or less.

Four strategies to start saving money:

- ☐ #1: Automate Contributions to a 401(k)
- ☐ #2: Automate Contributions to Multiple Tax-deferred Vehicles
- ☐ #3: Maximize Retirement Contributions and Start an Emergency Savings Fund
- ☐ #4: Maximize Retirement Contributions and Start a Scarcity Fund

Four strategies to manage debt wisely:

- ☐ #1: Pay Off High Interest Rate Debt First
- ☐ #2: Dave Ramsey's Snowball Method
- ☐ #3: Consolidate Your Debts
- ☐ #4: Pay Off Bad Debt and Add Good Debt

Four strategies for choosing a financial advisor:

- ☐ #1: Be Your Own Financial Advisor
- ☐ #2: Hire a Robo-Advisor
- ☐ #3: Choose a Fiduciary Advisor
- ☐ #4: Choose a Fiduciary Advisor with Advanced Credentials

00:20

CHAPTER SUMMARY

- Ability to delay gratification helps predict a person's future well-being.
- To put yourself on the right path to saving enough, we must first define how much is "enough."
- A good high-level benchmark for achieving financial freedom is saving between ten to twenty times your income.
- The first step of reverse budgeting is to max-out a retirement plan using automated contributions. You can automate saving for retirement by treating it like another monthly subscription.
- The earlier you start saving the better. Time is a critical driver of long-term compounding.
- In addition to 401(k) plans, other tax-advantaged savings vehicles include traditional and rollover IRAs, Roth IRAs, Health Savings Accounts (HSAs), and 529 plans.
- An emergency savings fund is a highly liquid account where you keep between six months to twelve months' worth of living expenses. In general, the more volatile your income is, the higher your emergency savings account should be.
- The purpose of a scarcity fund is to sustain you through any tough period when money grows scarce. But instead of keeping all the money in cash or cash-equivalent reserves, you invest approximately half in cash and the other half in scarce assets.
- There are only two requirements for including an asset into a scarcity fund: (i) the asset must be in scarce or limited supply, and (ii) you must enjoy owning it.

CHAPTER 9
HOW TO DISTINGUISH GOOD DEBT FROM BAD DEBT

Debt is one person's liability, but another person's asset.

—PAUL KRUGMAN

When Daniela Capparelli graduated from the University of Hartford in 2007, she planned to use her degree in economics and finance to land a good job. She was determined to set herself on a solid financial path.

Instead, she experienced one of life's U-turns.

Shortly after Daniela graduated, the 2008 financial crisis ensued, and the US unemployment rate surged. Daniela entered an ultra-crummy job market carrying $150,000 in student debt. To pay it off, she would owe $1,498 a month for thirty years.

Now thirty-five-years old, Daniela says, "My student loans have been the center of my financial world. I have always felt a huge weight on my shoulders because of this astronomical financial burden."

In Hillary Hoffower's *Business Insider* article titled, "How the American Millennial is Overcoming Debt, the Dollar, and the

Economy They Were Handed," it's made clear that Daniela's story is more of a rule than an exception. Millennials are only about 80 percent as wealthy as their parents were at a similar age, and the main reason is debt.

As of 2019, there was a staggering $1.5 trillion in outstanding student loan debt alone. Over the past forty years, the cost of attending college has doubled. Daniela would go on to spend the first five years of her postgraduation life devoting about 50 percent of her income to student loan payments. *Half* of her income—just to cover student debt!

To be fair, people with college degrees can expect to earn, on average, more than those with only a high school diploma. The median income for a full-time worker, aged twenty-two to twenty-seven, with a bachelor's degree is $52,000 according to a 2022 Federal Reserve Bank of New York study. For people with high school diplomas in the same age group, it's $30,000.

This wage gap is substantial, but so is the debt that often saddles college graduates for decades. There was a time in America when a college degree was considered a sensible, reliable ticket to an above-average income. Nowadays, though, evaluating the utility of advanced education requires more of a pro-and-con-style analysis. As the costs rise, so do the cons.

The takeaway from stories like Daniela's is troubling: millennials are on track to be the first generation *not* to exceed their parents' standard of living in terms of inflation-adjusted income. Many from this generation have had to delay key life milestones like buying a home, saving for retirement, and even getting married.

In a *Bloomberg* article titled, "Millennials Are Running Out of Time to Build Wealth," Olivia Rockeman and Catarina Saraiva offered a side-by-side comparison of the two mega-generations. In inflation-adjusted terms, millennials are lagging across a variety of key measurables.

	MILLENNIALS AT AGE 40	BOOMERS AT AGE 40
A year of college	$24,600	$10,300
Own a home	61%	66%
Cost of a home	$328,000	$216,000
Middle age net worth	$91,000	$113,000
Own stocks	14%	17%

■ ■

Unfortunately, student loan debt isn't the only liability millennials need to worry about.

In 2019, I interviewed *Wall Street Journal* columnist Joseph Sternberg on behalf of *Forbes*. I was intrigued by the title of his book, *The Theft of a Decade: How the Baby Boomers Stole the Millennials' Economic Future*.

Since the 1980s, the Baby Boom generation has been in charge of America's political agenda. But that will soon change as more millennials assume key leadership posts.

Mr. Sternberg, born in 1982, is himself a millennial. In his book, he outlines the economic challenges his generation has faced in the aftermath of the Great Recession of 2008. According to Mr. Sternberg, millennials want to get ahead economically like their parents did. They want to be able to buy a home, raise a family, and retire comfortably.

Baby Boomers' policy interests are narrower. Mainly, they want to retire comfortably and receive government benefits they've been promised for decades.

A key problem facing both generations, however, is the US government's debt burden, which stands at $29 trillion and counting. The official figure is huge, and it doesn't even count the true elephant in the room, which is the $160 trillion in unfunded liabilities needed to pay for entitlement programs like Social Security, Medicaid, and Medicare.

Here is an excerpt from my interview with Mr. Sternberg:

> **Me**: Do you think the ultimate solution will have to involve cutting benefits as part of a necessary compromise between the two generations?
>
> **Sternberg**: It's a discussion that's going to have to happen. And I think the Boomers are in real danger of regretting all the opportunities that they missed to reform these entitlement programs on their terms.
>
> There have been numerous discussions over the years about various ways one could tweak the programs. There were the Bush Era efforts to reform Social Security. And there's been occasional talk about means testing benefits to avoid draining the coffers.
>
> Boomers always shot those ideas down because they thought they had created an environment where everyone believed that entitlement reform was the political third rail, and that the generations after them would be equally afraid of touching it. Eventually, you run into a reality constraint where if Millennials can't pay these bills, we won't.
>
> **Me**: That's a pretty simple way of framing it.

Sternberg: This is the story of several canaries in the coal mine I point to in the book, at the state and local level. Places like Detroit discovered that after you reach a point where you're bankrupt and must make cuts somewhere, everything comes back on the table.

So, I do think Boomers are going to regret those missed opportunities. They're going to realize that the options were not to reform then, or draw down all these benefits. The options were to reform then on their terms, or reform at some point in the future on Millennials' terms.

In the years since the 2008 financial crisis, which many consider a debt-bubble, the US government has almost tripled the amount of debt it carries on its balance sheet. Meanwhile, the Congressional Budget office projects Federal Debt relative to GDP to keep rising into unchartered territory for the foreseeable future. Financial leverage is rampant across the US economy.

FEDERAL DEBT HELD BY THE PUBLIC AS A % OF GDP, 1900-2051

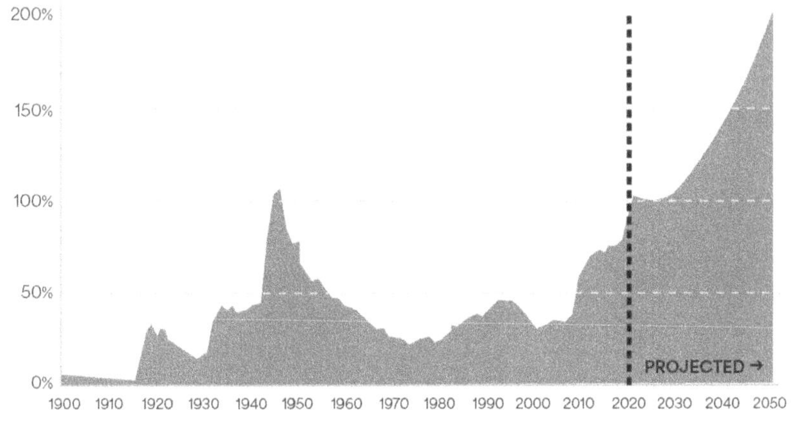

Source: Congressional Budget Office

The recent surge in US debt comes on the eve of entitlement expenses kicking into a higher gear. But what if the retirement system's habit of front-loading benefits and back-loading payments backfires someday? To understand why this is likely, all you have to do is run the math using the government's own numbers.

Per the Congressional Budget Office's projections, net interest on debt is expected to consume 27 percent of the total federal budget by 2051. That would cost more than all other discretionary spending *combined*, including important things like the defense, transportation, and education budgets.

This probably all seems quite harrowing, I know. But that's also the point. Taking stock of the shaky fiscal outlook should ignite your desire to strengthen your own balance sheet. Learning how to distinguish good debt from bad debt is a crucial step in this process.

Good Debt versus Bad Debt

> *Bad debt is debt that makes you poorer. I count the mortgage on my home as bad debt, because I'm the one paying on it. Other forms of bad debt are car payments, credit card balances, or other consumer loans.*
>
> —**ROBERT KIYOSAKI**

As we reviewed in the Retirement 101 chapter, there is an accounting relationship that everyone who wants to achieve financial freedom must understand:

Assets – Liabilities = **Equity**

Equity makes you richer. That's what increases your net worth. Unfortunately, we don't do a great job as a country in hammering this concept home. In fact, the opposite is true.

The federal government has many programs that encourage folks to borrow more. Federally funded student loan programs, FHA home loans, the ability to write off mortgage loan interest—all of these are programs designed to incentivize taking on more debt.

But is the most *indebted* person living on your block the richest? Probably not. The richest person on your block is whoever's assets exceed their liabilities by the widest margin.

To retire well, you need to learn how to intelligently manage your assets and liabilities to build up equity (i.e., your net worth). To build up more assets than liabilities, you need to know how to distinguish between the two.

Here is a simple litmus test:

- **Assets** put money *into* your pocket.
- **Liabilities** take money *out* of your pocket.

It's all about cash flow.

Many people wonder: Is a personal residence an asset or liability?

Your home is a liability because it costs you money to live there. It takes money out of your pocket.

On the other hand, if you own an investment property that generates positive cash flow, that would be an asset—because it's putting more money into your pocket than it's taking out.

To figure out where you stand, look at all your debt balances and label them either "good" or "bad" using the above definitions as a guide.

GOOD DEBT EXAMPLES

It's fitting that "debt" is a four-letter word because the debt narrative is mostly negative.

Even just the word … debt … has kind of a stomach-churning ring, doesn't it?

But it shouldn't be that way because debt isn't universally bad. In fact, some debt is actually good and worth having on your balance sheet. It depends on what type of debt it is, and how you're using it.

Good debt is any form of financial leverage you can use to derive a higher expected return than the cost of capital.

For example, if you have cash you can use to either pay off a mortgage with an annual interest rate of 4 percent or invest into a strategy with an expected annual return of 8 percent, which would you choose?

In this example, you can earn a positive return—and put money into your pocket—by keeping the mortgage debt and investing the money. This is because you're borrowing at a lower rate than you earn by investing the dollars—pocketing the difference.

Another example of good debt might be student loan debt for medical school. According to the American Medical Association, medical school debt often reaches $200,000 or more. That's a lot of money coming out of your pocket, but it should also generate a lot more money flowing in later. According to the Medscape Physician Compensation Survey of 2022, physician salaries on the low-end were $240,000/year, while on the high-end (for plastic surgeons) they reached $576,000 a year.

Bridge loans are another common type of good debt.

For instance, I have a retired client who recently wanted to buy a new home, and she was presented with two options.

1. Take out a bridge loan to buy the new house, knowing that her old house—once sold—would generate enough proceeds to pay off the new loan in full; or,

2. Sell investments to pay for the new house.

My client chose the first option because the economics were better.

The loan helped her avoid transaction costs, taxes, and the opportunity cost of selling investments. And since the interest rate on the bridge loan was relatively low, a minimal amount of money left her pocket in the process.

Which brings us to one of the biggest debt decisions a person will ever make: buying a home.

Owning a home provides the opportunity for price appreciation over time and experiential perks—such as a feeling of stability and freedom to make property improvements.

On the other hand, there are also costs associated with owning real estate. These include broker fees, moving expenses, property taxes, maintenance costs, and the opportunity cost of not being able to invest a down payment.

For people with long time horizons, many of these costs will eventually be outpaced by the benefits of price appreciation. But this takes time. Generally, you should only buy a property if you will be content living there for at least five years.

As for how much house you can afford, aim for a house payment that is 25 percent or less of your monthly take-home pay. That leaves room in your budget to cover maintenance costs while still saving for things like retirement. If you budget appropriately, steadily paying down principal allows you to gradually build up equity.

BAD DEBT EXAMPLES

One way to segment debt is by differentiating between installment debt and revolving debt.

- Installment debt is the kind you pay over a set period of time, like a student loan or a mortgage.
- Revolving debt is the kind with no end date—e.g., a credit card.

Tip: Revolving debt is almost always bad!

As I'm writing this, the average annual percentage rate (APR) on credit cards in the US is over 16 percent. Most credit card debt is used to buy stuff—e.g., furniture, home appliances, toys, food, gas, etc. Consumers rarely earn a return on such items, so they are sunk costs.

To turn credit card debt into good debt, you would have to buy something that reliably nets you a greater than 16 percent return. Good luck with that.

Car loans also have potential to become bad debt. It's safe to assume that the moment you drive a new car off the lot, it's worth 10 percent less than what you bought it for. Taking on debt to buy a depreciating asset like that strains your balance sheet.

As a general rule, try to own appreciating assets and rent depreciating assets.

Here's where a potential caveat comes into play: say you pay off a car loan in five years but keep the car for fifteen years. In that case, you've got ten years of no car payments other than repairs, registration, and insurance. No debt also qualifies as good debt.

However, if you pay off your car loan, then immediately decide to trade it in for a new one—and a whole new set of payments—you're likely to fall into a bad debt loop.

Thus, if you're the type of person who likes getting a new car every few years, you're probably better off leasing a vehicle.

Another form of bad debt is a reverse mortgage. A reverse mortgage doesn't feel like debt at all, since people with reverse mortgages have money going into their pocket. Thing is, that money is actually borrowed money that has to be paid back, with interest. So, it's just another form of debt.

Reverse mortgages are generally marketed to retirees, since older people tend to have a lot of built-up equity in their homes and frequently need extra sources of income. A reverse mortgage sounds appealing in these cases—simply withdraw equity from your home to boost your cash flows.

But it's not really that straightforward. "Withdrawing equity" in a reverse mortgage actually means taking out a loan and pledging your home equity as collateral. That gives the lender a stake in your home, or if you pass away, a potential stake in your heirs' assets. After all, all loans must be repaid eventually.

Most retirees should avoid taking on interest-bearing debt. No matter how you slice it, increasing debt will always increase your risk profile. Why potentially jeopardize your Golden Years? Plus, the whole point of wealth management is to build *equity* over time.

Here are four strategies to manage debt wisely.

#1: Pay Off High Interest Rate Debt First

Most debt obligations require a minimum monthly payment. To protect your credit score, you must honor those. However, any extra cash flow you can muster on top of those payments should be allocated toward debt reduction.

Not all debt is created equal. One way to pay off debt is to prioritize payments based on the interest rates. Debt with higher interest rates should be knocked out first. So, if you're saddled with car loans, credit card debt, or other forms of high interest debt, rank them by their respective interest rates. Then create a plan to pay off your high interest debt first.

NAME OF DEBT	TOTAL AMOUNT	APR	MINIMUM PAYMENT

For instance, if I had credit card debt of $30,000 with a 24 percent APR and a car loan of $8,000 with a 9 percent APR, I'd want to pay off the credit card first.

There's no sense in spreading your payments equally over all your debt accounts. Make the minimum payments on your "less bad" debt. After you pay off your debt with the highest interest rate, go to work on the next debt with the second highest interest rate, and so on.

Who Should Select This Option?

Readers who want to make the biggest dent possible in the amount of interest they pay.

#2: Dave Ramsey's Snowball Method

Dave Ramsey is one of the most successful personalities in personal finance today. He is the author of multiple *New York Times* bestselling books and hosts a nationally syndicated radio broadcast.

For Ramsey, helping people conquer their debt burdens is a very personal mission. In 1988, he became overleveraged with too many loans and lines of credit that suddenly came due. When he was unable to pay, he was forced to file for bankruptcy.

However, Ramsey quickly turned his adversity around and found a silver lining. That same year, he founded the Lampo Group, a financial counseling service. And in 1992, he wrote and self-published his first book, *Financial Peace.*

Ramsey knows how hard it is to climb out of debt. It can feel overwhelming. That is why Ramsey endorses a unique approach for paying off debt. His "Snowball Method" prioritizes paying off debts with the lowest balances first—rather than the highest interest rates—to help build psychological momentum.

So, let's say you have two credit cards with balances of $2,000 and $10,000, respectively.

- The card with the $2,000 balance has an APR of 16 percent.
- The card with the $10,000 balance has an APR of 19 percent.

Using Ramsey's approach, you would pay off the card with the $2,000 balance first. Even though this is financially inefficient because the interest rate is higher on the other card, being able to cut up and rid yourself of the smaller card can help provide a sense of accomplishment and motivational lift.

Who Should Select This Option?

Readers who often feel overwhelmed by their debt and like the idea of a mini-step approach to climbing out of debt.

#3: Consolidate Your Debts

Another possibility is getting a personal loan you can use to pay off all your bad debt at once.

Consolidating your debts into a single loan is a great way to streamline your finances. It reduces the number of payments and interest rates you have to worry about and provides one number you can focus on to get debt free. You also may be able to negotiate a more attractive interest rate compared to your other loans.

For example, if you have four credit cards with total debt of $45,000 and an average APR of 18 percent, and you can get a personal loan of $45,000 with an APR of 11.5 percent, it probably makes sense to take the loan and pay off all the credit cards.

Be advised, however, that debt consolidation can also entail added costs such as origination fees, balance transfer fees, and closing costs. So, if you choose to go this route, shop around for lenders, and make sure you understand the full costs before signing on the dotted line.

Who Should Select This Option?

Readers who want to simplify their debt payments. Also, if your credit score has improved since you took out your original loans, you may be able to qualify for debt consolidation at a lower interest rate.

#4: Pay Off Bad Debt and Add Good Debt

As we touched on earlier, some debts are good.

For example, if you're ready to settle down and start a family, buying a home may be a good idea. In that case, a mortgage can be beneficial.

Mortgages can act like a forced savings account. Over the last century, amortizing mortgages were the primary form of wealth accumulation for America's middle class. By steadily paying down principal, people build up equity. There are also tax deductions for mortgage interest.

One way to assess whether mortgage debt qualifies as a good debt is to compare the relative cost of owning versus renting in your local area. When it comes to real estate, each region has its own set of supply and demand factors to weigh. When it's cheaper to own versus rent, taking on mortgage debt to buy a home is inherently less risky because the potential for price appreciation is greater. Conversely, when it's relatively cheaper to rent in your area, taking on mortgage debt to purchase property is riskier.

Who Should Select This Option?

Readers who feel financially secure, have little or no revolving debt, and have a long enough time horizon (i.e., more than five years) to make a mortgage economically sensible.

■ ■

Now that we've covered how to think about debt, it's time for you to utilize this knowledge and practice taking action!

In twenty seconds or fewer, pick one of the four solutions to help you manage debt more wisely.

THE SAVINGS LAP

For each category, pick whichever of the four solutions is the best fit for you in twenty seconds or less.

Four strategies to start saving money:

- ☐ #1: Automate Contributions to a 401(k)
- ☐ #2: Automate Contributions to Multiple Tax-deferred Vehicles
- ☐ #3: Maximize Retirement Contributions and Start an Emergency Savings Fund
- ☐ #4: Maximize Retirement Contributions and Start a Scarcity Fund

Four strategies to manage debt wisely:

- ☐ #1: Pay Off High Interest Rate Debt First
- ☐ #2: Dave Ramsey's Snowball Method
- ☐ #3: Consolidate Your Debts
- ☐ #4: Pay Off Bad Debt and Add Good Debt

Four strategies for choosing a financial advisor:

- ☐ #1: Be Your Own Financial Advisor
- ☐ #2: Hire a Robo-Advisor
- ☐ #3: Choose a Fiduciary Advisor
- ☐ #4: Choose a Fiduciary Advisor with Advanced Credentials

00:40

CHAPTER SUMMARY

- Millennials are less wealthy than their parents due to increasing debt.
- The US government's debt and unfunded liabilities pose challenges for future generations.
- The richest person on your block isn't whoever has the most debt; it's whoever has the highest net worth.
- Assets put money into your pocket, whereas liabilities take money out of your pocket.
- Good debt examples include investments with higher returns than the cost of borrowing and student loans for high-paying careers.
- Bad debt examples include credit cards, car loans, and reverse mortgages.
- Try to rent depreciating assets and own appreciating assets.
- If you want to buy a house, make sure you intend to live there for at least five years, and aim for a housing payment that is 25 percent or less of your monthly take-home pay.
- Strategies to manage debt include paying off the highest interest rate debt first, using Dave Ramsey's Snowball Method, consolidating debts, and adding good debt.

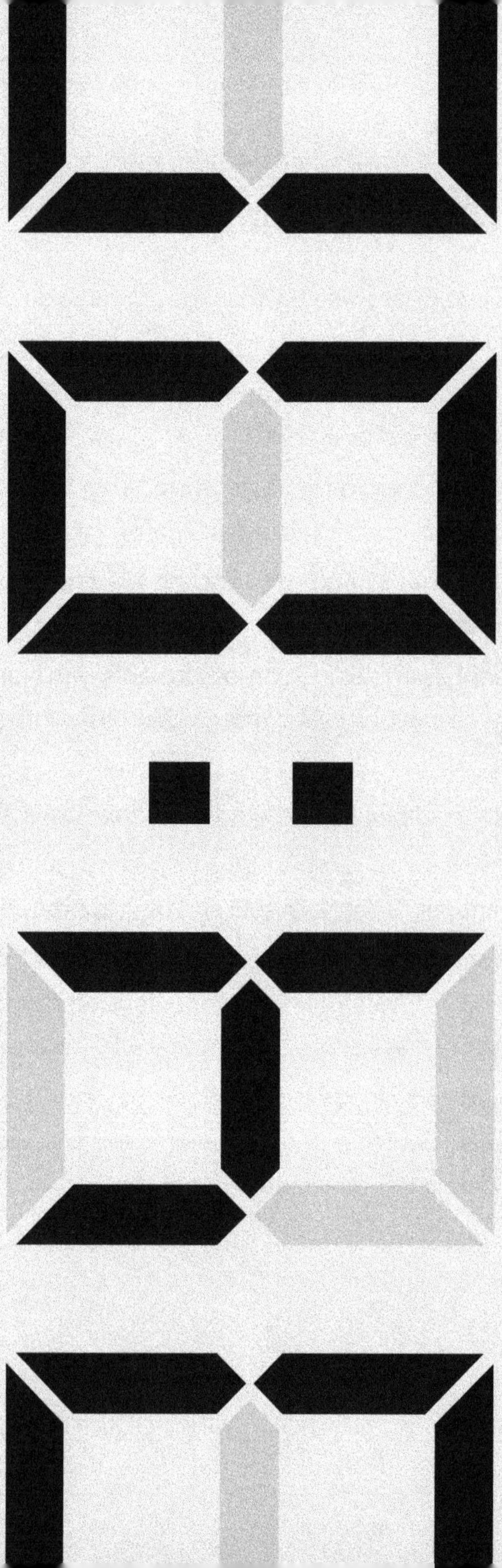

CHAPTER 10
FINDING FINANCIAL ADVISORS WHO PAY FOR THEMSELVES

It's hard to trust something you can't look in the eyes.

—JOHN GLENN

In 2008, I was a twenty-nine-year-old equity analyst for Fisher Investments. Back then, I covered a sizable list of stocks, but it was also my job to occasionally travel around the country and host investment roundtable meetings with groups of clients. The Global Financial Crisis was well underway, so a lot of the meetings lasted over three hours, and some got emotional.

That year, almost everyone was worried about the economy. Baby Boomers in particular felt like the crisis was just a pile-on to their already unsettled feelings about the future. Here's an excerpt from a June 2008 Pew Research Center survey. Keep in mind this survey was conducted *before* the actual crisis began:

> Members of the large generation born from 1946 to 1964 are more downbeat about their lives than are adults who are younger or older ... Not only do boomers give their overall

> quality of life a lower rating than adults in other generations, they also are more likely to worry that their incomes won't keep up with inflation – this despite the fact that boomers enjoy the highest incomes of any age group.
>
> More so than those in other generations, boomers believe it is harder to get ahead now than it was ten years ago. And they are less apt than others to say their standard of living exceeds the one their parents had when their parents were the age they are now.
>
> —Pew Research Survey, "Baby Boomers: The Gloomiest Generation"[30]

If this survey was taken before the biggest economic crash since the Great Depression, how do you think those Boomers felt *after* that?

Most clients wanted to know when the market would bottom—a question I obviously could not answer.

What I could do, however, was leverage my knowledge of markets and investor psychology to help folks better cope with the uncertainty they were feeling. That included looking people in the eye, being a good listener, and always empathizing before I attempted to educate someone.

One meeting in Dallas was particularly memorable. A gentleman in his fifties raised his hand and asked if he should sell his family's shares in General Electric. At the time, the stock was down over 70 percent from its high.

Before answering his question, I asked questions to learn more about his story. Along the way, he told me that GE wasn't just another position in his portfolio—it was a *big* position. GE shares were the cornerstone of his family's wealth and had been passed down through generations. This made him feel an extra sense of responsibility to do the right thing.

Once I understood the backstory, I knew I would try to convince him to hold the shares. Not because a computer model said so, and not because the stock's P/E was low. The reason I thought he should hold on was because he was emotionally conflicted, and that's almost never a good time to make a major financial decision. If he wanted to sell, there would be a better time to do so.

Rather than just telling him what I thought he should do, though, I probed more so he could figure it out for himself.

I asked, "Did your family own GE shares through the Depression?"

He said yes.

"How do you think your grandfather felt during that period?"

His demeanor shifted as he thought about it. I noticed his shoulders drop and his tone softened. "Not good," he calmly replied. That was my opportunity to start drifting toward logic.

Then we talked about why the economy in 2008 wasn't nearly as bad as it was during the Depression, and why I thought GE's balance sheet was stronger than Lehman Brothers' (which had recently gone bankrupt).

I'll never know for sure if the man in Dallas held onto his GE shares. But I do know he left that meeting in better shape to make the decision compared to when he arrived. And that's the role of a financial advisor—we help people make more informed decisions.

When someone is in a highly emotional state, logic has a hard time breaking through. You learn that when you're a real person, dealing with real people, during a treacherous bear market. You also learn that showing up, looking folks in the eye, and coupling empathy with education can help people make better financial decisions.

Financial Advisors Worth Hiring Pay for Themselves

Hiring a financial advisor is one of the most important financial decisions a person can make.

Top advisors can supercharge your efforts to grow wealth. For years, Vanguard has published research that seeks to quantify an "Advisor's Alpha," or how much additional *net* return a quality advisor can generate for a client—assuming the advisor follows best practices.[31]

The detailed breakdown below shows how advisors can have the most impact:

VANGUARD ADVISOR'S ALPHA STRATEGY	TYPICAL VALUE ADDED FOR CLIENT (BASIS POINTS)
Behavioral coaching	0 to > 200
Spending strategy (withdrawal order)	0 to 120
Asset location	0 to 60
Cost-effective implementation (expense ratios)	30
Rebalancing	14
Suitable asset allocation using broadly diversified funds/ETFs	> 0*
Total return versus income investing	> 0*
Range of potential value added (basis points)	**Up to, or even exceed, 3% in net returns**

** Value is deemed significant but too unique to each investor to quantify*

Source: Vanguard.

More than anything else, investors tend to benefit from behavioral coaching.

The investor's chief problem—and even his worst enemy—is likely to be himself.

—BENJAMIN GRAHAM

Investors make predictable mistakes. According to the research firm DALBAR, which has studied behavioral bias for decades, the average investor switches strategies too often ("chasing heat"), systematically under-allocates to equities, and usually sells at inopportune times. Poorly reasoned decisions pile up over time, causing significant underperformance.

For the thirty-year period spanning January 1991 to December 2020, DALBAR found the average equity fund investor achieved a 7.1 percent annual return, compared to a 10.7 percent annual return for the S&P 500 Index. Meanwhile, the average bond investor achieved a paltry 0.3 percent annual return compared to an annual 5.3 percent return for the Bloomberg US Aggregate Bond Index.[32]

Peter Lynch managed the Fidelity Magellan Fund from 1977 to 1990, generating about a 29 percent average annualized return. Yet, according to a study by Fidelity Investments, the average investor in the Magellan Fund managed to *lose* money over that period. The problem was investors tended to buy the fund after hot performance streaks and sell during cold streaks.

The DALBAR study and investors' experience with the Magellan Fund remind us that it's easy to mistime the market. Market cycles are an emotional roller coaster. And on this roller coaster, you often feel like doing the exact wrong thing at the exact wrong time.

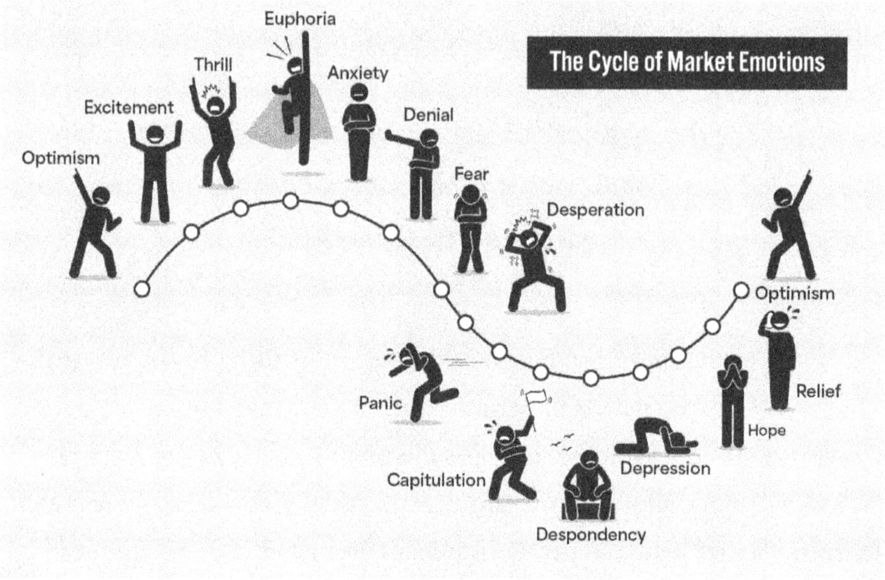

Source: iStock Getty Images

A financial advisor worth his or her salt will help prevent timing mistakes by providing perspective at every turn, reminding investors how emotional responses often work in direct opposition not only to logic, but also to your long-term interests.

Behavioral coaching was what the gentleman I met in Dallas needed. His problem wasn't really GE, nor the financial crisis. His problem was an emotional fog that clouded his judgment. My job in that moment was to help him find his way out of the fog so he could look at his investment more objectively, unencumbered from the survival mind.

That's also one of my goals for you with this book.

It's easy to underestimate how important the behavioral side of wealth management is. I'll give you one more example from recent history.

In the early depths of the 2020 COVID-19 pandemic, many investors became so frightened by the sharp and sudden market declines—paired with media hysterics—that they liquidated their funds just before the market bottom in March, locking in huge losses. As shown below, equity fund outflows surged just before the market turned up (at the exact wrong time). Behavioral coaching could have prevented this.

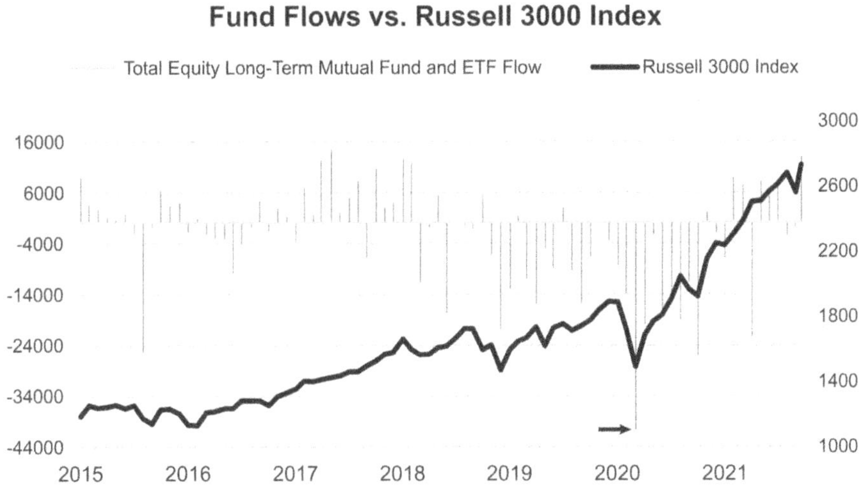

Source: Bloomberg

To sum up, an excellent financial advisor can add value that far exceeds what they charge in fees, and this should be your goal if you choose to work with one.

We've established that behavioral coaching is a key attribute to look for. Hiring an advisor with a defined strategy, a verifiable track record, and substantive experience also matters a lot.

But with 380,000 financial advisors in the US as of 2021, actually picking one can be a daunting task. With so many options to choose from, how do you pick the right advisor for you?

Four Strategies for Choosing a Financial Advisor

To steer your financial ship in the right direction and maximize the probability of landing at your target destination, someone always needs to be at the helm. Here are four strategies for putting the right person in charge of your portfolio.

#1: Be Your Own Financial Advisor

The first strategy is not to hire an advisor at all and assume all the responsibility yourself.

In this case, the job would be the same for you as it would be for a hired professional. You need to regularly evaluate your goals and financial position, select an appropriate asset allocation that is suitable for pursuing your objectives, and manage a portfolio of securities.

That means you must manage investments in your brokerage and other personal accounts (and those of your spouse, if applicable); run regular analysis to ensure you're on track to meet your goals; establish a research regimen and buy-sell disciplines; keep track of changes to tax laws and retirement account rules; and develop a strategy for generating income and cash flows later in life to fund retirement. Just to name a few of the responsibilities.

Most wealthy people don't want to take on all this. A CFA Institute survey of four thousand high–net worth households found that three out of four wealthy families presently work with a professional wealth manager, as most people find the above list of job responsibilities too time consuming, challenging, and important to do on their own.[33]

One reason why some people do choose to fly solo is to avoid fees. Here are some common advisory fees to watch out for:

Asset-based advisory fees. According to a 2021 study by McKinsey, revenues from asset-based fees comprise about three-quarters of the revenue generated by financial advisors. A Kitces.com study of financial advisor fees reveals the median advisor fee was about 1.0 percent of assets under management for account sizes up to $1 million. It's common to see tiered pricing models based on the level of assets being managed.

In addition to asset-based fees, there may be fees attached to the underlying investments an advisor chooses for you. Exchange traded funds (ETFs) and mutual funds typically have fees that range from 0.65 percent to 0.85 percent. After adding those fees into the mix, the range of "all-in fees" spans from about 1.30 percent per annum to 1.85 percent.[34]

Transaction-based commissions. Per McKinsey, about 41 percent of households who work with an advisor do so on a transaction-only model, which means they pay commissions to purchase investments recommended by the advisor. Meanwhile, 34 percent of households pay advisors based on a hybrid structure that includes a mix of transaction fees and asset-based fees. Advisors can receive commissions from a range of investment products. For example, there can be big incentives linked to insurance products and annuities. Some advisors may see commissions as high as 70 percent of the first year's premium. After that, they may receive an additional 3 percent to 5 percent of the premium per year as long as the policy is active. Annuity commissions are generally built into the price of the contract. Commissions usually range anywhere from 1 percent to 10 percent of the entire contract amount, depending on the type of annuity. For example, fixed-indexed annuities generally earn advisors a 4 percent commission.

Financial planning fees. About 25 percent of advisors charge extra standalone fees for financial planning. Per a study by Kitces.com, those fees typically range as follows:

- Tenth percentile: $1,000
- Fiftieth percentile: $2,500
- Nintieth percentile: $4,800

Once you include all the layers of potential fees, the total fees financial advisors charge can vary greatly. Sanity checking fees and expenses is important because even small differences in the short run will eventually compound into big differences over the long run.

Compound interest is the eighth wonder of the world.
He who understands it, earns it ... he who doesn't ... pays it.

—ALBERT EINSTEIN

Taking the DIY approach will save you money on advisory fees, but investors should also keep in mind the opportunity cost of missing out on the value that a solid advisor can provide.

Pros:

- Maintain full control of all financial decisions.
- Avoid advisory fees.

Cons:

- Susceptible to emotional responses to market volatility and economic uncertainty.
- Time-consuming and potentially stressful.

Who Should Select This Option?

Readers who are fee conscious or have a genuine interest in personal finance and are willing to devote the necessary time to the role.

#2: Hire a Robo-Advisor

If you're interested in keeping fees to a minimum but also want to limit your personal responsibility for overseeing your finances, a robo-advisor may be an option worth pursuing.

Robo-advisors use computer models and algorithms to construct a portfolio (usually of ETFs) that they manage on an ongoing basis, with little human intervention. The portfolio is tailored to each investor's risk tolerance, time horizon, desire for growth, and other inputs. And it's rebalanced periodically.

For an investor who just wants to set-and-forget their investments, pay relatively modest fees, and earn market-like returns, there are few drawbacks to the robo-advisor model. Investors who shop around can easily find a robo-advisor whose total fees are less than 1 percent per year. The fee structure generally ranges in the 0.25 percent to 0.50 percent range annually for management fees, plus the expense ratios associated with the ETFs that are chosen.

Because of the simplicity of the robo-advisor model—all handled online and with little-to-no service or personal attention to a person's full financial picture—it is generally marketed to younger investors just starting out.

Pros:

- The investment process is automated by a computer program, removing the possibility of emotionally triggered mistakes.
- Fees are generally lower compared to working with a human financial advisor.

Cons:

- A low-service model could mean no one is paying attention to your holistic financial picture.
- Most robo-platforms invest passively, meaning there is no active management to sidestep market downturns.

Who Should Select This Option?

Readers who are fee conscious but still want to delegate financial management responsibility.

#3: Choose a Fiduciary Advisor

The Latin root of the word "fiduciary" is "trust."

A fiduciary is legally required to put their client's best interests ahead of their own. This may seem like it should be a basic requirement to give people financial advice, but it isn't.

Advisors who are *not* fiduciaries—like many brokers and insurance agents—can recommend whatever financial products they like, including those with the highest commissions. If a financial product is loosely aligned with an investor's goals and has the right disclosures, it's fair game under the suitability standard.

A survey by Financial Engines found that 93 percent of Americans think advisors who provide retirement advice *should* be fiduciaries, but the unfortunate reality is many are not.

The difference between acting in a person's "best interests" versus recommending products that "align with their goals" may not seem significant, but it really is. If a broker can make more money selling certain products over others, they may not be motivated to find the best possible solution for your assets.

A fiduciary, on the other hand, must always pursue their client's best interests. The best fee structure, in my opinion, is a flat fee. This automatically puts advisors and clients on the same side of the table. If a client does well and their assets grow, the advisor also earns more. If a client's assets shrink, the advisor's compensation shrinks too. They win and lose together—as it should be.

The fiduciary test is an easy screen you can use to whittle down the field of potential advisors.

Tip: Apply the Fiduciary Test to any money manager you consider hiring.

1. Ask how the advisor is compensated. Are they fee-only or do they also receive commissions?
2. Who is their regulator?

If they are regulated by the Financial Industry Regulatory Authority (FINRA), they are probably not held to a fiduciary standard.[35] That means the advisor holds some type of securities license. You can use the BrokerCheck feature on FINRA's website to see if the advisor is in good standing or has complaints against them.

If the advisor is regulated by the US Securities & Exchange Commission (SEC), they are probably held to a fiduciary standard, which requires them to always act in your best interest.

Pros:

- Fiduciary advisors must always act in your best interest.
- It's easy to screen for a fiduciary—ask how they are compensated and who their regulator is.

Cons:

- Some advisors are dual registered, which makes it murky whether to trust them.
- Dual-registered advisors can receive commissions for annuities and insurance products.

Who Should Select This Option?

Readers who want to delegate financial management responsibility to a professional who is likely to act in their best interest.

#4: Choose a Fiduciary Advisor with Advanced Credentials

When comparing potential advisors, it's also important to consider *who* you will be working with. Is it a single advisor or a team? Who will make the investing decisions? Who will be your primary relationship contact? And do these people specialize in areas most relevant to you?

For instance, some advisors specialize in financial planning while others specialize in selling insurance products. If you want an insurance specialist, go with that type of firm. If you want someone to help you set up a 529 college savings plan and optimize your budget, then a planning-focused advisor would be more appropriate.

Just remember that anyone can call themselves a "Financial Advisor" or "Portfolio Manager," which makes comparing the quality of advice you are likely to receive from different advisors a challenge. In the financial sphere, there are more than a few generic titles that don't really mean anything, and way too many designations to keep track of.

Per FINRA, there are over two hundred professional designations used within the financial services industry, and 121 of those designations begin with the letter C.

Here are three of the most important ones:

Chartered Financial Analyst (CFA)

CFAs specialize in portfolio management and investment analysis. CFAs must take three challenging exams that require on average over one thousand hours of studying to pass. They must also have four years of relevant work experience and obtain several letters of professional reference.[36]

Certified Financial Planner (CFP)

CFPs typically offer fee-based financial planning services. To earn a CFP certification, you must pass a six-hour exam, and amass either six thousand hours of professional experience or four thousand hours of apprenticeship experience.

Certified Public Accountant (CPA)

CPAs fill a wide range of financial roles, managing and preparing financial records and tax-related documents for both companies and individuals. CPAs must satisfy both state and national requirements. The state requirement is to meet a minimum education threshold and a minimum amount of experience. The national requirement is to pass a four-part CPA exam.

Tip: Apply the Credentials Test to any money manager you consider hiring. This consists of the following key criteria.

1. How many years of experience does the advisor have?
2. Does the advisor specialize in areas that you personally care about?

3. As a test, ask the advisor to explain a financial concept to you and see if you understand them.
4. What unique qualifications or designations do they have?

Pros:

- If you want excellent results, it makes sense to hire an advisor with excellent qualifications.
- You can find an advisor who specializes in the areas you personally care about.

Cons:

- Fiduciaries with strong credentials may charge higher fees.
- The more selective you are, the longer it may take to find an advisor.

Who Should Select This Option?

Readers who want to delegate financial management responsibility to a top-notch professional and are willing to be selective to find the right match.

■ ■

Now that we've reached the end of the chapter, it's time to act.

In twenty seconds or less, pick one of the strategies we just reviewed that you think is the best advisory solution for you.

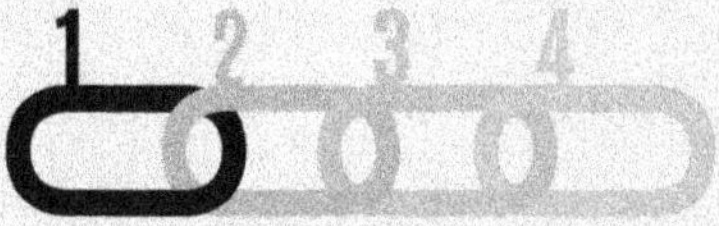

THE SAVINGS LAP

For each category, pick whichever of the four solutions is the best fit for you in twenty seconds or less.

Four strategies to start saving money:

- ☐ #1: Automate Contributions to a 401(k)
- ☐ #2: Automate Contributions to Multiple Tax-deferred Vehicles
- ☐ #3: Maximize Retirement Contributions and Start an Emergency Savings Fund
- ☐ #4: Maximize Retirement Contributions and Start a Scarcity Fund

Four strategies to manage debt wisely:

- ☐ #1: Pay Off High Interest Rate Debt First
- ☐ #2: Dave Ramsey's Snowball Method
- ☐ #3: Consolidate Your Debts
- ☐ #4: Pay Off Bad Debt and Add Good Debt

Four strategies for choosing a financial advisor:

- ☐ #1: Be Your Own Financial Advisor
- ☐ #2: Hire a Robo-Advisor
- ☐ #3: Choose a Fiduciary Advisor
- ☐ #4: Choose a Fiduciary Advisor with Advanced Credentials

01:00

CHAPTER SUMMARY

- Behavioral coaching can help investors make better decisions, especially during volatile times.
- Hiring a financial advisor can add significant value to your wealth management strategy.
- A solid financial advisor should be able to add more value than they charge in fees.
- Four strategies for choosing a financial advisor:
    1. Do it yourself: Handle all financial responsibilities yourself but be aware of the time and effort required.
    2. Hire a robo-advisor: Use a computer model for automated portfolio management at lower fees.
    3. Choose a fiduciary advisor: Look for an advisor who puts your best interests first and ask about their compensation and regulator.
    4. Choose a fiduciary advisor with advanced credentials: Look for advisors with specialized qualifications that match your needs.

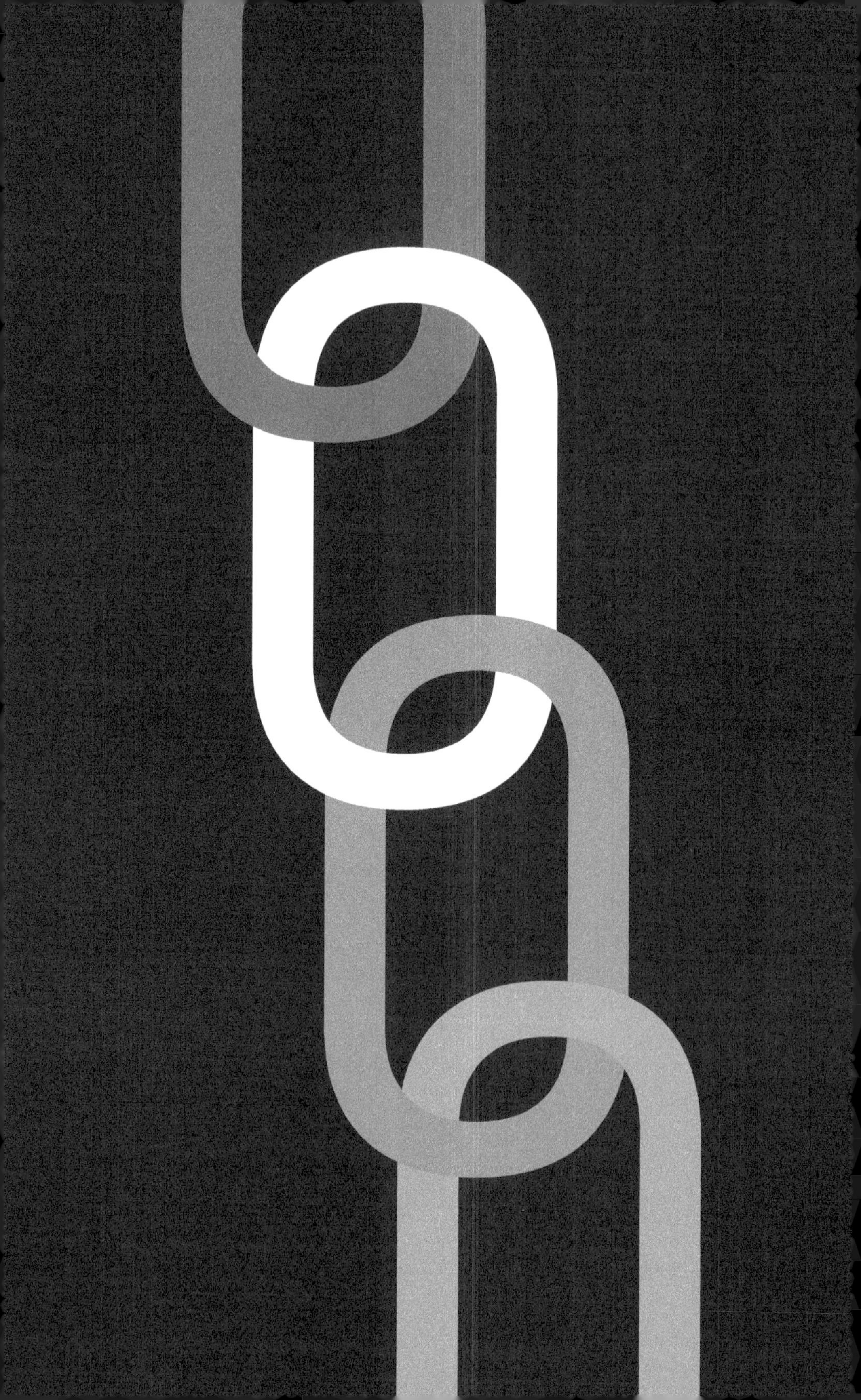

SECTION IV

THE INVESTING LAP

CHAPTER 11

THE FIRST RULE OF INVESTING IS SAFETY FIRST

There are old investors, and there are bold investors, but there are no old bold investors.

—HOWARD MARKS

Fear and greed are timeless. So is the story of Jesse Livermore.

Jesse was the Wall Street legend who inspired Edwin Lefèvre's fictional character in the 1923 classic, *Reminiscences of a Stock Operator*.

Jesse was a gutsy trader—the kind who thrives when most people shrivel.

In 1929, he correctly predicted the looming economic downturn and managed to play it beautifully. He shorted the market at the right time, covered well, and by the end of the Great Depression he was one of the richest people in the world.

Jesse could do well in any market environment. Bull or bear—he didn't care. His priority was making money. "Markets are never wrong, but opinions often are," he said.

Jesse learned to read and write by the time he was three and a half. At age five, he was reading newspapers. By the time he was fourteen, he began studying market trends as a Board Boy at Paine Webber. Back then, that meant standing in front of a chalkboard, refreshing stock quotes by hand as they were telegraphed.[37]

Around this time, Jesse also started a personal journal, where he meticulously tracked prices and began to notice patterns.

All through time, people have basically acted and reacted the same way in the market as a result of greed, fear, ignorance, and hope. That is why the numerical formations and patterns recur on a constant basis.

—JESSE LIVERMORE

It's unclear which "numerical formations" figured most prominently in his thinking. But his 1940 book, *How to Trade in Stocks,* may contain some hidden clues. Chapter 11 describes "Livermore's Secret Market Key."

> By continued close study of the many records I had kept, the realization struck me that the time element was vital in forming a correct opinion as to the approach of the really important movements. With renewed vigor I concentrated on that feature. What I wanted to discover was a method of recognizing what constituted the minor swings. I realized a market in a definite trend still had numerous intermediate oscillations. They had been confusing. They were no longer to be my concern.[38]

In the book, Jesse describes a dual counting system with two distinct color patterns. That part reminds me of a modern market timing tool I use called the DeMark Indicators.

Jesse learned it was futile to try and predict every short-term market move. He focused instead on getting the major market moves right. Another one of Jesse's trading rules was to only own the strongest stocks in a bull market, while avoiding or shorting the weakest stocks in a bear market.

Unfortunately, Jesse didn't always follow his own risk management rules, and the allure of big returns led him astray. Jesse traded too boldly, for too long. He would file for bankruptcy three times over the course of his career, losing a fortune that likely exceeded $100 million. His failures ultimately got the best of him—he took his own life in 1940.

Jesse pushed the boundaries of risk-taking, but the best long-term investors focus on taking prudent risks and avoiding permanent ruin. If we can do those two things well, the gains will take care of themselves—in any era.

Safety First: The Most Important Portfolio Management Principle

Investing trust in the wrong person or entity can be game over, even if you do everything else right. That's why identifying a trustworthy institution to safeguard your assets is *mission critical.*

You should only send money to name-brand financial institutions. A major financial custodian—like Charles Schwab, Fidelity, Pershing, or Morgan Stanley—is an institution that holds customers' assets to minimize risk of theft. These firms are regulated and insured, giving investors valuable layers of protection.

A hired money manager can be permitted to invest the funds in your Schwab or Fidelity account, but they cannot withdraw or move the funds without your explicit permission. You control the assets.

On the other hand, every Ponzi scheme you've ever heard of has one common denominator: someone gave a scammer full control of their funds. **Don't ever do this**.

Giving a manager direct custody (control) of your assets—or signing over a power of attorney—forfeits all mechanisms for oversight and accountability, which is precisely what you need in order to avoid fraud.

For example, famed Ponzi schemer Bernie Madoff ran the custody part of his business on a separate floor from his brokerage business. When investors hired Madoff to manage their money, they weren't sending funds to a third-party custodian like the ones listed above. They were sending money to bank accounts controlled by Madoff. His back-office created fictitious account statements and returns. Madoff didn't make a single trade in ten years. Investor money went straight into his personal bank account.

The very same red flags appeared more recently with the implosion of FTX, the now infamous cryptocurrency exchange. The cryptocurrency market has very few ties to the traditional world of finance, which also means that trading platforms like FTX don't work with third-party custodians or banks to hold customer assets.

Cryptocurrency exchanges are also largely unregulated, so there are no SIPC or FDIC insurance protections to speak of. In Section 2.10 of FTX's "Terms and Conditions," it explicitly states: "No deposit protection. Neither Digital Assets nor any fiat currency or E-Money held in your Account is eligible for any public or private deposit insurance protection."

The risks to investors were literally spelled out.

Celebrity endorsements and TV advertisements made FTX seem like it was a legitimate enterprise. But the minute you're asked to send money directly to an entity that isn't a regulated bank or third-party custodian, it's time to conduct serious due diligence. Investors who did would have noticed Section 2.10 of FTX's "Terms and Conditions" and walked away.

The goal of every fraudster is to gain *control* of your money. But if you only use a name brand custodian to open accounts registered in your name—which I call the "custody test"—then fraudsters will never gain control of your money.

Make the custody test your first line of defense in your risk management arsenal.

The Math of Risk Management

Rule number 1: Never lose money.

Rule number 2: Never forget rule number 1.

—WARREN BUFFETT

Finance theory frames risk and return as a trade-off decision, but it's not really a binary choice. The good news is you can actually achieve higher returns with below-average risk (cue the confetti!).

Think about it this way: Does it seem plausible Warren Buffett built a legendary investing track record by taking more risk than everyone else? Probably not. Anyone who has studied Buffett knows he's hardwired in the opposite direction.

Buffett has always been more of a risk manager than a risk taker. In Alice Schroeder's biography about Buffett, *The Snowball,* she describes him as a "cautious child, who kept his knees bent and stayed close to the ground when he learned to walk."[39] He walked that way on purpose to hedge the risk of falling down.

As an adult, Buffett became the Chairman and CEO of Berkshire Hathaway, the largest insurance firm in the world. Insurance companies make money by taking calculated risk and avoiding catastrophic losses. Successful investors think similarly.

Since 1988, Berkshire Hathaway shares have appreciated at a compounded annual growth rate of 13.9 percent. By comparison, the S&P 500 Index returned 8.2 percent per annum over the same period. In monetary terms, $100,000 invested in Berkshire stock in 1988 would currently be worth $11,790,338 compared to $1,520,183 for a similar size investment in the S&P 500.

Much of Buffett's outperformance has occurred during bear markets. Over the last three bear markets (2000, 2008, and 2020), Berkshire's average annualized return is -14.9 percent compared to -45.5 percent for the S&P 500.[40]

	BEAR MARKET AVG.	3/23/2000-10/09/2002	10/09/2007-3/09/2009	2/19/2020-3/23/2020
S&P 500	-45.5%	-47.4%	-55.2%	-33.8%
BERKSHIRE HATHAWAY	-14.9%	25.8%	-40.3%	-30.2%

Minimizing losses is critical because every loss requires a higher subsequent gain to breakeven. For instance, if an investor loses 25 percent, they'll need a 33 percent gain to break even. A 50 percent drawdown requires a 100 percent return, and so on.

DRAWDOWN	GAIN NEEDED TO BREAK EVEN
-10%	11.1%
-20%	25%
-25%	33.3%
-40%	66.7%
-50%	100%
-90%	900%

It's easy to make money in a bull market. But it's not how much you make in a bull market that counts; it's how much you *keep*. Every bear market repossesses a portion of a prior bull market's gains. And in severe cases, some bear markets wipe away all the gains (e.g., 1973, 2000, and 2008).

Throughout his career, Buffett won by investing prudently over the full market cycle. This allowed him to opportunistically risk-up when others were inclined to panic sell at low prices, and vice versa.

> *The less prudence with which others conduct their affairs, the greater the prudence with which we should conduct our own affairs.*
>
> **—WARREN BUFFETT**

In his book, *The Missing Risk Premium: Why Low Volatility Investing Works*, Eric Falkenstein shares many examples of other safety-first strategies that outperform:[41]

- Low-risk blue-chip stocks beat high risk penny stocks.[42]
- Low-risk horse racing favorites beat high risk longshots.[43]
- Low-risk in the money options beat high risk out of the money options.[44]
- Low-risk lotteries with the best odds beat high risk lotteries with the worst odds.[45]

Based on the mathematical laws of compounding, minimizing losses is the single most important part of investing. The best investors win long term by not losing as much as everyone else.

The Psychology of Risk Management

Another reason it's critical to control losses is because in our mind's eye—losses count more.

Daniel Kahneman and Amos Tversky originally coined the term "loss aversion" in their 1979 paper on subjective probability. According to the Nobel laureates, the pain of a loss is more than twice as powerful as the pleasure associated with an equivalent gain.[46]

Investors are regularly tripped up by loss aversion bias. Even though the goal of investing is to buy low and sell high, people are naturally inclined to do the opposite. In his book, *Thinking Fast and Slow*, Kahneman writes:

> When directly compared or weighted against each other, losses loom larger than gains. This asymmetry between the power of positive and negative expectations or experiences has an evolutionary history. Organisms that treat threats as more urgent than opportunities have a better chance to survive and reproduce.

To better understand the primal instincts involved here, imagine that you're seated in a dark theater. Suddenly, you hear someone in the back shout, "Fire!" Everyone around you begins to scurry toward the exit. But you don't personally see or smell any fire at all. In that moment, would you trust your own instincts and stay seated, or would you follow the herd?

Evolution has programmed you to cut and run.

Some call it the "survival instinct," while others call it "fight-or-flight syndrome." Most people would be inclined to follow the herd, because they would subconsciously perceive the risk of sitting still as too grave of a risk to bear.

That natural impulse to cut and run is useful sometimes—it can save your life. But it can also lead you to commit the cardinal sin of investing—selling low when everyone else is panicking.

In the end, bear markets can bring misery or opportunity. It all depends on how you're positioned. Strong investors use volatility to their advantage, usually at the expense of weaker investors who continually whipsaw themselves.

Here are four safety-first strategies to enhance your investing journey.

#1: Invest in a Low-Volatility Index Strategy

You can only manage things you measure. So if you want to become a better risk manager, you must learn how to measure risk intelligently. Thankfully, it's not hard to do.

One key measure of volatility is a portfolio's beta. This measures a portfolio's sensitivity to swings in the broader market.

For example, since the S&P 500 index is considered a proxy for the broad US equity market, it has a beta of 1.0. If your portfolio has a beta of 0.75, that means it's about 25 percent less volatile than the S&P 500. Conversely, if your portfolio has a beta of 1.25, that means it's about 25 percent more volatile than the S&P 500.

Even though a lot of finance theory is built upon the idea that investors must take extra risk to capture higher returns, history shows that is not true in practice. In fact, many lower volatility strategies have outperformed their respective benchmarks over time.

There are many ways an investor could build a low-volatility portfolio. One of the simplest ways is to invest in a low-volatility index.

From December 31, 1999 to December 31, 2022, the S&P 500 Low-Volatility Index outperformed both the S&P 500 Index and the S&P 500 High Beta Index, returning 539 percent (8.4 percent annually) compared to 304 percent (6.3 percent annually) for the S&P 500 and 65 percent (2.2 percent annually) for the S&P 500 High Beta Index.[47]

Even though you can't invest directly into an index, you can buy and hold an ETF that tracks the S&P 500 Low-Volatility Index, such as Invesco's S&P 500 Low-Volatility ETF (ticker: SPLV).

Like Warren Buffett's Berkshire Hathaway, the S&P 500 Low-Volatility Index has outperformed during past bear markets.

	BEAR MARKET AVG.	3/23/2000-10/09/2002	10/09/2007-3/09/2009	2/19/2020-3/23/2020
S&P 500	-45.5%	-47.4%	-55.2%	-33.8%
S&P 500 LOW-VOLATILITY INDEX	-22.0%	+11.8%	-42.1%	-35.7%

#2: Invest in a Low-Volatility Sector Strategy

A second way to buy and hold a low-volatility portfolio would be to purchase ETFs that track the three lowest volatility sectors in the S&P 500—health care, consumer staples, and utilities.

These three sectors are low volatility because demand for things like medical procedures, toilet paper, and electricity do not fluctuate much even as economic cycles change. Since demand stays relatively constant no matter the economic reality, earnings don't fluctuate too wildly. Below-average earnings risk translates to below-average stock volatility.

From a portfolio standpoint, you could invest one-third of your capital into the Health Care Select SPDR Fund (ticker: XLV), one-third into the Consumer Staples Select Sector SPDR Fund (ticker: XLP), and one-third into the Utilities Select Sector SPDR Fund (ticker: XLU). If you choose this approach, I'd recommend annually rebalancing your portfolio back to equal 33 percent weights to help maintain a consistent level of diversification.

From December 31, 1999 to December 31, 2022, an equal-weighted, low-volatility sector portfolio (33.3 percent XLV, 33.3 percent XLP, 33.3 percent XLU) returned +536 percent (8.4 percent annually) compared to +304 percent (6.3 percent annually) for the S&P 500.

Meanwhile, the annual volatility for the sector strategy over that timeframe was 14.4 percent compared to 19.8 percent for the S&P 500 index, and the sector strategy's beta was only 0.66.[48] Like Warren Buffett's Berkshire Hathaway, the Low-Volatility Sector strategy has outperformed during past bear markets.

	BEAR MARKET AVG.	3/23/2000-10/09/2002	10/09/2007-3/09/2009	2/19/2020-3/23/2020
S&P 500	-45.5%	-47.4%	-55.2%	-33.8%
LOW-VOLATILITY SECTORS	-24.4%	-12.9%	-34.5%	-25.9%

#3: Dollar-Cost Average

Legendary investor Benjamin Graham first coined the term "dollar-cost averaging" in his book, *The Intelligent Investor*. For many serious investors, this book is basically the investing bible.

The dollar-cost averaging (DCA) concept is simple and logical. A person commits to investing money at regular intervals, usually monthly, into a security or a portfolio of securities. That's it.

Every investor wants to buy low and sell high, and DCA helps achieve that. Without DCA, an investor is left trying to predict movements in markets and securities prices, which is extremely hard to accurately do over long periods of time.

With dollar-cost averaging, however, you don't need to worry about getting any timing decision exactly right. Since you're investing at regular intervals, you'll buy more shares when prices are low and fewer shares when prices are high. Graham wrote in his book that taking this approach would net an investor a "satisfactory overall price for his holdings."

The history of stock market cycles unequivocally shows you want to be a buyer during bear markets.

BUYING WHEN THERE IS BLOOD IN THE STREET WORKS

Forward returns for the S&P 500 after it has fallen 25% from all-time highs

PEAK	TROUGH	%DECLINE	+1 YEAR	+3 YEARS	+5 YEARS	+10 YEARS
12/12/61	6/26/62	-28.0%	31.2%	69.2%	94.8%	171.1%
11/29/68	5/26/70	-36.1%	32.2%	44.3%	27.9%	97.5%
1/11/73	10/3/74	-48.2%	1.4%	23.8%	42.0%	188.4%
11/28/80	8/12/82	-27.1%	43.9%	81.2%	238.6%	403.9%
8/25/87	12/4/87	-33.5%	14.7%	34.1%	96.8%	387.1%
3/24/00	10/9/02	-49.1%	0.2%	1.9%	21.5%	38.3%
10/9/07	3/9/09	-56.8%	-6.9%	3.7%	61.2%	209.6%
	AVERAGES	**-39.8%**	**16.7%**	**36.9%**	**83.3%**	**213.7%**

Source: Ben Carlson, YCharts

In a sense, younger investors should root for market selloffs. It just means they can buy in at more attractive levels, which boosts their long-term forward returns.

The best part about DCA is that it's super-easy to implement, and many readers may already be doing so. If you have money automatically invested into a 401(k) every month, that's DCA!

#4: Employ an Active Defensive Strategy

Every five to seven years people forget that recessions occur every five to seven years.

—MORGAN HOUSEL

In capital markets, a great time to get more defensive is when economic growth is likely to slow.

The economy goes through predictable seasonal patterns over time. The most important macro factors that influence prospective market returns are the rate of change in GDP growth and inflation.

Building on the research of firms like Bridgewater Associates and Hedgeye Risk Management, at my firm we use base rate analysis and a predictive tracking algorithm to nowcast the expected trajectory for growth and inflation. Then, using a four-quadrant framework, we tactically favor assets that have historically performed best in the most likely upcoming "economic season."

Economic seasons:

- Macro Spring: growth accelerating, inflation slowing.
- Macro Summer: growth accelerating, inflation accelerating.
- Macro Fall: growth slowing, inflation accelerating.
- Macro Winter: growth slowing, inflation slowing.

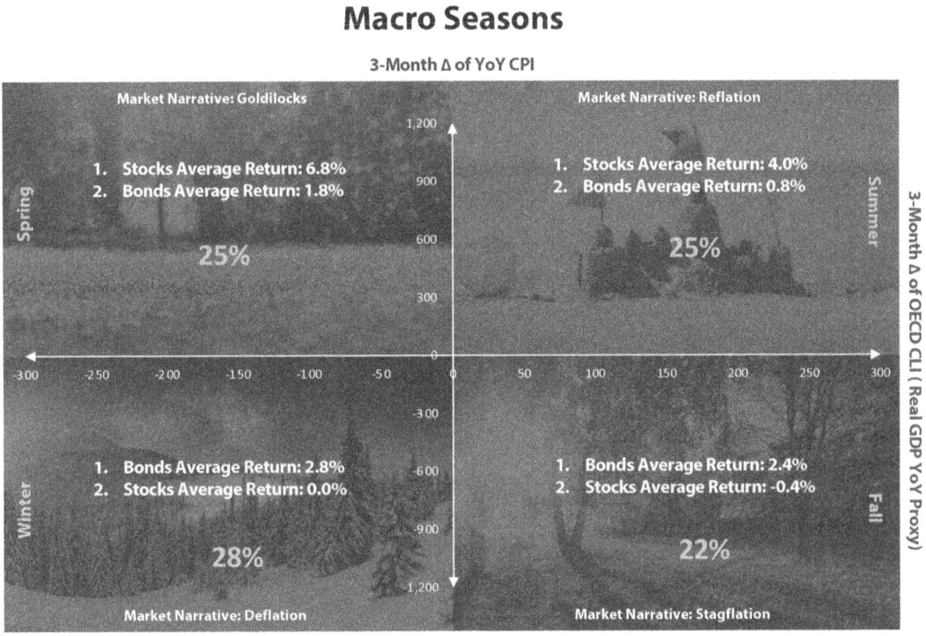

Percentages represent the number of months relative to the total period that the economy has been in one of the four macro regimes. Period of study: April 1980–January 2022. Data source: Bloomberg.

If you study the above graph, you will notice that virtually *all* the gains that equity investors have enjoyed since 1980 have come during the Spring or Summer macro seasons—when economic growth was accelerating. This has been the case about 50 percent of the time historically. The yellow percentages indicate the frequency of quarterly occurrences for each regime.

The S&P 500 has averaged a quarterly high return of +6.8 percent during the Spring macro regime, which is often referred to as a "Goldilocks" economic environment (not too hot, not too cold).

Conversely, in quarters when economic growth has decelerated (Macro Fall and Winter), bonds have historically outperformed stocks.

So, if you have a reason to believe economic growth is likely to decelerate in upcoming quarters, it's worth considering taking defensive actions in your portfolio.

One free way to monitor the GDP outlook is by following the Atlanta Fed's GDPNow forecast. It's publicly available on their website along with the underlying data. The Atlanta Fed's model does a fairly good job of incorporating the latest economic data to create a forecast for GDP.

Alternatively, if you don't mind paying a little for a lot of high-quality macro research, you can subscribe to Hedgeye Risk Management. Keith McCullough and his team map and model the GDP outlook better than most analysts on Wall Street, in my opinion.

Remember, it's the *rate of change* that counts most when you're trying to get a forward-looking read on a trend. Momentum is the most important variable in macro-economic forecasting.

The last time I went defensive for clients was in 2022. Entering that year, it became clear to me the US economy was going to slow considerably because it was about to lap some of the highest economic comparisons in a generation. To get defensive, I raised about 25 percent cash in client portfolios and overweighted a handful of "risk-off" sectors. By employing an active defensive strategy, Silverlight's Core Equity Strategy was only down 2 percent in 2022, which handily beat the 18 percent decline in the S&P 500.

Do you or your investment managers have a proactive defensive strategy?

To further illustrate that outperforming the market with below-average risk is indeed possible, I've included the ten-year track record for my firm's Core Equity Strategy in the Appendix section. Using many of the same principles you learned in this chapter, I was able to beat the market on a gross and net of fees basis, while running a portfolio beta of only 0.85. And I did that by sticking to a safety-first mindset!

Now it's your turn. Pick one of the solutions presented in this chapter and start building your safety-first portfolio.

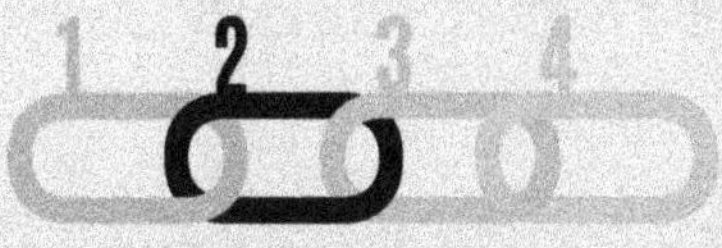

THE INVESTING LAP

For each category, pick whichever of the four solutions is the best fit for you in twenty seconds or less.

Four safety-first investing strategies:

- ☐ #1: Invest in a Low-Volatility Index Strategy
- ☐ #2: Invest in a Low-Volatility Sector Strategy
- ☐ #3: Dollar-Cost Average
- ☐ #4: Employ an Active Defensive Strategy

Four strategies to choose a benchmark:

- ☐ #1: Focus on Maximizing Long-Term Returns
- ☐ #2: Focus on Absolute Returns
- ☐ #3: Focus on a Volatility Threshold
- ☐ #4: Focus on Finding an Advisor

Four strategies to avoid the passive bubble:

- ☐ #1: Diversify with Equal-Weighted Portfolios
- ☐ #2: Blend Passive and Active Strategies
- ☐ #3: Self-Manage
- ☐ #4: Direct Indexing

01:20

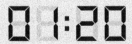

CHAPTER SUMMARY

- Markets are driven by fear and greed cycles.
- Only trust a name-brand financial institution to custody your assets.
- Minimizing losses is critical because each loss requires a higher subsequent gain to break even.
- Loss aversion bias suggests that losses are psychologically more powerful than gains.
- Historical market data shows lower volatility strategies often outperform over the long term.
- Safety-first strategies to enhance your investing journey:
    1. Invest in a low-volatility index strategy: For example, you could buy an ETF that tracks the S&P 500 Low-Volatility Index, such as Invesco's S&P 500 Low-Volatility ETF.
    2. Invest in a low-volatility sector strategy: For example, you could purchase ETFs that track the three lowest volatility sectors in the S&P 500—Health Care (XLV), Consumer Staples (XLP), and Utilities (XLU).
    3. Dollar cost-average: Since you're investing at regular intervals, this method guarantees you buy more shares when prices are low and fewer shares when prices are high.
    4. Employ an active defensive strategy: If you think economic growth will likely slow in upcoming quarters, it's worth considering defensive moves in your portfolio.

CHAPTER 12

CHOOSE YOUR OWN BENCHMARK

Always be a first-rate version of yourself, instead of a second-rate version of somebody else.

—JUDY GARLAND

It was a warm summer afternoon in 1990-something, and I was hitting practice putts at Sportsman's Country Club in Northbrook, Illinois. My grandmother, whom I called Nonny, motioned for me.

"We're playing with someone very special today," she said with a beaming smile. Then she told me we were randomly paired up to play eighteen holes of golf with legendary Chicago Bears running back Gale Sayers.

Sayers was the NFL's Rookie of the Year in 1968, and he became the youngest player ever to be inducted into the Pro Football Hall of Fame in 1977. He's also remembered for his special friendship with former Bears teammate, Brian Piccolo. After Piccolo passed away from cancer, Sayers was inspired to write an autobiography, which led to a famous film called *Brian's Song*.

My grandmother and I met Sayers and his playing partner, Steve, at the first hole. When I shook Sayers's hand, I noticed the immense size of his forearms.

Then Sayers made his way to the blue tee box—farthest from the hole—and he blasted a drive so far into the hazy sky, I lost sight of the ball.

Steve and I teed off next from the white tee box, which was a little closer to the hole. We hit OK shots. On our way back to the carts, Steve shared that this was a tune-up round for Sayers, who was scheduled to play in Michael Jordan's charity golf tournament the following week.

Last, it was my grandmother's turn. Normally a social butterfly, I could tell she was nervous as she made her way to the red tee box—closest to the hole.

After a couple practice swings, she squared her club to the ball, steadied her balance, and took one last look down the fairway. Then she shanked the ball straight into the bushes adjacent to the tee box. I don't know how, but she literally hit the ball sideways.

"Oh dear," she uttered.

Sayers encouraged her to try again, so she did. Another shank—straight into the bushes.

After her third attempt produced the exact same result, she was clearly embarrassed. So, we decided to just drop her next ball by mine. Technically that's against the rules, but oh well.

To his credit, Sayers wasn't the least bit annoyed by my grandmother's shank-fest. As we drove into the fairway, he made a self-deprecating joke that put her mind at ease. We played a fun round after that.

Here's a picture of the scorecard Sayers signed for me that day:

And here's the other side of the scorecard, showing how we stopped keeping score after the first hole.

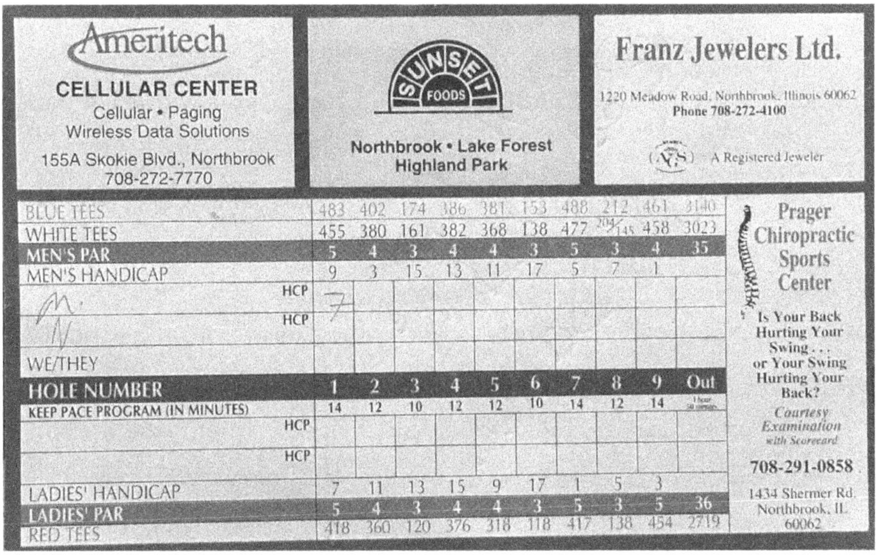

That day at Sportsman's, my grandmother's primary objective was to spend four uninterrupted hours with her grandson. Sayers's objective was tuning-up to play in front of a crowd alongside Michael Jordan. Point is: These were two people who belonged in different tee boxes.

People bring different skills and objectives to a golf course. There are multiple tee boxes and methods of competing so each golfer can customize for the game *they* want to play.

Nonny didn't have to keep a conventional golf score to win that day. After the first hole, she stopped mentally comparing her game to the NFL legend she happened to be playing with. Once she started playing *her* game, she was able to enjoy herself, despite hitting her first three shots into the bushes.

My grandmother was a true original. The last time I saw her, we met for lunch. All she ordered was a hot fudge sundae. Who does that? Well, Nonny did stuff like that all the time. She wasn't the world's best golfer, but I admire that she was never afraid to be herself—in any setting. She was a woman who lived by her own benchmarks.

Similarly, I encourage you to embrace your own individuality when choosing a portfolio benchmark. This chapter will teach you how to do that.

Portfolio Benchmarks

Benchmarks are like tee boxes in golf—they allow you to customize the game you want to play based on your personal situation and goals.

Investors use benchmarks to focus their investment strategy and journey. Benchmarks help structure a portfolio, monitor risk, and track performance. The most common benchmarks are major market indices, like the S&P 500 Index or Bloomberg US Aggregate Bond Index. These indices provide investors with decades of historical performance and risk data, as well as formal processes for what holdings are included and why.

This information not only helps you construct a portfolio, but it also provides a baseline of what you should expect from a performance and volatility standpoint over the course of your investing journey. Benchmarks give you a map to your destination.

One of the most important investing decisions anyone makes is asset allocation, and this is central to choosing an appropriate benchmark. Asset allocation is the process of dividing your investment portfolio among different asset categories, such as stocks, bonds, and cash. Many academic studies have shown that asset allocation plays a significant role in determining portfolio returns.

A great way to understand the real value of a benchmark is to think about what happens if you don't have one. Without a benchmark, an investor is left to wander aimlessly into the vast, complex world of investing. And because we're emotional creatures, that almost certainly leads to the trap of chasing the flashiest asset class and the highest possible return every year.

With this approach, failure is all but assured. Not benchmarking would be akin to my grandmother having a goal to outdrive Gale Sayers on every hole and turn in a better score than him. The likelihood of her reaching that goal was exactly 0 percent.

Instead, investors should think about benchmarking as a process of creating guidelines, targets, and a *framework* that makes success possible with the right kind of effort and diligence. Benchmarks also provide a safety net that prevents you from losing too much ground when you're wrong.

Roger Bannister's pace runners were like benchmarks—as long as he stayed with them or just ahead, he knew he'd accomplish his goal by the end of the race. But at the same time, falling a little behind didn't mean automatic failure. All he had to do was stay close, which would give him plenty of chances to get back ahead.

In this chapter, I'm suggesting that investors choose their own benchmark—whatever market index or combination of indices work best for you.

The first step in the benchmark selection process is to figure out a savings rate and target rate of return that are likely to fund your financial goals.

Tip: One technique I use to help clients forecast the odds of achieving their top three financial goals on time is called Monte Carlo simulations. You need software to run this analysis, but there are some affordable options available to individual investors.

Monte Carlo simulations are often used by financial advisors to stress test financial goals because they offer a probabilistic approach to assessing financial risk. The analysis generates many potential outcomes for a financial plan based on variables like investment returns, inflation, and lifespan. Since it runs thousands of scenarios, it allows you to see how likely you are to achieve your financial goals under different conditions and return paths. This helps you make more informed decisions when it comes to picking an appropriate benchmark.

The second step in the benchmark selection process is to establish which benchmarks are useful and well-constructed and which aren't. According to CFA Institute, "an appropriate benchmark is one that is specified in advance and is relevant, measurable, unambiguous, representative of current investment options, accountable, investable, and complete."

By these standards, the S&P 500 or the MSCI ACWI indices are solid benchmark choices. Each index has all the attributes set out by the CFA institute, with the S&P 500 giving investors a solid option for benchmarking against major US companies and the MSCI ACWI allowing for international equity diversification.

Major companies in the US and abroad are constantly creating value and generating profit, and if your goal is to track the growth and price appreciation of some of the best companies in the world over time—which is a great goal by the way—these are solid benchmarks to use.

Your neighbor's investment portfolio is an example of a bad benchmark. Your neighbor only mentions what's working well in their portfolio, not the duds. There's a term for this in behavioral finance called "regret avoidance," which describes an investor's refusal to admit poor investment choices. Your neighbor's regret avoidance could then give you a condition called "FOMO," which is almost always hazardous to your investing health.

Another example of a bad benchmark besieged by FOMO is cryptocurrency. Wild, unpredictable, and unexplainable swings in price make something like Bitcoin a poor benchmark. But it's also part of a new asset class that lacks sufficient history that investors can use to generate reliable risk and return assumptions.

This is not to say that Bitcoin or cryptocurrency as a category cannot be a good benchmark someday in the future. But it will take at least a few more market cycles, and probably several decades, to really understand how this asset class will likely behave long term.

In summary, it's important to always spread your money across different types of investments to minimize risk and maximize returns.

Choosing the right benchmark for your goals is a logical first step to begin this process.

Here are four strategies to choose the best benchmark for you.

#1: Focus on Maximizing Long-Term Returns

If you have a long investment time horizon, a simple asset allocation choice is to use an equity benchmark. This is because stocks have historically produced superior returns.

Here are annualized returns for the three major asset classes from 1928 to 2022:

- Stocks: 9.6 percent
- Bonds: 4.6 percent
- Cash: 3.3 percent[49]

A few points' difference in return may not matter a lot over a single year or two, but it compounds into *dramatically* different outcomes over the course of a typical investor's time horizon, which often spans several decades.

ANNUAL RETURN	30-YEAR RETURN
4%	224%
6%	474%
8%	906%
10%	1,645%
12%	2,896%

If you want to maximize your portfolio's long-term growth and you aren't rattled by short-term market volatility, the S&P 500 or the MSCI ACWI would be reasonable equity benchmarks to consider.

#2: Focus on Absolute Returns

Not everyone needs to maximize long-term returns. Some people have enough liquid assets to meet their lifetime needs. Or they may have little appetite for volatility.

Investing more conservatively is perfectly fine, assuming you can still satisfy your needs and objectives. Having a 5 percent target return, for example, would allow an investor to limit the percentage of stocks in their portfolio, which would also help limit overall volatility. A balanced benchmark that consists of stocks and bonds would likely be sufficient to accomplish this goal over time.[50]

Moving further down the required return scale, fixed annuities could also be worth considering. If you know you only need a 3.5 percent return to avoid running out of money and a fixed annuity is guaranteed to pay you that, it could function like a benchmark.

There's just one big issue with trying to use annuities as a benchmark. Currently, there aren't any major indices to track performance for annuities, which is a red flag and problematic for benchmarking purposes. If annuities' performance was strong, wouldn't the companies who distribute those products be incentivized to track and publish a composite return? Well, they don't.

Publishing the net return figures for annuities and allowing investors to easily compare them to other traditional asset classes wouldn't be flattering. The high fees embedded in annuities take a big bite out of their returns over time. Without more transparency into the net return history for the asset class at large, it's hard to draw a clear map to reliably fund your goals.

If achieving an absolute level of return matters most to you, you can choose whatever well-constructed benchmark has achieved that level of return historically with the least amount of volatility.

#3: Focus on a Volatility Threshold

Another way to configure your asset allocation strategy is to identify a maximum volatility threshold, or what I call a *risk budget*. This could take the form of an annualized volatility target or maximum drawdown threshold based on stress test scenarios.

If an investor doesn't need high growth and cringes at the thought of volatility, they should not overweight risk assets in their portfolio. Some might call this "the Sleep-at-Night-Factor." Regardless of your time horizon, comfort matters, because even the best strategy in the world is worthless if you can't stick with it.

One way to establish a risk budget is to imagine losing a percentage of your portfolio. If your 401(k) declined by 20 percent over the next year, would you be able to hold on? If your portfolio declined by 30 percent or even 50 percent, would you be able to sleep at night?

Try to define the boundary of your comfort zone in the form of a maximum drawdown threshold. That tells you what your risk budget is. From there, choose whatever asset allocation you think maximizes your long-term expected return within that risk budget.

#4: Focus on Finding an Advisor

If you're unsure which tee box you belong in, you can always ask a pro. The sheer number of available benchmarks—and possible combinations of benchmarks—can make the task of picking one daunting. It's OK to ask for help.

Experienced financial advisors are well-versed in what questions to ask and what information to get from you to help determine an appropriate benchmark.

The process usually begins with an information-gathering session, where the advisor will ask you to provide financial statements to paint the overall picture of your current situation. The conversation will then shift from where you are today to where you want to go.

Once they understand your risk tolerance and any investing constraints you may have (tax needs, asset classes or securities you want to exclude, liquidity concerns, etc.), an advisor can recommend a benchmark that matches your goals.

Tip: If you choose to delegate the responsibility of choosing a benchmark, make sure the portfolio you end up with has characteristics that resemble the benchmark from a risk perspective, and in terms of the allocation percentages, to different sectors, countries, styles, etc.

THE INVESTING LAP

For each category, pick whichever of the four solutions is the best fit for you in twenty seconds or less.

Four safety-first investing strategies:

- ☐ #1: Invest in a Low-Volatility Index Strategy
- ☐ #2: Invest in a Low-Volatility Sector Strategy
- ☐ #3: Dollar-Cost Average
- ☐ #4: Employ an Active Defensive Strategy

Four strategies to choose a benchmark:

- ☐ #1: Focus on Maximizing Long-Term Returns
- ☐ #2: Focus on Absolute Returns
- ☐ #3: Focus on a Volatility Threshold
- ☐ #4: Focus on Finding an Advisor

Four strategies to avoid the passive bubble:

- ☐ #1: Diversify with Equal-Weighted Portfolios
- ☐ #2: Blend Passive and Active Strategies
- ☐ #3: Self-Manage
- ☐ #4: Direct Indexing

CHAPTER SUMMARY

- Benchmarks help structure a portfolio, monitor risk, and track performance.
- Roger Bannister's pace runners were like benchmarks—as long as he stayed with them or just ahead, he knew he'd accomplish his goal by the end of the race.
- The first step in the benchmark selection process is to figure out a savings rate and target rate of return that are likely to fund your financial goals.
- Monte Carlo simulations offer a probabilistic approach to assessing financial risk and can help you pick an appropriate benchmark.
- The second step in the benchmark selection process is to establish which benchmarks are useful and well-constructed and which aren't.
- The most common benchmarks are major market indices, like the S&P 500 Index or Bloomberg US Aggregate Bond Index.
- Asset allocation is the process of dividing your investment portfolio among different asset categories, such as stocks, bonds, and cash.
- Four strategies to choose the right benchmark for you:
    1. Focus on maximizing long-term returns.
    2. Focus on absolute returns.
    3. Focus on a volatility threshold.
    4. Focus on finding an advisor.

CHAPTER 13

THE PASSIVE INVESTING BUBBLE

It is ludicrous to believe that asset bubbles can only be recognized in hindsight.

—MICHAEL BURRY

John Bogle was born in 1929, the same year his family—like many American families—lost everything in the market crash. Growing up poor in the Depression taught people how to live frugally and to control the cost of everything. For John Bogle, it would become his life's work and professional legacy. Bogle spent his career turning something expensive (professional investment management) into something cheap (passive index investing).

The vision began at Princeton, with a senior thesis laying out—in stunning detail—what The Vanguard Group would ultimately become. Bogle's thesis became a central document that guided his approach to money management throughout his career. It was so good it transcended the classroom and landed him an executive position at a premier investment firm, Wellington Management Company.

It was clear from the beginning that Bogle was the real deal. He quickly ascended up the corporate ladder and eventually replaced the founder, Walter Morgan.

Yet, in 1966, Bogle made a fateful error. He merged the Wellington Management Company with a high-flying group of traders from Boston (Thorndike, Doran, Paine and Lewis, Inc.), whose market-beating Ivest Fund's returns fizzled in the 1973-1974 bear market.[51]

After the normally conservative and value-focused Wellington Fund lost 50 percent of its value, Bogle was fired.[52]

Bogle had committed a classic investing error: he ignored valuations, chased heat, and got burned.

Nevertheless, getting fired proved to be a pivotal turning point in John Bogle's life—one that ultimately led to a more fruitful path. "Vanguard was conceived in Hell and born in strife," Bogle wrote in his 2018 book, *Stay the Course*.[53]

After being ousted as the CEO of Wellington Management, Bogle was still able to retain a position as President of Wellington Fund and its sister funds. These were the roots that Vanguard sprouted from. Under the new structure, Bogle was determined to restore the Wellington name to its prior glory. In a speech he gave to commemorate the Wellington Fund's seventy-fifth anniversary, Bogle said:

> Sometimes in life, we make the greatest forward progress by going backward. That is just what we did when we decided to take Wellington Fund back to its roots. The Board agreed to our policy recommendations: (1) Hold the equity ratio firmly within a range of 60 to 69 percent of assets; (2) Emphasize large blue-chip stocks, with a significant representation of both value stocks and growth stocks; (3) Sharply increase the Fund's dividend income, which, given the fund's mandatory position in high-grade bonds, would require the

> sale of many of the portfolio's low-yielding growth stocks, with the proceeds reinvested in higher-yielding value stocks.[54]

In other words, Bogle tried to improve Wellington by reemphasizing fundamental analysis. But that approach didn't last for long.

The Vanguard Group was also a vehicle for Bogle to freely pursue the philosophy he articulated in his senior thesis. Bogle believed "investment companies should be operated in the most efficient, honest, and economical way possible," and that "future growth can be maximized by reducing sales charges and management fees."

Thus, when Vanguard launched the first index fund in 1976, now called the Vanguard 500 Index Fund, the firm's focus began to drift toward minimizing costs. This meant eschewing traditional overhead costs such as research expenses. Since Vanguard's indexing products only sought to match a market index, they didn't need an army of analysts to do fundamental research.

Index investing is a passive strategy that blindly tracks the performance of a broad market index such as the S&P 500. In many ways, it's the antithesis of a fundamentally focused investment fund.

The indexing product was a flop in the beginning. Bogle sought to raise $250 million, but he was only able to attract $11 million. The disappointing launch was labeled "Bogle's Folly," and many on Wall Street openly chastised the indexing concept as "a sure path to mediocrity." Some even called Bogle's ideas "un-American."

Undeterred, Bogle doubled down. He began selling his service directly to investors, undercutting competitors who charged broker commissions ranging as high as 9 percent. Investors have been reaping the rewards ever since. And Bogle's ideas—once thought radical and absurd—gradually became mainstream.

Passive Funds Take over Retirement Portfolios

There are two basic categories of investors: active and passive.

Active investors try to identify investments likely to outperform a benchmark index.

Passive investors try to match the return of a benchmark index. Since their portfolio is predetermined by an index provider, there isn't any need to do fundamental research.

The active versus passive investing debate is relentless. Truth is, neither approach is perfect, and both offer certain advantages.

Many investors prefer a passive investing approach because it is a cheaper route that has historically outperformed most active funds. This explains why passive fund flows have outpaced active flows for ten years in a row.

In 2013, 34 percent of domestic equity funds were invested passively (mutual funds and ETFs), whereas today that figure stands at 60 percent.[55]

Passive strategies that invest like the S&P 500 have become pervasive in retirement portfolios. One of the most common places where people hold passive investments is in target-date funds.

Target-date funds currently manage around $3.3 trillion. They started becoming more popular after legislation was introduced in 2006 by the Department of Labor, which established target-date funds as the "Qualified Default Investment Alternative" for individual 401(k)s.[56]

Target-date funds are mutual funds that make automatic rebalancing decisions based on your estimated date for retirement. Nearly 85 cents of every retirement dollar that is invested nowadays goes into a target date fund. According to Vanguard, target-date funds are offered by nearly 90 percent of employer-sponsored defined contribution plans like 401(k)s.

Passive investors have spent years crowding into the same funds while asking few questions. Hopefully this chapter will encourage readers to ask more.

The Passive Bubble Hides in Plain Sight

Most passive funds are market capitalization driven, which means they automatically buy the biggest, most valuable companies in whatever their coverage universe is. That's it.

When stocks outperform, they receive higher proportional weights, while those that lag receive lower weights. Passive funds don't typically consider how much profit a company earns, or its valuation. If a stock went up a lot in the past, that's good enough.

With over half of domestic funds now invested passively, capital markets have become more inefficient. Passive investors lower the market's IQ. Market cap-focused passive investors are a homogenous group that allocates capital purely based on past price momentum. That means they ignore changes taking shape in the economy and within individual companies.

■ ■

In 1906, a man named Sir Francis Galton visited a livestock fair. The statistician and cousin of Charles Darwin asked a crowd of eight hundred people to guess the weight of an ox. The average guess was 1,197 pounds, which missed the true weight of the ox by less than 1 percent. The result shocked Galton, but it was no fluke.

In *The Wisdom of Crowds*, James Surowiecki uses stories like this to show how diverse groups are typically better problem solvers, forecasters, and decision-makers than individuals or an elite few.

Surowiecki writes, "If you can assemble a diverse group of people who possess varying degrees of knowledge and insight, you're better off entrusting it with major decisions rather than leaving them in the hands of one or two people, no matter how smart those people are."

If a wise crowd is typified by independent actors, then it's obvious why widespread passive investing is problematic: it promotes mindless herding behavior! The so-called "wisdom of the crowd" is diluted when less investors bother to do any fundamental research. This hinders the market's ability to estimate future outcomes, and leads to inefficient capital allocation.

Capital markets are the foundation of our financial system. As investors, do we really want to invest in a manner that systematically rewards the richest companies based solely on their past accomplishments? How does that type of investing promote progress? How does that type of investing promote common prosperity?

One thing too much passive investing does promote is asset bubbles.

In March 2016, James Ledbetter wrote the following in a piece for *The New Yorker* titled, "Is Passive Investment Actively Hurting the Economy?"[57]

> It's not hard to imagine large-scale passive investments warping the stock market in similar ways. Typically, stocks are indexed by market capitalization—the value of a firm's share price times the number of shares—from highest to lowest. A market with more passive investors than active ones will continue to push money into the largest firms, whether these companies are actually performing strongly or not.

> Timothy O'Neill, the global co-head of Goldman Sachs' investment-management division, told me that essentially every new indexed dollar goes to the same places as previous dollars did. This "guarantees that the most valuable company stays the most valuable, and gets more valuable and keeps going up. There's no valuation or other parameters around that decision," he said. O'Neill fears that the result will be a "bubble machine"—a winner-take-all system that inflates already large companies, blind to whether they're actually selling more widgets or generating bigger profits. Such effects already exist today, of course, but the market is able to rely on active investors to counteract them. The fewer active investors there are, however, the harder counteraction will be.

There is a limit to passive investing somewhere. Even John Bogle understood this.

In November 2018, months before his passing, Bogle wrote an editorial for the *Wall Street Journal* titled, "Bogle Sounds a Warning on Index Funds." He wrote: "If historical trends continue, a handful of giant institutional investors will one day hold voting control of virtually every large US corporation. Public policy cannot ignore this growing dominance, and must consider its impact on the financial markets, corporate governance, and regulation. These will be major issues in the coming era."

Is there evidence of a "bubble machine" that is wildly inflating the values of the largest companies? Yes.

The harmful effects of passive funds growing too big are already showing up. A massive amount of passive money is flowing into the biggest companies of major indices, providing a cost of capital advantage that helps make the richest companies richer.

Here's one startling fact: as of this writing, Apple Inc.'s market capitalization of $2.7 trillion exceeds the entire Russell 2000 index of small-cap stocks. A key reason why Apple is worth more than all of those 2,000 firms combined is because the company from Cupertino has benefited from an ever-expanding valuation premium.

In 2013, before the passive bubble started to hyper-accelerate, Apple was worth about $420 billion, whereas the combined value of the 2,000 companies populating the Russell 2000 was about $1.7 trillion. Back then, Apple shares traded at 2.5 times sales compared to a 1.1 times sales multiple for the Russell 2000 index.

Today, Apple trades at 7.2 times sales while the Russell 2000 index still only trades at 1.1 times sales! In my view, this valuation divergence is a byproduct of the passive bubble.

The steady rotation of capital away from active managers and into market-cap weighted target-date funds disproportionately hurts small value stocks and helps large growth stocks. If this trend continues unchecked, Apple will eventually be worth more than all of the mid-cap companies combined.

Where will society draw the line? Sure, we all love our iPhones, but do we really want to see so much wealth inequality? Not everyone can get stock grants to work at Apple.

The academic community is starting to sniff out the problem. In a paper titled, "Tracking Biased Weights: Asset Pricing Implications of Value-Weighted Indexing," Hao Jiang, Dimitri Vayanos, and Lu Zheng found that "Flows into funds tracking the S&P 500 index raise disproportionately the prices of large-capitalization stocks in the index relative to the prices of the index's small stocks."

In the last decade, as passive went from being 34 percent of domestic funds to 60 percent, the S&P 500 large cap index that is most favored by passive investors consistently outpaced the performance of smaller cap indices. Since 2013, the S&P 500 has returned 13.2 percent annually, compared to a 11.7 percent return for the S&P 400 mid cap index, and a 10.0 percent return for the Russell 2000 small cap index.

We can also see further evidence of price distortions under the surface of the market. For example, the median valuation of the ten largest stocks in the S&P 500 index has risen at a much faster rate since 2010 compared to the smallest fifty stocks in the index.

Since 2010, the median price-to-sales multiple of the ten largest companies in the S&P 500 index has gone up +356 percent, rising from 2.1 to 9.4. Over the same period, the bottom fifty names in the S&P 500 index saw their price-to-sales multiple rise +90 percent, rising from 1.1 to 2.0. (Source: Bloomberg)

So, we've established that big firms are inflating in value faster than smaller firms. Now let's shift gears and talk about why overvaluation in popular retirement benchmarks like the S&P 500 is problematic for everyone.

The problem is: *when valuations go up, future expected returns go down.*

Over the long-term, equity market prices are a function of two things: (i) corporate earnings, and (ii) the valuation multiple investors assign to those earnings.

Martin Schmalz is a professor of finance and economics at the University of Oxford who published a paper in 2023 titled, "Index Funds, Asset Prices, and the Welfare of Investors." According to Schmalz, "The presence of the index fund tends to increase stock market participation and thus increase asset prices and decrease expected returns from investing in the stock market."[58]

After building a model and running many simulations, Schmalz found that even though individuals may benefit in the short run by migrating to a lower cost, passive form of investing, wide-scale adoption of this investing style presents problems, because it drives up the valuation of popular passive investments and erodes their future return potential.

Given how pervasive passive investing has become, investors ought to consider diversifying how much active and passive exposure they carry in their portfolio going forward.

Here are four strategies you can use to sidestep the passive investing bubble.

#1: Diversify with Equal-Weighted Portfolios

Thankfully, there are ways to invest passively that aren't based on market capitalization criteria. One way is to invest in an equal-weighted index.

If you are someone who generally favors a hands-off, passive approach to investing, but you are also rightfully concerned about the valuation risks highlighted in this chapter, you could diversify your investments by putting 50 percent into traditional market-cap weighted passive funds and 50 percent into passive equal-weighted funds (or some other ratio you're comfortable with).

In an equal-weighted index, each stock is given an equal weight, regardless of the company's market capitalization. This means that each company in the index has the same impact on the overall index performance, regardless of its size.

For example, if an equal-weighted index contains ten stocks, each stock would have a weight of 10 percent.

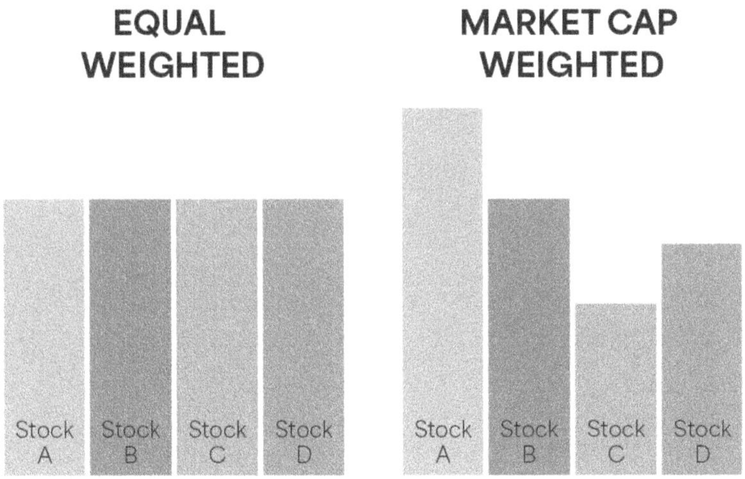

Examples of equal-weighted indices include the S&P 500 Equal Weight Index and the Russell 1000 Equal Weight Index.

You can invest in an equal-weighted portfolio using a variety of ETFs. These include the Invesco S&P 500 Equal Weight ETF (ticker: RSP) and Invesco's Russell 1000 Equal Weight ETF (ticker: EQAL).

One drawback to be aware of is that equal-weighted funds typically have slightly higher expense ratios compared to market-cap weighted passive funds.

That said, an equal-weighted portfolio can be a useful tool for investors who want to achieve greater diversification and potentially higher returns when the passive bubble reverses someday in the future.

#2: Blend Passive and Active Strategies

To perpetually ignore fundamentals 100 percent of the time invites tail risk into your portfolio. A better idea is to construct your retirement portfolio using a blend of passive and active funds.

Let's say you want to keep 30 to 50 percent of your portfolio passive. To complement that, you'll need to find some actively managed funds.

Here are examples of different active investing strategies, and the top three exchange traded funds (ETFs) for each category ranked by assets under management:

- **Value investing**: This strategy involves identifying undervalued stocks and buying them in anticipation that they will increase in value over time.

  ETF Examples: JPMorgan Equity Premium Income ETF (JEPI), Dimensional US Core Equity 2 ETF (DFAC), Dimensional US Marketwide Value ETF (DFUV)

- **Growth investing**: Growth investing focuses on buying stocks of companies that are expected to grow faster than the overall market.

  ETF Examples: Nuveen Growth Opportunities ETF (NUGO), Capital Group Growth ETF (CGGR), Capital Group Global Growth Equity ETF (CGGO)

- **Sector-based investing**: Sector-based investing involves investing in specific sectors of the economy, such as technology, healthcare, or energy.

  ETF Examples: ARK Innovation ETF (ARKK), First Trust North American Energy Infrastructure Fund (EMLP), ARK Genomic Revolution ETF (ARKG)

- **Global investing**: Global investing involves investing in companies located around the world to diversify a portfolio and potentially capture opportunities in different regions.

ETF Examples: Dimensional World Ex US Core Equity 2 ETF (DFAX), JPMorgan International Research Enhanced Equity ETF (JIRE), Dimensional International Value ETF (DFIV)

- **Income investing**: Income investing aims to provide investors with regular income through dividends or interest payments.

  ETF Examples: JPMorgan Equity Premium Income Fund (JEPI), Amplify CWP Enhanced Dividend (DIVO), Capital Group Dividend Value ETF (CGDV)

- **ESG investing**: ESG stands for environmental, social, and governance, and this strategy involves investing in companies that meet certain criteria related to sustainability and social responsibility.

  ETF Examples: BlackRock US Carbon Transition Readiness ETF (LCTU), BlackRock World Ex US Carbon Transition Readiness ETF (LCTD), Dimensional US Sustainability Core 1 ETF (DFSU)

In building out a portfolio, investors should try to pick several strategies that work well over time, but at different times.

For example, when value strategies outperform, growth strategies typically don't and vice versa. This type of diversification helps smooth out performance.

You can implement active strategies directly through a reputable online broker or indirectly by working with an advisor.

Here are additional criteria to consider when evaluating active investing strategies:

Performance. Investors should look for strategies with a strong track record of performance over an extended period.

Investment philosophy. Investors should seek to understand the investment philosophy of the fund manager or investment team behind the strategy, and make sure the investment is aligned with their goals and risk tolerance.

Investment process. Investors should look for strategies with a clear and disciplined investment process that can be consistently applied. This process should include criteria for security selection, portfolio construction, and risk management.

Fees. Investors should evaluate the fees associated with any strategy, including management fees, performance fees, and other expenses.

Transparency. Investors should look for strategies that provide transparency into their holdings and investment decisions.

Tip: If you want to compare funds based on risk-adjusted returns, two useful metrics favored by institutional investors are the Sharpe Ratio and Sortino Ratio.

If I was going to consider employing an active investment manager, I'd screen the initial pool by identifying managers with unusually high Sharpe and Sortino Ratios. Then, I'd ask the final contenders three questions:

1. What are your net returns?
2. What is your investment process?
3. Why is your process repeatable?

That's it. The manager who answers those questions best would likely win my business.

#3: Self-Manage

If you want to invest actively but don't want to do deep research or pay management fees, you can rebalance your portfolio once a year by following a simple factor formula.

My favorite investing book of all-time is *The Little Book That Beats the Market*, by Joel Greenblatt. In the book, Greenblatt explains how to invest according to a "magic formula" that has outperformed the market long-term. You can find stock screeners online that publish lists of his magic formula stocks, which you can use to construct your own portfolio.

Another effective strategy that's easy to implement is called the Dogs of the Dow. This stock-picking method was popularized in a book written by Michael B. O'Higgins in 1991, and it involves buying and holding for one year the ten highest dividend-yielding stocks in the Dow Jones Industrial Average. The theory behind the strategy is that blue-chip companies with a long history of paying dividends are stable and profitable. Hence, their stock prices should eventually rise consistent with their earnings and payouts. Similar to Greenblatt's magic formula, there are tools online that can help you build your own Dogs of the Dow portfolio.

In 2018, I introduced *Forbes* readers to the Dobermans of the Dow, which is a stock screen I invented as an alternative to the Dogs of the Dow strategy. Whereas the Dogs of the Dow only ranks stocks by their dividend yield, the Dobermans screen favors high quality companies trading at attractive valuations. The screen is based on two factors:

1. Rank the thirty Dow stocks by Return on Equity (ROE), keep the top twenty.
2. Rank the remaining twenty names by Free Cash Flow Yield, keep the top ten.

Those final ten stocks are your Dobermans.

Weighing quality against price is a pragmatic way to shop for anything, including common stocks. My preferred investing style is "Quality at a Discount." A high-quality asset is one whose intrinsic worth reliably grows at an attractive rate. Over the long term, quality assets generate quality investment returns. If you buy quality assets when they are temporarily marked down and cheap, you do even better.

I've written numerous articles for Forbes over the years describing the Dobermans' historical outperformance. If you like this approach, you could literally rebalance your portfolio once a year while sitting at the beach sipping a Mai Tai. And since I just gave you the formula for free, it's even cheaper to implement than buying a passive fund!

#4: Direct Indexing

One problem with index funds is you don't really know what you own under the hood. Direct indexing fixes that by allowing you to choose individual securities for your portfolio in an affordable manner. Direct indexing is an investment strategy that involves buying the individual securities that comprise an index, instead of just purchasing a fund that tracks the overall index.

The main benefit of direct indexing is that it provides investors more control over their investments. Investors can choose which stocks to include or exclude from their portfolio. This level of customization allows you to avoid the highest valuation stocks, or companies you just don't personally care for.

Direct indexing also offers tax advantages compared to traditional passive investing. With direct indexing, investors can sell individual stocks that have lost value during the year and use those losses to offset gains in other parts of their portfolio, reducing their overall tax liability.

Some specific offerings for direct index investing strategies include the following:

- **Wealthfront's Direct Indexing**: Allows investors to customize their portfolio based on their tax-objectives and invest in individual stocks.
- **BlackRock iShares**: Offers several ETFs that use direct indexing strategies, such as the iShares Enhanced US Large Cap ETF (IELG) and the iShares Russell 1000 Growth ETF (IWF).
- **Parametric Custom Core**: Provides customized index-based portfolios tailored to each client's unique investment objectives and preferences.

■ ■

Some may wonder: When will the passive bubble end?

The passive bubble will end when the passive share of the market starts receding. That may not happen for years. But when it does, it will likely ignite the mother of all mean reversion trades. Until then, I expect to see high volatility to the upside and downside in shares of the biggest passive beneficiaries.

Many of the biggest retirement funds today do almost no fundamental research. Think about that for a moment … one can imagine how silly that statement may sound someday in the future when market historians look back at this period.

In May 2017, John Bogle said, "If everybody indexed, the only word you could use is chaos, catastrophe ... The markets would fail."

As of this writing, 60 percent of US equity funds are invested in passive products according to Bloomberg. Between here and 100 percent, when exactly should we worry? Where is the tipping point? And most importantly—who is actively monitoring that?

What we do know is the more passive markets become, the more inefficient they will be. This exacerbates volatility and may help explain some of the wild price swings in recent years. Like when a quarter of the global bond market traded at negative yields in 2019, followed by a spike in yields that brought about the biggest treasury bond bear market ever. Or when crude oil traded at negative prices in 2020, before spiking to over $100 a barrel in 2022. Or when the S&P 500 fell 34 percent in twenty-three days in 2020, before staging the fastest 100 percent rally in history the following year.

These are extreme price movements that have never happened before.

Inefficient markets also create unproductive economies. This impacts everyone, because if we want to collectively achieve a higher standard of living over time, we must collectively invest in ways that promote progress. Market-cap driven passive investing does not promote progress. Rather, it's a system that rewards the richest companies for their *past* achievements.

To protect your retirement savings and promote efficient markets, I encourage you to diversify at least some of your portfolio outside of passive investments. This chapter has provided four ways to do that.

THE INVESTING LAP

For each category, pick whichever of the four solutions is the best fit for you in twenty seconds or less.

Four safety-first investing strategies:

- ☐ #1: Invest in a Low-Volatility Index Strategy
- ☐ #2: Invest in a Low-Volatility Sector Strategy
- ☐ #3: Dollar-Cost Average
- ☐ #4: Employ an Active Defensive Strategy

Four strategies to choose a benchmark:

- ☐ #1: Focus on Maximizing Long-Term Returns
- ☐ #2: Focus on Absolute Returns
- ☐ #3: Focus on a Volatility Threshold
- ☐ #4: Focus on Finding an Advisor

Four strategies to avoid the passive bubble:

- ☐ #1: Diversify with Equal-Weighted Portfolios
- ☐ #2: Blend Passive and Active Strategies
- ☐ #3: Self-Manage
- ☐ #4: Direct Indexing

02:00

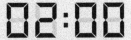

CHAPTER SUMMARY

- John Bogle revolutionized the investment industry by introducing low-cost passive investing.
- Bogle's senior thesis at Princeton became a central document that guided his approach to money management throughout his career.
- Passive investing has grown significantly, with 60 percent of domestic equity funds now invested passively.
- The higher the passive share of the market, the less efficient the market becomes.
- Target Date Funds (TDFs) are common places for holding passive investments.
- Passive funds' growth can lead to overvaluation and a dangerous feedback loop for large companies.
- Equal-weighted portfolios can offer benefits like greater diversification and lower concentration risk.
- You can implement active strategies directly through ETFs or indirectly with an advisor.
- Simple factor strategies like the Magic Formula and Dobermans of the Dow can help you actively self-manage a portfolio.
- Direct indexing allows investors to choose individual securities instead of index funds.

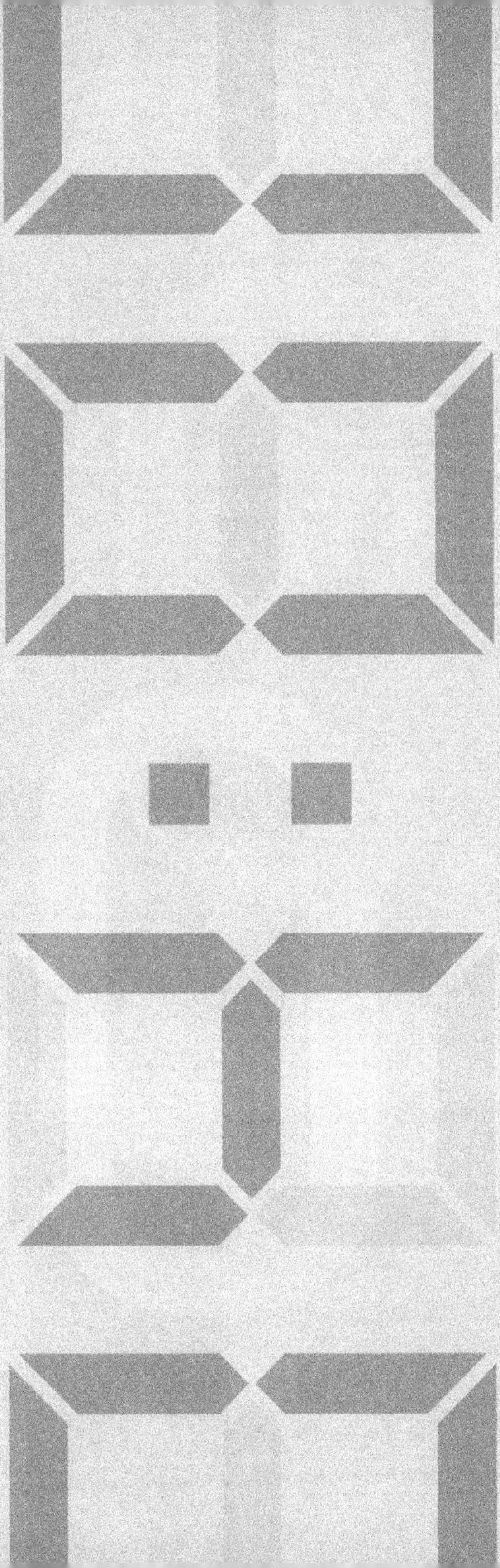

SECTION V

THE LIFESTYLE LAP

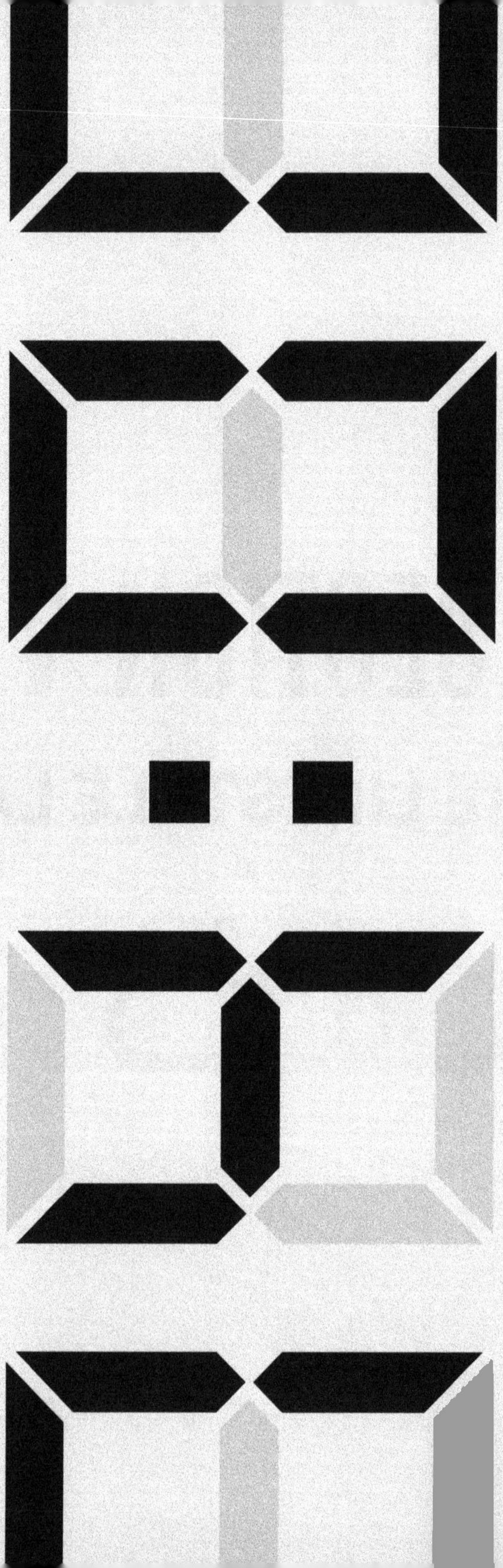

CHAPTER 14

DECIDING WHERE TO LIVE IN RETIREMENT

It is not the shortage of time that should worry us, but the tendency for the majority of time to be spent in low-quality ways.

—RICHARD KOCH

A former insurance industry executive and friend, Don Hurzeler, learned about "The 80/20 Rule" while completing an Executive MBA course at Harvard Business School. He described the experience in his book, *The Way Up*.

> Each day we had different business professors, some of the finest minds in the world. Each day for the entire three weeks, we were told that the dean of Harvard Business School would join us. Each day he had to cancel because he had to take a call from the president of the United States or make an emergency trip to Saudi Arabia or something else equally impressive.

> On the last day of class, the dean made his appearance. His introduction took about fifteen minutes as the professor in charge of the program listed his various degrees, notable engagements, and the books he had written. He came onto the stage to warm applause. We all wanted to hear from this guy.
>
> The dean had his glasses propped up high on his forehead. He had his sleeves rolled up. Under one arm he had a hundred slides he planned to show on the overhead projector (this being the days before PowerPoint). We settled in for a long last day in the classroom.
>
> The dean put down his slides. He faced the audience. He looked up in the air for a bit and stood silently. Just before it got really uncomfortable, he said, "I can tell you everything I know about business in one sentence: The 80/20 Principle works."
>
> At that, he grabbed his slides, pulled the glasses back down onto his nose, and exited stage left.
>
> That was the end of my Harvard education. It was also the most important business lesson of my life.

The 80/20 rule has been around for over a century. In 1896, an Italian economist named Vilfredo Pareto was gardening and noticed that 20 percent of his pea pods produced 80 percent of the harvest. Then he zoomed out and noticed that 20 percent of Italians owned 80 percent of the land. The pattern was so prevalent everywhere he looked that it eventually became the 80/20 Rule, also known as "The Pareto Principle."

The 80/20 rule says that roughly 20 percent of actions, decisions, or inputs lead to 80 percent of results.

For example, it's common for about 20 percent of a company's customers to account for 80 percent of its sales.

In everyday life, the 80/20 rule is all about time management and focus. Creating a massive to-do list isn't the answer. When we narrow our focus and remember that 20 percent of the things we do account for 80 percent of our output, we not only feel more fulfilled—we actually get more done too!

Choosing where to live is a key decision where the 80/20 rule applies. It's one of those big decisions you really want to get right.

Think about all the downstream implications of a single decision about where to live: the walkability of your neighborhood can make you more or less likely to exercise; your surrounding community can make you more or less likely to socialize; proximity to a nearby airport can make you more or less likely to see family regularly; the list goes on.

In retirement, you should strive to live in the best surroundings possible, while still getting a good deal. It's all about balancing quality of life and cost of living. Here are four potential choices for where to live in retirement.

#1: Age in Place

According to a survey by AARP, 77 percent of adults fifty and older wish to remain in their homes for the long-term, indicating that retiring in place is a popular choice among seniors.[59]

A home is more than just a place to live. It's where we make memories and feel the most safe and secure. If you love living where you are now, aging in place might be for you. Retiring where you currently live can offer several benefits, including:

- **Familiarity**. You're already familiar with the area, the people, and the amenities. This can help reduce stress and anxiety during the retirement transition. Plus, you're already familiar with your existing expenses for things like food, taxes, insurance, maintenance, and entertainment.
- **Social Connections**. You likely have an established social network in your current town, including friends, family, and community groups. Maintaining these connections can help provide a sense of belonging and purpose in retirement.
- **Cost Savings**. Moving to a new location is expensive, so retiring where you live now helps save money on moving costs and real estate fees.
- **Access to Reliable Health Care**. If you already have established healthcare providers in your current town, retiring there can help ensure continuity of care.

If you think aging in place might be for you, there are a few issues worth considering.

First, you may want to make some adjustments to your home over time. "The first step in an aging-in-place plan is to run a complete safety check of your home to identify hazards," says Stacey Watson, head of life event planning at Fidelity. "The good news is that many of the improvements that make it safer to stay in your house can be relatively easy and inexpensive."[60]

As we age, it's inevitable that our vision, hearing, and cognitive functioning will be challenged. But that doesn't need to derail our happiness if we take the proper precautions. Some easy tweaks that make it easier to stay in a residence well into retirement include:

- Add extra lighting to halls, closets, and dark rooms.

- Remove nonessential furniture that could pose a hazard.
- Add a shower chair and grab bar.
- Replace doorknobs with lever-style handles.
- Install a device to automatically turn off the stove.
- Get a home monitoring service.
- Find a wearable medical alert device.

Second, it's important to consider how mobility changes over time. The ability to drive a car is a key aspect of aging in place. If there comes a point where you can no longer drive yourself, how will you get around?

Third, aim to maintain strong social connections before and after retirement. Isolation is no way to spend retirement. Stay in touch with the people who count and be open to discovering new social connections.

#2: Home Sharing or Multigenerational Living

If you're old enough to remember the 1980s TV sitcom *Golden Girls*, you're familiar with the benefits of home sharing.

In recent years, home sharing has become a more popular concept. This is when a group of several seniors—who may or may not already know each other—pool resources to buy a home and share responsibilities for cooking, cleaning, and shopping.

Services that match people looking for compatible roommates include Senior Homeshares, Silvernest, Homeshare International, Roommates4Boomers, Golden Girls Network, and Nesterly.

Multigenerational living is another option for home sharing that's worth considering for similar reasons. This is a living arrangement where different generations of a family all live under the same roof, and it can include grandparents, parents, and children.

Multigenerational living is becoming more popular in recent years, but it has been a part of many cultures for centuries. The Pew Research Center estimated in 2021 that 18 percent of Americans lived in multigenerational households.

The upside to multigenerational living is that it provides an ongoing sense of companionship and shared economics. You can help your family while they help you.

Donna Butts, executive direction of Generations United, a Washington DC organization that advocates for programs that connect generations, says extended families living together can be a beautiful win-win solution. "There was a stigma that formed around the middle of the twentieth century we call 'the John Wayne Syndrome' in which people felt like it wasn't strong, and it was wrong if they needed each other," she says. "What people didn't realize is we sometimes need support and that makes us stronger."[61]

If this idea sounds appealing based on your family's circumstances, talk to your family members about it, and consider speaking to a real estate agent who specializes in multigenerational homes.

Home sharing and multigenerational living can bring many benefits for retirees, including companionship, financial relief, easier home maintenance, and enhanced safety and security.

#3: Retire to a Retirement Mecca

For lifestyle goals, it helps to picture yourself engaging in particular activities.

For example, imagine having a view of the Manhattan skyline, a private movie theater, and an in-house Mediterranean restaurant. And this isn't a luxury hotel; it's a retirement home.

High-end retirement facilities like this are springing up across the country, including in places like New York. Here, people pay a premium to engage in activities outside of things like bingo and shuffleboard. They get to regularly enjoy organized activities like Tai Chi, book clubs, and personal development classes (e.g., memoir writing and meditation).

The Villages is another type of retirement community. Located near Orlando, Florida, this unique enclave was the fastest growing metropolitan area in the United States between 2010 and 2020.[62]

A master-planned community like The Villages is great for retirees who value activities such as golf, tennis, pickleball, archery, volleyball, basketball, swimming, or fishing. There are also many clubs for activities such as birdwatching, billiards, and wine tasting. The number of offerings is nearly limitless.

Designed to serve the needs of seniors aged fifty-five and over, The Villages is mostly laid out in suburban blocks where golf carts are as common as cars. There are also assisted living facilities nearby for those who require a step-up in the level of ongoing care. More than eight hundred thousand Americans currently reside in assisted living communities, which is roughly 2 percent of seniors over the age of sixty-five.

One advantage of retirement communities is they can help streamline expenses. The cost-of-living factor is also transparent, so you know with fairly high precision what your monthly and annual spending will be and what you'll get for it.

How much you spend can depend on community type, level of care being offered, whether it's a luxury outfit with high-end amenities and accommodations, and/or whether you're buying or renting.

Tip: Retirees should avoid putting a large down payment on a retirement home residency because it can tie up a significant portion of savings in a single illiquid asset, which limits financial flexibility. Moreover, a large down payment may be unnecessary since most retirement homes offer a range of flexible payment options that can help retirees manage their cash flow and preserve their savings.

Pros of living in a retirement mega community:

- Many opportunities for socialization and activities with peers.
- Access to amenities such as fitness centers, pools, and golf.
- Maintenance-free living with on-site services such as landscaping and home repairs.
- Sense of security with gated entrances and security patrols.
- Potential for a sense of community and belonging.

Cons of living in a retirement mega community:

- Limited diversity in age and lifestyle.
- Potential for cliques and exclusion of certain individuals.
- High cost of living, including HOA fees and amenities.

- Limited privacy with close proximity to neighbors.

Here are the top five most popular retirement mega communities:

1. The Villages: Located in Florida, boasting over 120,000 residents and numerous amenities.
2. Sun City: Located in Arizona, offering many golf courses and fitness centers.
3. Laguna Woods Village: Located in California, known for its mild climate and outdoor activities.
4. Del Webb at Dove Mountain: Located in Arizona, featuring luxury homes and mountain views.
5. Cresswind at Lake Lanier: Located in Georgia, offering lakefront homes and outdoor recreation.

#4: Relocate to a New State or Country

Some retirees choose to move to a new location and start fresh. AARP reports that about 234,000 retirees moved to a new state in 2022.

Many retirees are attracted to places with a lower cost of living or better climate. Have you ever wondered if your favorite vacation spot would be the best place to retire? If you're thinking about retiring in a different state or country, the first step is to identify potential areas that make the most sense for you.

Quality of life is largely in the eye of the beholder. Not everyone needs to live walking distance from a beach to be happy, and some people may just want to garden and read books all day, which you can do just about anywhere. If family time is what gives you the most fulfillment, your decision on where to live in retirement might be one of the most straightforward ones you ever make.

The cost-of-living consideration is different, however. It can matter a great deal if you live in a high-tax state versus a low-tax state, or if you choose to live in a city where everything from groceries to gas to gym memberships tends to be more expensive than they would be elsewhere.

For those eager to spread their wings in retirement, here are some cost-of-living considerations to weigh as part of your decision-making process.

SOME STATES TAX SOCIAL SECURITY INCOME

There are currently twelve states that could potentially tax your Social Security income (in addition to federal income taxes). The mechanisms that trigger the tax vary by state.

In Colorado, for instance, taxes on Social Security income may apply to people under the age of sixty-five, but not those older. In Missouri, your Social Security income will be taxed only if you make more than $85,000 a year ($100,000 for married couples).

The twelve states that may currently tax your Social Security income are: Colorado, Connecticut, Kansas, Minnesota, Missouri, Montana, Nebraska, New Mexico, Rhode Island, Utah, Vermont, and West Virginia.

HOUSING AFFORDABILITY CAN SHIFT OVER TIME

If you're planning to retire in ten or twenty years and you already have a destination picked out, just remember that housing costs can change a lot over time. A recent boom in some cities like Austin, Nashville, and Orlando has driven up the cost of housing so significantly that many middle-class families are being priced out. A good idea is to track housing prices in your top choices and monitor how trends play out over time.

Property taxes are another key factor to consider when moving to a new place. Some states like Texas have no income taxes but property taxes are relatively high.

Like anything, there are pros and cons to consider related to the prospect of relocating in retirement.

Pros:

- **Cost of living**. Depending on where you move, you may be able to achieve a lower cost of living to stretch your retirement savings further. Also, depending on where you move, you may be able to take advantage of tax breaks.
- **Climate**. If you live in a place with harsh winters or sweltering summers, moving to a new state or country with a better climate could offer a big lifestyle upgrade. For instance, many retirees move to places like Florida, Arizona, or Costa Rica for the weather.
- **New experiences**. Moving to a new place offers a chance to try new things, meet new people, and explore new cultures. Every place you live changes you. You take a piece of it with you. And the richer your experiences are, the richer your life will be.

Cons:

- **Leaving family and friends**. The biggest downside to relocating for retirement is distancing yourself from loved ones.
- **Adjusting to a new place**. Moving to a new state or country can be stressful and it takes time to adjust to new surroundings.
- **Cost of moving**. Moving can be expensive, especially if it's a long distance. You'll need to budget for the cost of hiring

movers, shipping your belongings, and possibly buying new furniture and appliances.

So, where do most people want to retire?

According to the United States Census Bureau, the top five states for incoming retirees are Florida, Arizona, North Carolina, South Carolina, and Nevada. Many retirees are attracted to warm weather, lower cost of living, and strong healthcare systems. These are prime factors that influence a retiree's quality of life.

THE LIFESTYLE LAP

For each category, pick whichever of the four solutions is the best fit for you in twenty seconds or less.

Four choices for where to live in retirement:

- ☐ #1: Age in Place
- ☐ #2: Home Sharing or Multigenerational Living
- ☐ #3: Retire to a Retirement Mecca
- ☐ #4: Relocate to a New State or Country

Four distinct stages of life:

- ☐ #1: Early Adulthood (twenties to early thirties)
- ☐ #2: Pre-retirement (mid-thirties to fifties)
- ☐ #3: Early Retirement (late fifties to mid-sixties)
- ☐ #4: Late Retirement (mid-sixties and beyond)

Four withdrawal strategies:

- ☐ #1: The 4 Percent Rule
- ☐ #2: The Dynamic 5 Percent Rule
- ☐ #3: The Guyton-Klinger Rule
- ☐ #4: The Yale Endowment Spending Rule

02:20

CHAPTER SUMMARY

- The 80/20 Rule (Pareto Principle) states 20 percent of actions lead to 80 percent of results.
- Choosing where to live is the type of big decision you really want to get right.
- Retirement decisions should focus on balancing quality of life and cost of living factors.
- Four retirement living options to consider:
    1. Age in place: Staying in your current home offers familiar surroundings, social connections, and cost savings. If you go this route, consider making the appropriate safety adjustments to your home.
    2. Home sharing or multigenerational living: Sharing resources and responsibilities with other seniors or family members offers companionship and financial relief.
    3. Retire to a retirement mecca: High-end retirement communities offer luxurious amenities and organized activities.
    4. Relocate to a new state or country: The top five states for retirement based on warm weather, cost of living, and healthcare are Florida, Arizona, North Carolina, South Carolina, and Nevada.

CHAPTER 15

MILESTONES ON YOUR RETIREMENT JOURNEY

Life moves pretty fast. If you don't stop and look around once in a while, you could miss it.

—FERRIS BUELLER

Ossie Dahl's retirement didn't go as planned.

The sixty-four-year-old hospital executive had just put the finishing touches on a forty-year career at White Plains Hospital in New York. Moments after giving a speech at his retirement party—he collapsed and passed away.

"His last moments were spent expressing love, gratitude and happiness, surrounded by his closest family, friends and colleagues," the obituary said.

Of course, Mr. Dahl never planned on dying at the age of sixty-four. But there is a bright side to this story—before his unexpected passing, Dahl had lived a happy and fulfilling life.

Based on the way his family described him, Dahl had a past positive mindset. He maintained an open-door policy at his Ogden

Avenue home, where he and his wife raised their children in the same house his father and grandfather built. Dahl enjoyed hosting family events and reminiscing over a glass of wine.

"His face literally lit up when he was around family, especially his kids and grandkids," Dahl's family said. "He loved interacting with them—chatting, drinking, eating, and laughing with his kids; playing hide and seek, gardening and doing 'marching band' with his grandsons."

Dahl also had a future positive personality. Relatives describe him as an around-the-house handyman, whose signature catchphrases included "we will make it work," and "measure twice, cut once."

Dahl's positive attitude also helped him excel at his job. According to the *White Plains Examiner*, the hospital Dahl worked at experienced major growth during his tenure. Before he retired as vice president of facilities, Dahl helped oversee a string of renovations. In 2016, he was recognized with a certificate of appreciation and made an honorary member of the White Plains Department of Public Safety.

Mr. Dahl also had a present hedonistic side. He enjoyed regular Monday night card games with friends. He drank Stoli martinis straight up with a twist, and he possessed a dapper sense of style—often wearing paisley ties and hats that only he could pull off. Dahl loved going to Bruce Springsteen concerts, college basketball games, and vacationing at his Aunt Gloria's spring lake house.[63]

Dahl was a man who valued hard work, family, and fun, and he planned well enough to retire right on time. Unfortunately for Dahl and everyone reading this book, we don't know how long we're retired for. Some retirements last only a few minutes, while others can last decades.

Even though everyone's time horizon is ultimately different, many of the key planning milestones are the same. For instance, there is a minimum age for when we are allowed to obtain our first credit card or sign up for things like Medicare and Social Security.

To customize the best path to your ideal retirement—whenever that is—this chapter outlines the most important priorities for each stage of your time horizon.

Understanding Your Time Horizon

In financial planning, your time horizon helps determine an appropriate asset allocation and investment strategy. Generally, the longer your time horizon is, the more aggressive you can afford to be in your portfolio, and vice versa.

If you're saving money for a down payment on a home a few years down the line, that money would have a relatively short time horizon. There isn't much room for risk taking because there isn't a lot of time to recover from short-term losses. This is why stable assets like short duration treasury bonds are normally appropriate for short-term investing.

Saving for retirement typically involves a long time horizon, which allows you to pursue more growth in that part of your portfolio. You'll probably need that growth, too, if you happen to live a long time.

In the year 1900, the average life expectancy was just forty-seven years. Today, it's much longer. For a couple that are both the age of 65, the chance of at least one of them living to the age of 90 is about 50 percent.

IF YOU'RE 65 TODAY, THE PROBABILITY OF LIVING TO A SPECIFIC AGE

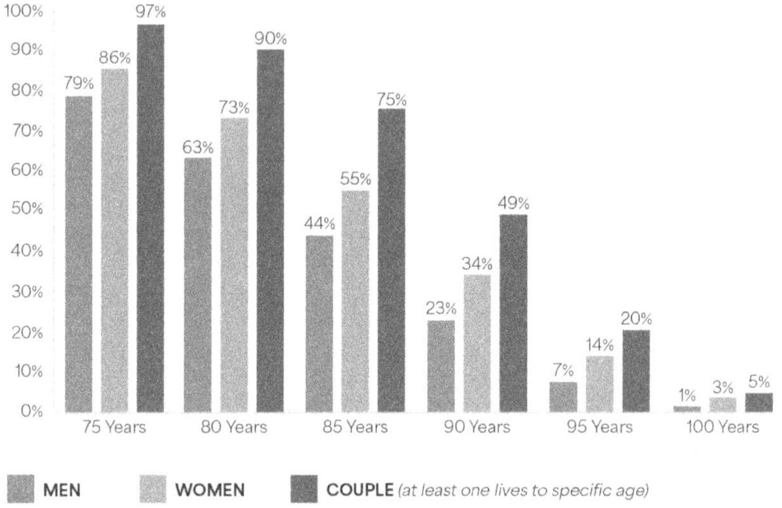

Source: Social Security Administration, as of 12/2/19. Period Life Table 2016.

The greatest threat to a peaceful retirement is running out of money. Therefore, a healthy 60-year-old should plan a thirty-year time horizon. COVID-19 delivered a temporary setback to life expectancy numbers, but with medical advances and the deployment of AI into drug research, life expectancy will continue to go up over time.

In addition to supporting us for longer, our money also needs to keep up with inflation and other costs that tend to rise as we age, like healthcare.

According to Fidelity Benefits Consulting, a sixty-five-year-old couple probably needs close to $280,000 in today's dollars (after tax) to fully cover estimated medical expenses in retirement. Big number! Many folks aren't currently factoring any extra health care costs into their retirement savings plans.

Medicare begins at age sixty-five, but it doesn't cover everything. The average retiree should expect to pay thousands of dollars per year in extra costs for supplemental insurance and out of pocket expenses.

If you're still working and have a qualifying health plan, you can get ahead of the curve by contributing to a Health Savings Account (HSA). This type of plan allows you to save more pretax dollars that you can grow and withdraw tax free if you use the funds for qualified medical expenses. There's no time limit for using the funds, and an HSA can follow you if you switch jobs.

Clearly, there is quite a lot to keep track of over the course of our financial lives. To summarize, here is a timeline of all the key birthdays that impact people financially:

- Age sixteen: This is the age when most teenagers can legally work.
- Age eighteen: This is when young adults can vote, sign contracts, and open credit card accounts without a cosigner. However, in many states they are still considered minors when it comes to certain financial decisions, such as investing in stocks.
- Age twenty-one: This is the age when most states consider people to be legal adults, which means they can access their own credit reports and take out loans in their own name. Opening investment accounts or taking control of custodial accounts opened in someone's name also becomes legal in many states.
- Age fifty: At this age, people can start making catch-up contributions to certain types of retirement accounts, such as IRAs and 401(k)s.

- Age fifty-five: This is the age when people can start taking penalty-free withdrawals from their 401(k) if they retire or leave their job.
- Age fifty-nine and a half: At this age, people can start taking penalty-free withdrawals from their IRAs and other retirement accounts.
- Age sixty-two: This is the earliest age at which people can start collecting Social Security retirement benefits, but their monthly payments will be reduced if they do so.
- Age sixty-five: This is the age when people become eligible for Medicare, which helps save money on healthcare costs.
- Age seventy: The maximum age you can wait to start taking Social Security Benefits, which also maximizes the monthly amount you're eligible to receive.
- Age seventy-three: This is the age at which people must start taking Required Minimum Distributions (RMDs) from their traditional IRAs and 401(k)s.

■ ■

Over time, our financial goals and priorities naturally change. Since people from different age groups are reading this, the rest of the chapter will highlight the key financial priorities in four distinct stages of life: early adulthood, pre-retirement, early retirement, and late retirement.

#1: Early Adulthood (Twenties to Early Thirties)

Early adulthood is the time to start building a solid financial foundation that paves the way for future success. Here are some top financial planning priorities for this life stage.

Establish Financial Goals. Establishing clear financial goals is the first step in financial planning. Whether it is saving for a down payment on a home, paying off student loans, or building an emergency savings fund, it's essential to identify your priorities so you can create a targeted plan.

Create a Budget. Creating a budget is a vital part of achieving your financial goals. Start by tracking your expenses and income, and then create a budget that is realistic and achievable.

> **Tip**: As of this writing, some popular budgeting apps I am a fan of include: Quicken Simplifi, YNAB, and Copilot.

Reduce Debt. Managing debt wisely is a key priority in early adulthood. Try to pay off high-interest debt, such as credit card debt and personal loans, as soon as possible. If you can't immediately pay off bad forms of debt, try consolidating with a low-interest rate loan, or consider a credit card that has a temporary 0 percent APR attached to it.

Save for Retirement. It's never too early to start saving for retirement. Begin contributing to a 401(k) or IRA as soon as possible to take advantage of compound interest and long-term growth potential.

Build Diverse Skills. With the ever-changing job market, having a range of skills can help young adults stay competitive and gain access to better opportunities, higher salaries, and greater financial security.

You can think of human capital as future earnings potential, which is typically worth a lot more early on in someone's career compared to their financial capital (i.e., savings). Strong human capital makes it easier to build financial capital.

We can improve our human capital by developing a diverse array of skills. You can do this by experimenting with different types of jobs, furthering your education, and connecting with value-added mentors.

If you think about it, super successful people are usually good at more than one thing.

For example, Jennifer Lynn Lopez (nicknamed "J. Lo") has come a long way since she started out as a Fly Girl dancer on the TV program, *In Living Color*. Since then, she's transformed herself into a multi-dimensional entertainment mogul with a net worth exceeding $400 million.

> *You have to remember the value of your individuality—that you have something special and different to offer that nobody else can.*
>
> **—JENNIFER LOPEZ**

J. Lo is a unique "triple threat." After succeeding as a dancer, she then landed the starring role in the film, *Selena*. Two years later, she released her first studio album.

What makes J. Lo such an elite entertainer? Is she the *best* dancer, actress, or singer in the world? Probably not.

J. Lo has built an antifragile career in a notoriously fragile industry by *combining* her talents synergistically. Being skilled at acting, singing, and dancing creates more opportunities to win, providing her a competitive advantage over most single threat entertainers.

As J. Lo told *Adweek*, "It's about being the scarce asset." In the early adulthood phase, this is especially sound advice.

Anyone can be a triple threat in anything. For instance, instead of just being a personal trainer, you could be a trainer who also understands nutrition and how to leverage social media marketing strategies.

Envisioning yourself as a triple threat is a simple formula anyone can use to enhance the ROI from their human capital. Instead of just being an expert at X (fill in the blank), be one who also understands Y (fill in the blank) and Z (fill in the blank).

#2: Pre-Retirement (Mid-Thirties to Fifties)

The pre-retirement phase is when you should start evaluating your progress towards achieving long-term goals and adapting your plan accordingly. Here are some key financial planning priorities for this stage.

Review Your Retirement Plan. Regularly review your retirement plan so you stay on track toward your retirement goals. If you start to fall behind schedule, consider increasing your savings and upgrading your investment strategy.

Pay Down Mortgage. Paying off your mortgage can provide significant financial security and reduce your monthly expenses in retirement. When you receive unexpected windfalls, consider making extra payments toward your mortgage or refinancing to a shorter amortization schedule (e.g., moving from a thirty-year fixed rate to a fifteen-year fixed rate).

Create a Will and Estate Plan. Creating a will and estate plan helps ensure that your assets are distributed per your wishes. Consider working with an estate planning attorney or service to create an estate plan.

Life Insurance. Purchasing life insurance in mid-life is beneficial for several reasons. First, life insurance ensures that financial obligations, such as mortgage payments or college savings, can be met in the event of an unexpected death. Second, life insurance can provide a source of income replacement for a spouse or dependents, especially if the insured was the primary breadwinner. Third, life insurance offers peace of mind, helping people feel more secure about their financial future.

According to a study conducted by LIMRA, an insurance industry research group, more than half of households in the United States are underinsured, with an average coverage gap of $200,000. This suggests that many individuals are not adequately prepared for unexpected events, such as premature death.

The cost of life insurance tends to increase with age, making mid-life an ideal time to purchase a policy. By purchasing life insurance in mid-life, you can take advantage of lower premiums and lock in a rate before any significant health issues arise.

There are two main types of life insurance: term and whole life insurance.

Term life insurance provides coverage for a specific time period, such as ten, twenty, or thirty years. If the policy holder dies within the term, the beneficiaries receive the death benefit payout. After the term ends, the policyholder typically has an option to renew the policy, but the premiums will increase based on their age and health status.

Whole life insurance provides coverage for the holder's entire lifetime. Whole life insurance policies also have a cash value component that grows over time, and the policyholder may be able to borrow against it or withdraw the cash value. However, the premiums paid for whole life insurance are generally higher because of the lifetime coverage and cash value component.

I generally recommend term life insurance over whole life insurance because it provides coverage when you most need it (mid-life) at a lower cost. Since the primary purpose of life insurance is to replace income in the event of an unexpected death, term life insurance is the most straightforward and cost-effective way to achieve that goal.

When buying life insurance, how much coverage should you get? As a general rule of thumb, I think it's wise to have a life insurance policy that covers around ten times your annual income.

Disability Insurance. Disability insurance protects you from the financial hardship of lost income if you become disabled and can no longer work.

The ideal age to purchase disability insurance is typically in your thirties or forties, when most people are in good health and have a lower risk of developing a disability. By purchasing disability insurance at a younger age, you can lock in lower premiums and ensure that you have coverage in place. Waiting until you're older or have a health condition can make it more difficult to obtain coverage and will increase the cost of your premiums.

Your disability benefit should be about 60 percent of your pretax annual income. To obtain that coverage, expect to pay between 1 percent and 3 percent of your annual salary.

#3: Early Retirement (Late Fifties to Mid-Sixties)

Early retirement is an exciting time, but you need to make sure you have enough income to support your lifestyle. Here are some key financial planning priorities for this stage.

Evaluate Your Income Sources. Evaluate your income sources, including Social Security, pensions, and retirement accounts, to determine if they will be enough to support your lifestyle in retirement.

Manage Your Portfolio. Manage your investment portfolio to ensure that it is aligned with your retirement goals, risk tolerance, and time horizon. Consider working with a financial advisor to create a diversified portfolio that meets your needs.

Plan for Healthcare Costs. Healthcare costs can be a significant expense in retirement. Consider purchasing supplemental insurance or exploring other ways to cover healthcare costs.

Long-term Care Insurance. Long-term care is assistance to individuals who are unable to perform everyday activities on their own due to a prolonged illness, injury, disability, or aging. Long-term care services may include help with activities of daily living such as bathing, dressing, eating, and medication management.

Long-term care insurance is a type of insurance policy that covers the cost of long-term care services. The best time to buy long-term care insurance is when you are young and relatively healthy, typically in your fifties or early sixties. The earlier in life you buy a policy, the lower the premiums.

According to the American Association for Long-Term Care Insurance, the cost of long-term care insurance increases by about 8 to 10 percent for every year you delay purchasing a policy. Also, the likelihood of being approved for coverage decreases as you age, and pre-existing medical conditions may make it more difficult to obtain coverage.

It's important to note that long-term care insurance may not be the best option for everyone. Generally, I think it makes the most sense for people who want to plan conservatively and have a history of longevity in their family.

Tap Into Senior Discounts. Senior discounts are free money!

Here are some examples of discounts available to senior citizens, along with the age requirements: [64]

- Retail Discounts—Age 55+
  Example: Kohl's offers a 15 percent discount every Wednesday to shoppers aged sixty and over.
- Restaurant Discounts—Age 55+
  Example: Denny's offers a 15 percent discount to customers aged fifty-five and over.
- Travel Discounts—Age 50+
  Example: Marriott Hotels offers a 15 percent discount to seniors aged sixty-two and over.
- Entertainment Discounts—Age 60+
  Example: AMC Theatres offers a senior discount on movie tickets to customers aged sixty and over.
- Prescription Drug Discounts—Age 50+
  Example: Walgreens offers a discount on prescription drugs to customers aged fifty-five and over through their "Balance Rewards for Seniors" program.

- Public Transportation Discounts—Age 65+
  Example: New York City's Metropolitan Transportation Authority offers reduced fares on buses and subways to seniors aged sixty-five and over.
- Health and Wellness Discounts—Age 65+
  Example: SilverSneakers offers free gym memberships to seniors aged sixty-five and over at participating fitness centers.
- Financial Discounts—Age 50+
  Example: Bank of America offers a discount on safe deposit box rentals to customers aged sixty-two and over.
- Utility Discounts—Age 60+
  Example: Pacific Gas and Electric Company offers a discount on gas and electric bills to seniors aged sixty and over through their "CARE" program.

#4: Late Retirement (Mid-Sixties and Beyond)

Late retirement is a time to enjoy the fruits of your labor and to focus on your legacy. Here are some key financial planning priorities for this stage.

Manage Your Withdrawals. Manage your retirement account withdrawals to ensure you do not run out of money in retirement. Consider working with a financial advisor to create a withdrawal strategy that meets your needs.

Review Your Estate Plan. Review your estate plan regularly to make sure it reflects your current wishes and circumstances.

Focus on Your Legacy. Focus on your legacy and consider charitable giving or other ways to leave a lasting impact.

Optimize Social Security Timing. If you're healthy, it's almost always best to wait as long as possible to claim Social Security Retirement Benefits.

When you delay claiming Social Security income, your benefits increase by about 8 percent per year until you reach the age of seventy. This increase is due to what's called "delayed retirement credits" (DRCs). From your full retirement age (FRA)—which can be between sixty-six and sixty-seven depending on your birth year—until the age of seventy, you accumulate DRCs for each month you delay claiming benefits.

So, if you start taking benefits at age sixty-two, you'll receive a lower monthly benefit, but you'll receive benefits for a longer period of time. If you wait until age seventy, you'll receive a higher monthly benefit, but you'll receive benefits for a shorter period of time. The break-even point is typically around age eighty, so if you expect to live longer than that, it likely makes sense to delay taking benefits.

Here is a breakdown of the factors to consider when making the Social Security timing decision:

- **Health**. If you have health issues or a family history of shorter lifespans, you may want to consider taking Social Security earlier, as you may not live long enough to see the full benefit of waiting until age seventy.
- **Financial Situation**. If you have sufficient savings to cover your expenses, you can delay taking Social Security and receive a higher benefit later on. Conversely, if you need the income now to cover your expenses, you may want to start taking Social Security earlier.
- **Spousal Benefits**. If you're married, you may be able to take advantage of spousal benefits, which allow you to receive up to half of your spouse's benefit if it's higher than your own.

- **Work Status.** If you're still working and earning income, your Social Security benefit may be reduced if you take it before your full retirement age (FRA). However, once you reach your FRA, you can earn as much as you want without affecting your benefit.

Consider Delaying Retirement. Last, consider working later into your retirement years.

The US Bureau of Labor Statistics projects workforce participation among people seventy-five and older will climb to 11.7 percent by 2030 from 8.9 percent in 2020.[65]

John Tamny, author of *The Future of Work*, is optimistic about the future of work for people of all ages. He thinks many people will voluntarily delay retirement. "Guaranteed income won't be necessary simply because the work of tomorrow will be something *we can't not do,"* he writes. "And since work will be defined by joy, retirement will be what more and more of us avoid."[66]

Tamny sees jobs in the future becoming ever more tailored to fit our personal interests and goals. In many ways, this would be similar to how occupational choices have expanded compared to one hundred years ago. If what you do in the future doesn't feel like "work," you may find it personally rewarding.

For example, Jayne Burns is a one-hundred-year-old who *chooses* to still work four days a week. Burns says there's no secret to living a longer, happier life, but "working has helped." For twenty-six years, she has worked as a part-time fabric cutter at Joann Fabric and Crafts store.

The centenarian, who was a bookkeeper for most of her career, tried retiring several times in her seventies and eighties. She quickly unretired because she missed the routine of being around coworkers.

"I enjoy talking to everybody I work with, and meeting the customers who are very nice," she says, "even if some of them are surprised to see me at the cutting table."

Over her long career, Burns has learned that there's one trait the best jobs have in common: nice coworkers. "It's important to find people who are friendly and kind," she says.

At Joann's, Burns is friends with younger coworkers, including a college student who introduced her to TikTok videos during a coffee break.[67] The pair have made several TikToks together, dancing in the store's breakroom and chatting about some of Burns's favorite memories (like how she met her husband). One of their videos has over nine million views.[68]

Here are the top reasons why people choose to keep working in retirement.

REASONS PEOPLE CHOOSE TO WORK IN RETIREMENT

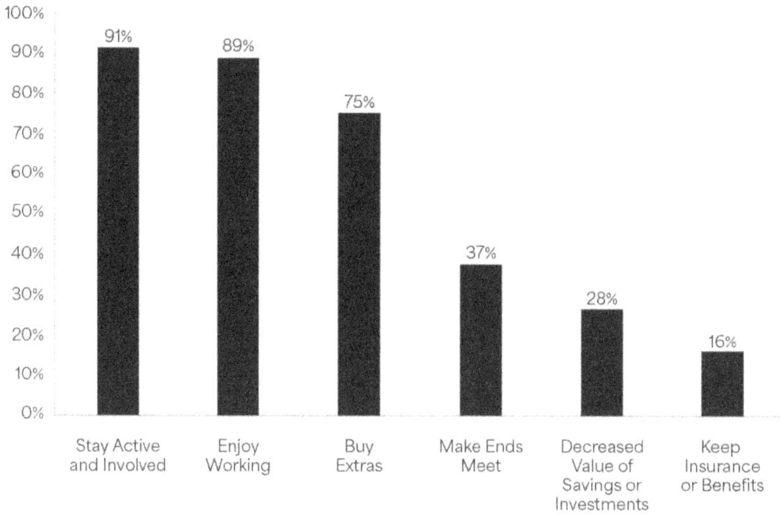

Source: Employee Benefit Research Institute, as of 4/13/20. 2019 Retirement Confidence Survey. Respondents could select multiple reasons that apply to their situation.

THE LIFESTYLE LAP

For each category, pick whichever of the four solutions is the best fit for you in twenty seconds or less.

Four choices for where to live in retirement:

- ☐ #1: Age in Place
- ☐ #2: Home Sharing or Multigenerational Living
- ☐ #3: Retire to a Retirement Mecca
- ☐ #4: Relocate to a New State or Country

Four distinct stages of life:

- ☐ #1: Early Adulthood (twenties to early thirties)
- ☐ #2: Pre-retirement (mid-thirties to fifties)
- ☐ #3: Early Retirement (late fifties to mid-sixties)
- ☐ #4: Late Retirement (mid-sixties and beyond)

Four withdrawal strategies:

- ☐ #1: The 4 Percent Rule
- ☐ #2: The Dynamic 5 Percent Rule
- ☐ #3: The Guyton-Klinger Rule
- ☐ #4: The Yale Endowment Spending Rule

02:40

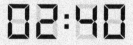

CHAPTER SUMMARY

- Understanding your time horizon is crucial in financial planning.
- Early adulthood (twenties to early thirties) priorities
  - Establish clear financial goals and plan accordingly.
  - Create a budget and manage expenses effectively.
  - Reduce high-interest debt and start saving for retirement.
- Become a triple threat to enhance your human capital.
- Pre-retirement (mid-thirties to fifties) priorities
  - Review your retirement plan and adjust contributions if needed.
  - Pay down the mortgage and create a will/estate plan.
  - Purchase life and disability insurance for protection.
- Early retirement (late fifties to mid-sixties) priorities
  - Evaluate income sources like Social Security and pensions.
  - Manage investment portfolio according to goals and risk tolerance.
  - Plan for healthcare costs, including long-term care insurance.
- Late retirement (mid-sixties and beyond) priorities
  - Manage retirement withdrawals to avoid running out of funds.
  - Review and update the estate plan as necessary.
  - Consider charitable giving and focus on leaving a legacy.
  - Optimize Social Security timing.
  - Consider delaying retirement to stay active.

CHAPTER 16
STAY RICH OR DIE TRYIN'

Concentrate on your money. Try to hold your paper.

—50 CENT

Before 2002, Jack Whittaker was known in his small West Virginia community as the owner of a successful company called Diversified Enterprises Construction. The business did well, and so did Jack—his net worth was estimated to be $17 million.

Then came a fateful Christmas Eve that would change Jack's life forever.

On a frigid morning, Jack stopped at a C&L Super Serve for a breakfast sandwich and one hundred Quick Pick lottery tickets. It wasn't that Jack was a manic lotto player or a serial gambler. He once said that he only played when the jackpot exceeded $100 million. It was at $315 million that day, so Jack rolled the dice. And he won.

It was the largest single-ticket jackpot in history, which should have made it the best day of Jack and his family's life, right?

Unfortunately, winning the lotto would set into motion a full unraveling of Jack's life.

A guy who had once been grounded by hard work and responsibility would ultimately be ravaged by the temptations of fortune. Driving his Lamborghini around the neighborhood, throwing cash out of the windows, and traveling around with suitcases full of cash turned Jack into a person he would later regret becoming.

Jack particularly loved to spoil his beloved granddaughter. However, two years after Jack cashed in his winning ticket, she died of a drug overdose. Five years later, her mother—Jack's daughter—also died. And during the intervening years, Jack was robbed and sued multiple times, often by acquaintances.

Jack's story is sad but not uncommon. Studies show that lotto winners are more likely to declare bankruptcy than non-winners, and there's a relatively high incidence of lotto winners who struggle with depression and divorce.

According to economist Jay L. Zagorsky, a columnist for *US News and World Report*, "studies found that instead of getting people out of financial trouble, winning the lottery got people into more trouble."[69]

Jack Whittaker was certainly one of these people. In an interview with *Time* magazine a few years after winning the lottery, Jack said, "I wish we had torn the ticket up."

Truth is, you can have all the money in the world yet be completely miserable. And it's because no matter how much money we have, we still need a well-balanced time perspective to be happy.

Jack's problem wasn't winning the lotto. His problem was that he allowed his present hedonism to go into overdrive, which created extra stress in his life. Then, after he lost two people he loved, he fell into a pit of past negative despair. It could happen to anyone.

Wouldn't it be nice if Jack had tools to coach him through that web of emotions? Maybe writing and reviewing the story behind his financial plan could have helped with that.

On the financial side, Jack's story illustrates that getting rich and staying rich are two very different things. Accumulating wealth certainly doesn't mean being wealthy forever. In fact, becoming rich may just expand a person's blind spots, making them more vulnerable.

As my grandmother used to say, "A fool and his money will soon part."

In this chapter, I want to help you understand that wealth accumulation is only the first step to long-term financial success. You also need to take steps to preserve your wealth after you retire.

Sequence of Returns Risk

Reckless spending habits and bad investments can ruin anyone's fortune, but timing can also make a huge difference. Not many people realize it, but *when* you choose to retire can have a huge impact on how far your money takes you.

That brings us to one of the most important—yet also least understood—topics associated with retirement planning: sequence of returns risk.

To illustrate why the timing of your retirement matters so much, let's assume two investors have portfolios valued at $500,000.

Each investor withdraws $25,000 in the first year and then increases the withdrawal amount by 3 percent annually to account for inflation. We'll also assume both investors average a 6.6 percent return over a thirty-year time horizon, but they take different paths for achieving that result (i.e., their returns each year are different).

Basically, we're assuming the two investors retire at different times, and in different market cycles.

As shown in the table below, Investor A runs out of money in year twenty, while Investor B still has plenty of money left after thirty years.

SAME RETURNS, DIFFERENT RESULTS

Year	Annual Returns (Investor A)	Portfolio Value (Investor A)	Annual Withdrawal	Year	Annual Returns (Investor B)	Portfolio Value (Investor B)	Annual Withdrawa
1		$500,000		1		$500,000	
2	*-11.2%*	*$419,000*	$25,000	2	15.8%	$554,000	25,000
3	*-18.5%*	*$315,735*	$25,750	3	22.1%	$650,684	25,750
4	*-2.9%*	*$280,056*	$26,523	4	12.6%	$706,148	26,523
5	4.5%	$265,341	$27,318	5	-3.5%	$654,114	27,318
6	8.8%	$260,553	$28,138	6	13.4%	$713,628	28,138
7	1.2%	$234,698	$28,982	7	21.1%	$835,222	28,982
8	17.4%	$245,684	$29,851	8	2.3%	$824,580	29,851
9	5.2%	$227,712	$30,747	9	9.0%	$868,046	30,747
10	7.6%	$213,349	$31,669	10	16.3%	$977,868	31,669
11	5.5%	$192,464	$32,619	11	-4.2%	$904,178	32,619
12	19.9%	$197,167	$33,598	12	9.2%	$953,765	33,598
13	8.6%	$179,517	$34,606	13	6.5%	$981,154	34,606
14	11.2%	$163,979	$35,644	14	4.3%	$987,699	35,644
15	6.3%	$137,596	$36,713	15	-2.0%	$931,232	36,713
16	8.5%	$111,477	$37,815	16	15.0%	$1,033,102	37,815
17	15.0%	$89,250	$38,949	17	8.5%	$1,081,966	38,949
18	-2.0%	$47,347	$40,118	18	6.3%	$1,110,012	40,118
19	4.3%	$8,062	$41,321	19	11.2%	$1,193,013	41,321
20	6.5%	-$33,975	$42,561	20	8.6%	$1,253,051	42,561
21	9.2%	-$80,939	$43,838	21	19.9%	$1,458,570	43,838
22	-4.2%	-$122,692	$45,153	22	5.5%	$1,493,639	45,153
23	16.3%	-$189,198	$46,507	23	7.6%	$1,560,648	46,507
24	9.0%	-$254,128	$47,903	24	5.2%	$1,593,899	47,903
25	2.3%	-$309,313	$49,340	25	17.4%	$1,821,898	49,340
26	21.1%	-$425,398	$50,820	26	1.2%	$1,792,941	50,820
27	13.4%	-$534,746	$52,344	27	8.8%	$1,898,375	52,344
28	-3.5%	-$569,944	$53,915	28	4.5%	$1,929,888	53,915
29	12.6%	-$697,290	$55,532	29	*-2.9%*	$1,818,389	55,532
30	22.1%	-$908,589	$57,198	30	*-18.5%*	$1,424,789	57,198
31	15.8%	**-$1,111,060**	$58,914	31	*-11.2%*	**$1,206,298**	58,914

How is this outcome possible? Didn't the investors both average the same returns over thirty years?

Even though the two investors average the same annual returns, they do so *in reverse order*. Take a closer look at the Annual Returns columns in the above chart. Investor A earns negative returns in the first three years, whereas Investor B doesn't see a string of poor returns until the final three years of their time horizon. The impact of this timing luck is enormous.

Unfortunately, nobody controls how their retirement timeline will precisely unfold in relation to market cycles. But we can hedge sequence risk by being more cautious at the onset of retirement—when sequence risk can do the most damage.

Many people mistakenly assume they should steadily invest more conservatively the older they get, but this isn't always the case. I generally recommend investing the most conservatively in the first few years of retirement. If you can make it through the first five years of retirement without a major hiccup, for example, the probability of your assets surviving throughout your lifetime goes way up.[70]

Negative returns early in retirement severely compromised Investor A's long-term success, but they didn't have to. Had Investor A made some adjustments early on, like reducing or delaying withdrawals, the portfolio could have weathered the storm.

So, in addition to reducing portfolio risk at the onset of retirement, investors should also be armed with a time-tested income strategy that enhances the probability of preserving wealth.

Here are four withdrawal strategies to consider.

#1: The 4 Percent Rule

The Four Percent Rule for retirement originated in the 1990s based on a study by a financial advisor named William Bengen. He found that if a retiree withdrew 4 percent of their retirement savings in year one, and then adjusted the amount for inflation each year thereafter, their savings would likely last at least thirty years.

Here's an example of Bengen's rule in action. Let's say you have $1 million saved up for retirement. In the first year, you would withdraw

4 percent of that, which is $40,000. If inflation is 2 percent the next year, you would increase your withdrawal by 2 percent, making it $40,800 ($40,000 x 1.02). Pretty simple.

The Four Percent Rule was based on an analysis of historical market data. It provided a simple rule of thumb to help retirees avoid running out of money.

Bengen, an MIT graduate, reviewed actual market returns from 1926 through 1992. He assumed withdrawals were made at the end of each year and the portfolio was rebalanced annually.

For the purposes of this book, I've updated the study to include actual market returns from 1926–2021. As shown below, if someone had invested in a 100 percent equity portfolio that mimicked the S&P 500 Index, there was a 95 percent chance their money would have lasted them over a thirty-year retirement using the 4 Percent Rule.[71]

Four Percent Rule Study: 1926-2021

WITHDRAWAL RATES (2% INFLATION)

	3%	4%	5%	6%	7%	8%	9%	10%	11%	12%
100% STOCKS										
20 YEARS	100%	97%	93%	89%	80%	67%	53%	51%	37%	31%
25 YEARS	99%	96%	94%	93%	80%	63%	53%	41%	30%	19%
30 YEARS	98%	95%	94%	89%	75%	62%	48%	38%	28%	14%
60% STOCKS, 40% BONDS										
20 YEARS	100%	100%	97%	93%	80%	56%	45%	29%	15%	5%
25 YEARS	100%	99%	96%	89%	67%	50%	30%	14%	9%	1%
30 YEARS	100%	97%	94%	80%	57%	35%	20%	12%	2%	0%

Keep in mind: The 4 percent withdrawal rate *only* applies to year one of retirement. After that, inflation decides the amount you should withdraw each year, because the goal from that point on is to simply maintain your purchasing power.

It's important to remember that with any withdrawal strategy, there is never a 100 percent guarantee of success.

Tip: If the Four Percent Rule sounds appealing, you can also use it to reverse engineer the amount of retirement savings you need to maintain your target lifestyle.

To do so, follow these steps:

- **Calculate your annual expenses**. Determine the total annual expenses you expect to have during retirement, which should include housing, utilities, food, healthcare, transportation, and other personal expenses.
- **Adjust for other income sources**. If you have income sources during retirement like Social Security, pensions, or rental income, subtract these amounts from your annual expenses to find your net annual expenses.
- **Apply the Four Percent Rule**. To estimate the total amount needed in retirement savings, divide your net annual expenses by 0.04 (4 percent).

For example, if your net annual expenses are $40,000, applying the Four Percent Rule to calculate how much you need at the beginning of retirement would mean dividing $40,000 by 0.04, which equals

$1 million. In this case, you would need approximately $1 million in retirement savings to maintain your current lifestyle. Keep in mind this is a rough estimate, and individual circumstances may vary.

Here are some pros and cons associated with the Four Percent Rule.

Pros:

- Easy to understand and apply.
- Provides an income stream that adjusts for inflation to maintain purchasing power.

Cons:

- Based on historical market data, which may not accurately predict future performance.
- Doesn't account for changes in personal circumstances over time, or unexpected expenses that may arise in retirement.

The Four Percent Rule is ideally suited for people who expect to have a long retirement and want a simple withdrawal strategy.

#2: The Dynamic 5 Percent Rule

Another popular withdrawal strategy is called the Dynamic 5 Percent Rule.

It's a simple approach where you withdraw the same percentage of money each year. Dynamic withdrawal strategies are designed to adjust annual retirement withdrawals based on market performance and the rate of inflation.

For instance, if the market is up, then the withdrawal amount will increase. However, if the market is down, then the withdrawal amount will decrease. Since you're always withdrawing 5 percent, the amount you take home each year can vary quite a lot depending on how the portfolio performs.

Here's how it works: imagine someone taking 5 percent in their first year of retirement from a $1 million nest egg. This would give them $50,000 as a withdrawal and leave $950,000 as a nest egg.

In the second year of retirement, let's say the $950,000 portfolio experiences a nice up year, returning +35 percent with 0 percent inflation. As seen in the illustration below, the 5 percent withdrawal in that year would amount to $64,125.

Withdrawal Rate (5%) ↓

$$\$64{,}125.00 = \$950{,}000.00 * 1.35 * 0.05$$

↑ **Nest Egg** ↑ **Return (35%)**

In year three of this retirement, let's say the portfolio returned +10 percent and inflation was 5 percent for the year. In this case, with the same 5 percent withdrawal rate, the retiree would pull $70,361 from the account.

Withdrawal Rate (5%) ↓

$$\$70{,}361.16 = \$1{,}218{,}375.00 * 1.10 * 0.05 * 1.05$$

↑ **Nest Egg** ↑ **Return (10%)** ↑ **Inflation (5%)**

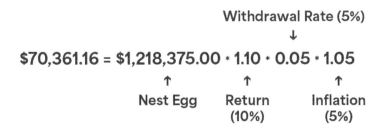

So, what happens if the market plunges 30 percent in the next year?

In that case, taking a withdrawal of 5 percent adjusted for inflation would amount to only $45,778. As you can see, there can be a lot of volatility when it comes to how much you'll be able to withdraw in any given year (study the Withdrawal Amount column closely).

Hypothetical illustration of the Dynamic 5 Percent Rule:

YEAR	RETIREMENT NEST EGG	WITH-DRAWAL RATE	WITH-DRAWAL AMOUNT	WITH-DRAWAL (INFLATION ADJUSTED)	NEW RETIRE-MENT NEST EGG	PORTFOLIO RETURN	INFLATIC RATE
1	$1,000,000	5%	$50,000	-	$950,000	35%	0%
2	$1,282,500	5%	$64,125	$64,125	$1,218,375	10%	5%
3	$1,340,213	5%	$67,011	$70,361	$1,269,852	-30%	3%
4	$888,896	5%	$44,445	$45,778	$843,118	20%	2%
5	$1,011,742	5%	$50,587	$51,599	$960,143	-	-

Here are some pros and cons associated with the Dynamic 5 Percent Rule.

Pros:

- Maintain your purchasing power as inflation is considered.
- Higher initial withdrawal rate compared to other strategies.

Cons:

- Dramatic changes in withdrawal amounts from one year to the next.

- More complex to understand and implement compared to other strategies.

The Dynamic 5 Percent Rule is ideally suited for people who want a flexible withdrawal strategy. It allows you to spoil yourself a little more after bull market years, but also requires you to be able to cut spending after bear market years.

#3: The Guyton-Klinger Rule

The Guyton-Klinger Rule is a retirement withdrawal strategy invented by financial planners Jonathan Guyton and William Klinger in 2006. It focuses on flexibility—namely the ability to adjust withdrawals based on the performance of your investments.

Here's how it works:

- **Initial withdrawal**. At the beginning of your retirement, you withdraw a specific percentage of your total savings, usually around 4–5 percent.
- **Inflation adjustment**. Each year, you adjust your withdrawal amount based on inflation, so your purchasing power stays constant.
- **Portfolio performance**. If your investments perform well, you can increase your withdrawals. If your investments perform poorly, you may need to reduce your withdrawals.
- **Withdrawal rules**. The Guyton-Klinger Rule has specific guidelines for when to increase or decrease your withdrawals. For example, if your withdrawal rate becomes too high (above 6 percent or so), you should cut back. If your withdrawal rate

becomes too low (below 4 percent), you can increase your withdrawals.

The Guyton-Klinger Rule also uses what are known as "guardrails" to adjust annual withdrawals. These guardrails help prevent a retiree from running out of money while maintaining their standard of living.

The Guyton-Klinger Rule calculates annual withdrawal amounts based on three guardrails:

1. Withdrawal rule: Withdrawals increase each year with inflation except when the portfolio has a negative return and the current year's withdrawal rate is higher than the initial withdrawal rate.
2. Prosperity rule: The withdrawal rate is increased by 10 percent if the current withdrawal rate falls below 20 percent of the initial withdrawal rate.
3. Preservation rule: The withdrawal rate is decreased by 10 percent if the current withdrawal rate exceeds 20 percent of the initial withdrawal rate.

For the Guyton-Klinger Rule, an initial withdrawal rate of 5 percent, with guardrails of 4 percent and 6 percent is recommended.

Altogether, in the first year a retiree could spend 5 percent of their portfolio. Each subsequent year they would adjust the prior year's withdrawal rate for inflation. However, if the withdrawal percentage violates the guardrails, then adjustments will be made that obey either the prosperity rule or the preservation rule.

Hypothetical illustration of the Guyton-Klinger Rule:

YEAR	RETIREMENT NEST EGG	WITHDRAWAL RATE	WITHDRAWAL AMOUNT	NEW RETIREMENT NEST EGG	PORTFOLIO RETURN	INFLATION RATE	PRESERVATION & PROSPERITY RULE
1	$1,000,000	5.0%	$50,000	$950,000	35.0%	0.0%	-
2	$1,282,500	3.9%	$50,000	$1,232,500	10.0%	5.0%	10.0%
-	$1,282,500	4.3%	$55,000	$1,227,500	-	-	-
3	$1,350,250	4.3%	$57,750	$1,292,500	-30.0%	3.0%	-
4	$904,750	6.4%	$57,750	$847,000	20.0%	2.0%	-10.0%
-	$904,750	5.7%	$51,975	$852,775	-	-	-
5	$1,023,330	5.2%	$53,015	$970,315	-	-	-

In the above table, we can see that, in year two, we need to recalculate our withdrawal amount because $50,000 (3.9 percent) is below the lower bound of our guardrail (3.9 percent < 4 percent). Therefore the propserity rule is triggered, and we adjust the withdrawal up by 10 percent.

On the other hand, in year four we see the initial withdrawal rate is calculated to be 6.4 percent. Since this number exceeds our 6 percent guardrail, we must recalculate our withdrawal rate. So we decrease it by 10 percent.

It is also worth pointing out that in year four, the previous year's portfolio return was negative (-30 percent) and the current year's withdrawal rate (5.7 percent) is higher than the initial withdrawal rate (5.0 percent), which means we would *not* adjust for inflation in year four because the withdrawal rule was triggered.

Did you get all of that?

Clearly, the Guyton-Klinger Rule is a more complicated withdrawal method than those previously mentioned. However, it's also robust. A financial advisor can help you apply the Guyton-Klinger Rule or help verify your work if you enjoy crunching numbers.

Pros:

- Offers a steadier stream of income compared to the Dynamic 5 Percent Rule.
- The guardrails help ensure that a retiree doesn't run out of money in retirement.

Cons:

- More complex to implement compared to other popular withdrawal strategies.
- Potential for reductions in withdrawal rates depending on market conditions.

The Guyton-Klinger Rule is ideally suited for people who are comfortable adjusting their annual withdrawals based on several dynamic variables. It might be a great fit for a detail-oriented engineer, but it's probably not the best route to go if you're seeking a simple solution.

#4: The Yale Endowment Spending Rule

The Yale Endowment Strategy for retirement withdrawals is a method that originates from the investment strategies used by Yale University's endowment fund. It is designed to provide a steady income while providing principal protection.

University endowments face similar challenges as retirees. Endowments generally seek to withdraw as much money as possible while avoiding a depletion trajectory. Sustainability is paramount.

While the specifics for how annual distributions are calculated under this method have varied over time, one approach involves three straightforward steps.

1. Take 70 percent of the amount of the distribution from the previous year and adjust for inflation.
2. Then, take 30 percent of the moving average of the principal balance over the past three years, multiplied by a spending rate such as 4 percent.
3. Add the two figures together to determine that year's withdrawal amount.

Readers who (understandably) felt slightly overwhelmed by the complexities of the Guyton-Klinger Rule may be raising some eyebrows here too. But an example may help bring the Yale Endowment strategy into clearer focus.

Let's say a retiree has a portfolio of $1 million, and in year one of retirement they decided to withdraw 4 percent, or $40,000.

For year two, the figures needed to calculate that year's withdrawal would be the inflation rate for the year and the three-year moving average of the portfolio's value. Let's say inflation was 2 percent and the three-year moving average of the portfolio is $1.1 million.

Here's how the math would work:

1. Step 1: Take 70 percent of the previous year's withdrawal adjusted for inflation. So, 0.7 x $40,000, or $28,000. Then, adjust for inflation: $28,000 x 1.02 = $28,560

2. Step 2: Take 30 percent of the three-year moving average of the portfolio's value multiplied by a 4 percent spending rate. In this case, that's 0.3 x $1.1 million x 0.04 = $13,200

3. Step 3: Add the two figures together for that year's withdrawal: $28,560 + $13,200 = $41,760

Reasonably straightforward, but we're not done quite yet!

There are also "guardrails" with the Yale Endowment Strategy, to ensure the university (or in our case, retiree) isn't spending too much or too little in any given year. The test a retiree can apply is to determine what percentage of the total portfolio the amount $41,760 represents.

Here's what a 4 percent low-end and 6 percent high-end guardrail scenario would look like. If the portfolio value in year two is $1.25 million, that means the retiree is only withdrawing 3.3 percent that year. It would be OK in this case to bump the withdrawal to 4 percent, or $50,000—no wonky math required.

On the other hand, if the portfolio value in year two had dropped to $600,000 in a big bear market, the $41,760 would amount to a 6.96 percent withdrawal—too high. In this case, the retiree would scale back to a 6 percent withdrawal, or $36,000.

Pros:

- Preserves retirement savings by only withdrawing a small percentage.
- Adjusts for inflation, so withdrawals maintain their purchasing power.

Cons:

- May not provide enough income if your expenses increase significantly.

- Not as flexible as other withdrawal methods.

The Yale Spending Rule is most suitable for people who have a moderate to large retirement portfolio and want a conservative approach to preserve their investment capital.

In summary, any of the withdrawal strategies profiled in this chapter can work if you follow them consistently. It's important to consider your individual financial situation and goals when choosing the best method for you.

THE LIFESTYLE LAP

For each category, pick whichever of the four solutions is the best fit for you in twenty seconds or less.

Four choices for where to live in retirement:

- ☐ #1: Age in Place
- ☐ #2: Home Sharing or Multigenerational Living
- ☐ #3: Retire to a Retirement Mecca
- ☐ #4: Relocate to a New State or Country

Four distinct stages of life:

- ☐ #1: Early Adulthood (twenties to early thirties)
- ☐ #2: Pre-retirement (mid-thirties to fifties)
- ☐ #3: Early Retirement (late fifties to mid-sixties)
- ☐ #4: Late Retirement (mid-sixties and beyond)

Four withdrawal strategies:

- ☐ #1: The 4 Percent Rule
- ☐ #2: The Dynamic 5 Percent Rule
- ☐ #3: The Guyton-Klinger Rule
- ☐ #4: The Yale Endowment Spending Rule

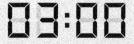

03:00

CHAPTER SUMMARY

- Wealth accumulation is just the first step; preserving wealth is equally important for long-term financial success.
- Guard against sequence of returns risk by being cautious at the start of retirement when bear markets can have the most negative impact on your long-term savings.
- Consider the following withdrawal strategies to enhance the probability of preserving wealth after retirement:
  1. The 4 Percent Rule: Withdraw 4 percent of retirement savings in the first year and adjust for inflation each year thereafter.
  2. The Dynamic 5 Percent Rule: Withdraw a constant 5 percent each year, adjusting based on market performance and inflation.
  3. The Guyton-Klinger Rule: Adjust withdrawals based on portfolio performance and guardrails to protect against running out of money.
  4. The Yale Endowment Spending Rule: Calculate withdrawals by considering previous year's distribution adjusted for inflation and a three-year moving average of the portfolio value.
- Understand the pros and cons of each strategy before choosing the one that best suits your financial situation and goals. Consider seeking help from a financial advisor if needed.

SECTION VI

THE LEGACY LAP

CHAPTER 17

ACTIVELY MANAGE YOUR ESTATE PLAN

Where there's a will–there's a relative!

–RICKY GERVAIS

Prince Rogers Nelson, known to just about everyone in the world as "Prince," was an iconic musician, singer, and songwriter.

Prince was a musical prodigy. By the age of fifteen, he could play over two dozen instruments. During his career, he sold over 100 million records, won seven Grammy awards, and received an Academy Award for Best Original Song Score for his work on the soundtrack of the film *Purple Rain*.

Prince was extraordinarily disciplined, detail-oriented, and meticulous as a musician. He knew exactly what he wanted, right down to the color of the last piano bench he ever bought.

Shortly before his passing in 2016, Prince worked with Yamaha on the design of a custom purple Yamaha C7Z grand piano, which he planned to make the centerpiece of his Piano & a Microphone

Tour. According to Chris Gero, VP/Founder of Yamaha Entertainment Group, Prince was "remarkably meticulous and in control of his own environment," noting how he corresponded with the Yamaha team multiple times a day about the piano's construction.

Prince was also a perfectionist in the recording studio, where he would spend long hours and personally play every instrument on a track. He also worked hand in hand with designers to make custom outfits for his performances, ensuring every detail synced perfectly with his intended brand and stage presence. No detail was too small. Prince micromanaged the production process.[72]

Even though Prince was detail-oriented in managing his career, he made a major oversight when it came to managing his personal affairs.

Prince died without a will.

Perhaps he thought he had more time to get his affairs in order. Or maybe it was just an honest mistake.

It's not like Prince didn't care about money. During his career, he battled with record labels and the media to maintain control over his work. He infamously changed his name to an unpronounceable symbol in 1993 as a strategic move during a dispute with Warner Bros.

Whatever the reason, Prince's failure to create a will led to a prolonged probate process. Per Minnesota law, his estate was divided equally among his surviving siblings. However, the situation was complicated by multiple people asserting to be his heirs. A lengthy legal battle ensued.

In the end, the largest beneficiary of Prince's estate was the IRS, followed by attorneys.

Prince's case isn't unique. Only 34 percent of American adults have a formal estate plan, according to a study by Caring.com. People die every day without a will, which creates a complex problem that someone has to clean up. Usually, that responsibility falls to a close family member.

There are common challenges to creating an estate plan. The number one challenge is the urge to procrastinate. If you wake up feeling good in the morning, do you really want to spend a lot of time thinking about how your assets should be divided when you die?

The thinking might be, "I don't really have much of an estate yet, so why do I need an estate plan?"

The answer is that having an estate plan will increase the odds for peace and stability in your family.

"If you hate the people in your family, leave unclear instructions and no will," says personal finance expert, Dave Ramsey. "Because they will all fight for the rest of their lives over your crap."[73]

Ramsey is right.

When someone dies without a will, it can take over a year to resolve their financial matters. In the meantime, families get stuck with bills that can rise quickly. For example, funerals cost on average about $7,900. On top of that, other debts and legal matters must be addressed, which are often complicated by varying state laws and tax situations. The average family spent $4,967 on probate matters in 2022.

This can be a lot to handle all at once—especially when family members are grieving. When emotions are running high, it's easy for families to quarrel over expensive decisions. Tense disagreements and failures to arrive at consensus are common, and these tensions can shatter family relationships.

Having a will and an estate plan in place may not prevent disagreements, but at least it makes the process unambiguous. Your wishes are your wishes, whether your family likes it or not.

Estate planning should be *dynamic*, meaning your plan should evolve as your life evolves. Many people mistakenly approach estate planning with more of a "set it and forget it" type of attitude, but it's actually a set of decisions and documents that should be revisited every few years.

After you first create a will, a lot can change. You could get married, have children, or experience a major change in your financial situation. Regularly updating your estate plan ensures that it continues to meet your goals and protects your loved ones. It also allows you to take advantage of new tax or estate planning strategies that can benefit your family.

Every estate is different because every family is different. But there are certain planning best practices everyone can follow. Here are four ways to actively manage your estate plan and enrich your legacy.

Estate Planning 101

Estate planning is the decision-making process that determines how your assets and property will be distributed after you pass away. Forming a plan can ensure your loved ones are taken care of, and it can minimize the time and expense associated with probate (the legal process of distributing your estate).

Here are the most important issues to address when creating an estate plan.

Inventory your assets. Make a list of everything you own, such as real estate, bank accounts, investments, and personal belongings. This will help you understand the size and complexity of your estate.

Tip: Everyone should create a "digital vault." This is a secure online storage system used to protect, manage, and organize sensitive data and digital assets. A digital vault is a place where you can store key account information and passwords so your loved ones can easily access important accounts.

When creating your digital vault, you should include the following information:

1. List of accounts (email, online banking, investment accounts, insurance, social media, etc.) with usernames and passwords.
2. Important documents stored digitally (will, insurance policies, tax records, etc.).
3. Contact information for key people (lawyer, financial advisor, executor, etc.).
4. List of digital assets (photos, videos, music, eBooks, cryptocurrencies, etc.).
5. Instructions for managing and distributing digital assets.
6. Information about any encryption tools or two-factor authentication used.

The digital vault should be stored in an encrypted digital file, and it should be shared with a trusted person or executor.

Determine your beneficiaries. Decide who you want to receive your assets after you pass away. Most people choose family members, friends, or charities. Be specific about who gets what and consider their individual needs and circumstances.

Choose an executor. Select a responsible person you trust to manage your estate and carry out your wishes. This person, called the executor, will handle tasks like paying debts, filing taxes, and distributing assets.

Create a will. A will is a legal document that outlines your wishes for distributing your assets. It names your executor and beneficiaries and provides instructions for managing your estate.

Set up a trust. Trusts can help you protect assets, reduce taxes, and provide for loved ones with special needs. A trust is a legal arrangement where a trustee holds and manages assets for the benefit of beneficiaries.

Plan for incapacity. In case you become unable to make decisions for yourself, you can designate someone to make medical and financial decisions on your behalf through documents like a durable power of attorney and a living will.

Consider taxes. Estate taxes can bite. Work with a professional(s) to minimize taxes and maximize the value of your estate for your beneficiaries.

Review and update your estate plan regularly. As your life changes, so should your estate plan. Review your plan about every three years to ensure it still reflects your wishes and meets the needs of your family.

That's a solid framework for building your estate plan and checking all the key boxes.

Below, I'll get more specific by outlining four estate planning solutions that can propel you into action.

#1: Engage a Low-Cost Legal Service

In the past, estate planning services were expensive and time consuming. Not anymore.

Three popular online options for simple estate planning needs are LegalZoom, Rocket Lawyer, and Trust & Will.

LegalZoom is an online legal service provider that offers estate planning services at an affordable price. The company's software can help you create a will and testament in less than 15 minutes. They provide a range of services, including the creation of wills, living trusts, and power of attorney documents. LegalZoom also offers packages that combine these services for a discounted price.

Approximate Cost: In 2023, a basic will starts at around $89, while their more comprehensive estate planning bundles cost up to $249.[74]

Rocket Lawyer is another popular online legal service platform that offers estate planning solutions. This platform allows you to create wills, living trusts, and power of attorney documents using their step-by-step document builders. Rocket Lawyer also offers ongoing legal advice through their attorney network, which is helpful for customers who want to pose questions to real-life lawyers via phone, email, or online chat.

Approximate Cost: $39.99 monthly access fee, which includes unlimited access to all their legal documents and discounted attorney services.

Trust & Will is an online platform specifically focused on estate planning services. They offer customizable wills, trusts, and guardianship documents. Trust & Will also has a guided process to help users navigate the estate planning experience and create their documents with ease.

Approximate Cost: A basic will starts at $159 per individual or $259 for couples, and a comprehensive package that includes a living trust and other documents can cost up to $599 for individuals and $699 for couples.

Any of these low-cost legal services can handle standard estate planning needs. If you have a more complex situation, it may be worth consulting an attorney who can design a more sophisticated and customized plan.

#2: Engage a Full-Service Legal Professional

Hiring a full-service estate planning attorney may be warranted if your situation is complex. There are a variety of circumstances when this tends to be the case.

High net worth. Individuals with significant wealth and complex financial holdings, including real estate, investment portfolios, and business interests, may require the expertise of an attorney to develop a comprehensive estate plan that minimizes taxes and ensures proper distribution of assets.

Blended families. In situations where there are multiple marriages, stepchildren, or adopted children, an estate planning attorney can help navigate the complexities of inheritance rights and protect the interests of all family members.

Special needs dependents. If a family member has a disability or requires long-term care, an attorney can help create a "special needs trust" to ensure their financial needs are met without jeopardizing eligibility for government benefits.

Family conflicts. When there is potential for disputes among family members, an experienced attorney can help prevent conflicts by drafting a clear and legally enforceable estate plan.

Business succession. Business owners may need assistance in planning the transfer of ownership and management of their business to successors, along with minimizing tax implications and ensuring continuity.

International assets. If an individual has assets in multiple countries, an attorney with expertise in international tax and estate law can help create an estate plan that addresses the unique legal and tax implications.

Charitable giving. Those who wish to incorporate philanthropy into their estate plans may require an attorney's guidance to establish charitable trusts or foundations.

Hiring a full-service estate planning attorney isn't always necessary, but for individuals with complex situations, it's usually worth paying up for personalized guidance and expert advice.

#3: Create a Trust Agreement

While a will can determine how your assets are to be distributed, a trust adds a much deeper level of control and specificity for how, when, and to whom your assets flow.

There are several different types of trusts, each designed to meet varying estate planning goals. Whether your goals are charitable giving, tax management, controlling how assets are invested, or something very specific like a monetary gift to your grandchildren, a trust can likely accomplish your intention.

Trust agreements offer several advantages.

Probate avoidance. Trusts can help avoid the time-consuming and expensive probate process, which is the legal process of validating a will and distributing assets.

Privacy. Trusts are not subject to public record, unlike wills, which ensures the privacy of your estate and its beneficiaries.

Tax benefits. Trusts can provide tax benefits by minimizing estate and inheritance taxes, especially for larger estates.

Control and flexibility. Trusts allow you to control and manage the distribution of assets to beneficiaries according to your wishes and can be customized to accommodate specific situations or needs.

Asset protection. Some trusts may protect assets from creditors and legal claims for both the grantor and beneficiaries.

Management during incapacity. A trust can provide a seamless transition of asset management if the grantor becomes incapacitated, ensuring financial affairs are handled according to their wishes.

Long-term planning. Trusts can provide ongoing support for minor children, disabled beneficiaries, or beneficiaries who may not be financially responsible, by distributing assets over time or under specific conditions.

Overall, trust agreements offer a wide range of benefits. Here's a quick overview of the most common types of trust agreements:

- **Revocable trust**. Also known as a living trust, this type allows you to maintain control over your assets during your lifetime. You can change or revoke the trust at any time, but your assets may be subject to probate and estate taxes upon your death.
- **Irrevocable trust**. Once created, this trust cannot be changed or revoked. Assets placed in an irrevocable trust are generally not subject to estate taxes and are protected from creditors.

- **Testamentary trust.** This type of trust is created by your will and becomes effective after your death.
- **Charitable trust.** This trust is established to benefit a charitable organization. It can provide tax advantages for the donor and support a cause they care about.
- **Special needs trust.** Designed to provide financial support for a beneficiary with disabilities, this trust allows them to receive assistance without jeopardizing their eligibility for government benefits.

Depending on the level of customization required, you can establish a trust with a low-cost online solution or by engaging a full-service estate attorney.

#4: Give with Warm Hands

A client named Julie taught me the saying, "It is better to give with a warm hand than a cold one."

The saying is an old proverb that suggests it is better to give or share while you are alive (a warm hand) rather than waiting until you have passed away (a cold one).

Giving with a warm hand allows you to experience firsthand the joy and satisfaction that comes from helping others.

Julie is a thrifty grandma who loves saving money more than spending it. In fact, being pennywise is a big reason why she's a multimillionaire. Julie was born just after the Great Depression and grew up learning how to save by watching her parents, both of whom she admired. That said, Julie does spend money on *some* things.

Not long ago, Julie paid for a week-long vacation for her family. They rented a cabin in Lake Tahoe. Her family's positive memories from that week are now part of her legacy, and that makes her happy.

Another way to give with warm hands is by gifting an early inheritance. Heirs who are in their thirties, forties or fifties usually face higher household operating expenses due to mortgages, raising a family, and other significant financial responsibilities. Providing an early inheritance can offer your loved ones financial support at a time in their life when they need it most.

Gifting assets can also help reduce the potential tax burden on your estate and simplify the probate and estate administration process. To determine whether this makes sense for you, it's wise to consult a tax and estate planning professional, since tax laws change frequently.

As of 2023, the annual gift tax exclusion is $17,000 per recipient. This means you can give up to $17,000 to any number of people each year without incurring gift tax. Married couples can combine their exclusions to give up to $34,000 per recipient per year.[75]

Finally, early gifting your assets to heirs offers them an opportunity to learn about financial management and responsibility. Personal finance expert, Suze Orman, suggests, "By giving your children an early inheritance, you can watch them learn from their mistakes and grow into financially responsible adults."[76] Early gifting can also facilitate open communication and foster stronger family relationships.

■ ■

As you review this section of the book, it's important to remember that your story doesn't end after your final breath. We live on in the memories of our loved ones, and that's why it's important to leave a positive legacy. You can take a step in that direction now by choosing to adopt one of the strategies we just covered for actively managing your estate plan.

THE LEGACY LAP

For each category, pick whichever of the four solutions is the best fit for you in twenty seconds or less.

Four estate planning solutions:

- ☐ #1: Engage a Low-Cost Legal Service
- ☐ #2: Engage a Full-Service Legal Professional
- ☐ #3: Create a Trust Agreement
- ☐ #4: Give with Warm Hands

Four strategies to maximize philanthropy:

- ☐ #1: Select High-Impact Charities
- ☐ #2: Use Tax-Efficient Giving Methods
- ☐ #3: Establish a Giving Plan
- ☐ #4: Make Philanthropy a Family Affair

Four ways to positively shape your legacy:

- ☐ #1: Start a Traditional Foundation
- ☐ #2: Become a Teacher
- ☐ #3: Actively Contribute to a Club
- ☐ #4: Write a Memoir or Record an Oral History

03:20

CHAPTER SUMMARY

- Only 34 percent of American adults have a formal estate plan.
- Estate planning is essential for ensuring peace and stability for your family.
- Important steps in estate planning include taking inventory of your assets, determining beneficiaries, choosing an executor, creating a will, setting up a trust, planning for incapacity, considering taxes, and regularly updating the estate plan.
- Three estate planning solutions for simpler needs include low-cost legal services like LegalZoom, Rocket Lawyer, or Trust & Will.
- Hiring a full-service legal professional may be necessary for complex situations like high-net worth families, blended families, special needs dependents, family conflicts, business succession, international assets, or charitable giving.
- Trust agreements provide various benefits, such as probate avoidance, privacy, tax benefits, control, asset protection, and management during incapacity.
- Giving with warm hands allows you to experience the joy of helping others and can reduce the tax burden on your estate.
- Early gifting to heirs offers financial support, teaches financial responsibility, and can foster stronger family relationships.

CHAPTER 18

CHARITABLE GIVING AND PHILANTHROPY

We make a living by what we get. We make a life by what we give.

—WINSTON CHURCHILL

At the beginning of the book, I shared a story about the day I was unexpectedly fired from my job. Now, I'd like to share a story about how that day ended.

A few days prior, the local Make-a-Wish chapter sent out an email asking for a Wish Granter who could volunteer to present at a wish party. The child was three years old, nonverbal, and it was an "emergency wish." In the parlance of the Make-a-Wish Foundation, that's code for "time may be running out, so we need to make this wish happen right away."

At the time, I had only been volunteering as a wish granter for a few months. The role is to meet with children and their families, and to help the children brainstorm their true and most authentic wish. After that, you usually host a wish presentation party, which is followed by whatever the wish might entail.

Some children want to go to Disneyland, some ask for a shopping spree, and some want to meet their favorite celebrity. Every child's story is different.

After receiving the tough news earlier in the day, I briefly thought about canceling my participation at the event. But I knew it wouldn't be easy to find a substitute at the last minute, so I went anyway. In retrospect, I'm very glad I did.

The Wish Presentation Party was held at Dave & Buster's. When I arrived, several family members were already there. I could tell from talking to the boy's uncles and grandparents they were a close-knit group. After exchanging a few pleasantries, my Wish Granter partner and I began to decorate the tables and get everything ready. About fifteen minutes later, the boy and his parents arrived.

Every time I've met the parents of a Make-a-Wish kid, I've been awed by their strength. In this case, it was obvious the mother was the rock of her family. Still only in her mid-twenties, this young woman had already been to hell and back. Her son couldn't easily communicate. He drooled and frequently experienced seizures. Despite all she had been through with him, she showed up that night determined to put on a brave face and make the best of the situation.

Her son's wish was to go to Disneyland and meet the characters from *Toy Story*, his favorite movie. According to his uncle, he lit up every time he saw Woody, his favorite character. The boy had a treasured Woody stuffy he slept with. Even though he was too sick to ride any of the rides at Disneyland, his family thought he would love to meet an oversized Woody character in person.

As is customary at these events, many of the family members went out of their way to thank me for my help making the wish come true. Truth is, I did very little. The foundation does the hard work of raising the money and awareness to make all the magic memories happen. I feel like I get way more out of the experience of being a Wish Granter than I contribute.

That night, I gained perspective on how lucky I was to have healthy children, and I was inspired by a family that was strong enough to gather and celebrate a child's life—even in the direst of circumstances.

Before I arrived at Dave & Buster's that night, I thought I had problems. By the time I left, I knew my problems were just short-term obstacles. They were fixable. I regained determination to make the best of my circumstances, rather than lament them.

Volunteering my time for a worthy cause helped me tremendously that night, and academic research suggests I'm not alone—volunteering can improve everyone's happiness and well-being.

A study titled, "Doing Well by Doing Good: The Relationship between Formal Volunteering and Self-Reported Health and Happiness" examined data to see how volunteering affects well-being.[77] The author, Francesca Borgonovi, writes: "Drawing on data from the USA, our estimates suggest that people who volunteer report better health and greater happiness than people who do not, a relationship that is not driven by socio-economic differences between volunteers and non-volunteers."

As more time and resources become available to you in retirement, it makes sense to pursue activities that inspire you. This chapter is about how to find a philanthropic cause that touches your heart, and how to maximize the mileage of your philanthropic efforts.

Choosing the Right Type of Philanthropy for You

A great way to start thinking about philanthropy is to connect the dots between your core values and different causes. You can use the story behind your financial plan as a launchpad to brainstorm ideas.

For example, I was drawn to Make-a-Wish because the organization helps sick children and their families. I know personally what being an immediate family member of a sick child feels like. During the toughest year of my childhood, my family and I spent a lot of time in the pediatric intensive care unit unit after my youngest brother was born prematurely and suffered complications. My brother eventually recovered, thankfully. But meeting the other families who weren't so lucky changed me forever.

My friend and fellow board member for the Boys & Girls Clubs of Capistrano Valley, Janice Frechette, also enjoys helping kids.

In addition to the Boys and Girls Club, Janice also helped Tarek El Nabli and Arda Kardjian launch the Parentis Foundation. Its mission is to empower older adults to leverage their talent and wisdom to provide one-on-one tutoring and mentoring to children who need help improving their reading skills and positive social development. They connect seniors and students on Zoom calls, so the seniors can listen while the children practice reading aloud to them.[78]

With the caring support of their adult volunteers, youth build self-confidence and can realize a brighter future through the lifelong benefits of academic achievement. Additionally, Parentis Foundation's intergenerational programs ensure families benefit from personalized support for their children which is essential during their most critical learning years, while older adult volunteers gain rich social connections and a higher sense of purpose.

Per the organization's website, the Parentis Foundation was founded on the core values of Responsibility, Respect, Knowledge, and Care.

Janice was attracted to help launch the foundation because the founders' vision aligned with her personal core values. Early in life, Janice's parents and grandparents instilled in her a spirit of service, which she nurtured by volunteering to help handicapped children as a teenager.

When she was twenty-six, her mother became terminally ill with cancer and entered hospice care. Even though that experience was very difficult at the time, Janice now views it as a gift, because it helped her develop a new passion for senior advocacy.

When Janice met the founders of the Parentis Foundation during her work with the Boys & Girls Club, she was touched by their vision and saw an opportunity to bridge two of her passions: helping children and seniors simultaneously.

To help you brainstorm philanthropic causes that may inspire you, take a minute to review the core values you came up with in chapter 5. Then, try to think of potential causes that are linked to your values.

Next, we'll cover four strategies you can use to enhance the ROI you derive from whatever philanthropic causes you choose to pursue.

#1: Select High-Impact Charities

When researching charities, try to identify organizations that effectively create positive change.

This process requires evaluating a charity's transparency, cost-effectiveness, track record, and need for more funding. Here are the key steps:

1. **Define your cause**. Determine the social issue or causes you are most passionate about (e.g., education, health, environment) to narrow your search.

2. **Compile a list**. Search for charities by leveraging databases like GuideStar, Charity Navigator, and GiveWell. These provide comprehensive information on charities' missions, financials, and impact.

3. **Assess transparency**. Look for charities that are transparent about their activities and finances and that provide annual reports and impact assessments on their websites.

4. **Evaluate cost-effectiveness**. High-impact charities maximize the good they do per dollar spent. GiveWell and The Life You Can Save are two organizations that identify and recommend cost-effective charities based on rigorous research.

5. **Examine track record**. Choose charities with a proven record of achieving tangible outcomes. Review their past projects, success stories, and third-party evaluations to assess their effectiveness.

6. **Consider if there is room for more funding**. Select charities with a demonstrated need for additional funding to ensure your donation has a significant impact.

7. **Verify findings with expert opinions**. Get insights from experts in the field, consult charity evaluators, and read up on articles or reports discussing the charity's work.

One expert on the subject, Peter Singer, author of *The Life You Can Save*, states, "Effective altruism is about asking, 'How can I make the biggest difference I can with the resources available to me?' and then using reason and evidence to act on that question."[79]

#2: Use Tax-Efficient Giving Methods

Tax-efficient charitable giving allows donors to maximize the impact of their contributions while minimizing their tax liability. There are several methods that can be used to achieve this goal, such as donating appreciated securities, using a donor-advised fund, gifting through an IRA, and establishing a charitable trust or foundation.

- **Donating appreciated securities**: Donors can contribute stocks, bonds, or mutual funds that have appreciated in value. By doing so, they avoid paying capital gains tax on the appreciation, and the charity receives the full value of the asset. This method is especially beneficial for donors in higher tax brackets.
- **Donor-advised fund (DAF)**: A donor-advised fund is like a savings account for charitable giving. You put money into the account and get a tax deduction for your donation. The money in the account is invested, so it can grow over time. DAFs are managed by sponsoring organizations, which handle the investments and make sure the grants go to eligible charities.
- **Qualified charitable distribution (QCD) from an IRA**: Individuals aged 70.5 or older can transfer up to $100,000 per year directly from their IRA to a qualified charity. The QCD is excluded from taxable income and counts toward the required minimum distribution (RMD).
- **Charitable trust or foundation**: Establishing a charitable trust, such as a charitable remainder trust (CRT) or charitable lead trust (CLT), or a private foundation, allows donors to make significant philanthropic commitments while receiving potential tax benefits. These options are more complex than

the strategies cited above, so you should work with a financial advisor and tax professional to set them up.

To summarize, tax-efficient charitable giving methods allow you to optimize the impact of your contributions while enjoying tax benefits. Choosing the best method depends on your individual circumstances and goals.

#3: Establish a Giving Plan

A giving plan is a strategic approach to philanthropy that helps individuals, families, or organizations maximize the impact of their charitable contributions. Establishing a giving plan involves setting goals and evaluating the performance of supported organizations.

Here are some best practices for creating an effective giving plan.

1. **Define your philanthropic mission**. Identify the values and principles that drive your philanthropy and use these as guidelines for selecting causes and organizations to support.
2. **Set clear and achievable goals**. Establish short-term and long-term goals for your giving plan, ensuring they are specific, measurable, attainable, relevant, and time bound (SMART).
3. **Research causes and organizations**. Research potential charities to ensure they align with your mission and have a proven track record of making a positive impact.
4. **Allocate your resources strategically**. Determine the amount you can realistically give each year and allocate your funds based on your priorities.

5. **Diversify your giving methods**. Consider different ways to support your causes, such as cash donations, in-kind gifts, volunteering, or leveraging your professional skills.
6. **Engage with recipients**. Establish relationships with the organizations you support, seeking opportunities for collaboration and learning.
7. **Monitor and evaluate the impact**. Regularly assess the performance of recipient organizations and the progress towards your giving goals.
8. **Share your experiences and insights**. Encourage a culture of philanthropy by sharing your lessons learned with friends, family, and peers.

As philanthropy expert Paul Brest notes, "Designing a giving plan is as much an art as a science, but it is informed by a deep understanding of the problems you are trying to solve, the organizations you are supporting, and the resources you bring to bear."[80]

#4: Make Philanthropy a Family Affair

Philanthropy is a powerful way to teach core values such as empathy, kindness, and gratitude. Making philanthropy a family affair can help raise socially responsible adults and strengthen family bonds. Here are some best practices.

- **Start early**. Introduce age-appropriate philanthropy concepts to your children as early as possible. For young children, simple acts of kindness and sharing can help lay the foundation. As they grow, involve them in more complex charitable activities.

For example, Fidelity Charitable recommends establishing a donation jar for yourself and your kids. Encourage them to contribute to the jar with spare change, gift money, or allowance money. Then, set up a meeting to discuss where they want to donate the jar's contents.[81]

- **Lead by example**. Children learn by observing their parents. Be a positive role model and involve your spouse or partner to create a unified message.
- **Engage in conversation**. Discuss the importance of giving back with your children. Explain why your family chooses to support specific causes and encourage kids to express their thoughts and feelings about charity.
- **Encourage volunteerism**. Participate in volunteer activities as a family. Choose projects that align with your children's interests.
- **Set family goals**. Establish charitable goals as a family, such as donation targets or a certain number of volunteer hours per year. This promotes teamwork and accountability.
- **Involve kids in the decision-making**. Let your children participate in selecting the causes or organizations your family supports. This fosters a sense of ownership and responsibility.
- **Share stories**. Share stories and experiences about the impact of your family's philanthropic efforts. This helps children understand the real-world consequences of their actions.
- **Celebrate achievements**. Acknowledge and celebrate your family's philanthropic milestones. This reinforces the importance of giving back and creates lasting memories.

- **Foster gratitude**. Encourage your children to reflect on their blessings and express gratitude for what they have. This cultivates a mindset of abundance and generosity.
- **Make it fun**. Find creative ways to make philanthropy enjoyable for your children. This could include hosting fundraisers, participating in charity events, or creating handmade items for donation.

By making philanthropy a family affair, you can positively shape your children's core values and strengthen your legacy.

THE LEGACY LAP

For each category, pick whichever of the four solutions is the best fit for you in twenty seconds or less.

Four estate planning solutions:

- ☐ #1: Engage a Low-Cost Legal Service
- ☐ #2: Engage a Full-Service Legal Professional
- ☐ #3: Create a Trust Agreement
- ☐ #4: Give with Warm Hands

Four strategies to maximize philanthropy:

- ☐ #1: Select High-Impact Charities
- ☐ #2: Use Tax-Efficient Giving Methods
- ☐ #3: Establish a Giving Plan
- ☐ #4: Make Philanthropy a Family Affair

Four ways to positively shape your legacy:

- ☐ #1: Start a Traditional Foundation
- ☐ #2: Become a Teacher
- ☐ #3: Actively Contribute to a Club
- ☐ #4: Write a Memoir or Record an Oral History

03:40

CHAPTER SUMMARY

- Look for a charitable cause whose mission represents your core values.
- Studies have shown a correlation between volunteering, happiness, and well-being.
- Four strategies to maximize the impact of your philanthropic efforts:
    1. Select high-impact charities: Evaluate transparency, cost-effectiveness, track record, and need for more funding.
    2. Use tax-efficient giving methods: You can donate appreciated securities, use a donor-advised fund, or make qualified charitable distributions from an IRA.
    3. Establish a giving plan: Set clear goals, research causes, allocate resources strategically, and monitor impact.
    4. Make philanthropy a family affair: Involve children in age-appropriate philanthropic activities, lead by example, encourage volunteerism, and set family goals.

CHAPTER 19

YOU DON'T HAVE TO BE A BILLIONAIRE TO START A FOUNDATION

We get one opportunity in life, one chance at life to do whatever you're going to do and lay your foundation and make whatever mark you're going to make.

—RAY LEWIS

A few years ago, a man stood before an audience, bewildered. He said he never imagined that he'd someday be employed by "the argumentative young boy who grew up in my house, eating my food and using my name."

To say the boy was a handful would be an understatement. He refused to clean his room and he was constantly late for dinner. When he was twelve, he got into such a heated argument with his mother that his father was compelled to throw a glass of water in his face.

Describing the incident later to a counselor, the boy proclaimed, "I'm at war with my parents over who is in control."

The man who gave the speech is Bill Gates, Sr. The boy, of course, was Bill Gates, Jr., who would later become the richest person in the world.

Today, Bill Gates controls one of the largest private foundations in the world, which he established in 2000 with his then-wife Melinda French Gates. The Bill & Melinda Gates Foundation began with a $28 billion endowment from the Gates family, which has grown to over $50 billion.

Per the Gates Foundation's website, its mission is to improve the quality of life for individuals around the world by focusing on three key areas: global health, global development, and US education.

Some of the foundation's primary achievements in these areas include:

Global Health. The foundation has played a significant role in reducing child mortality rates, improving vaccination coverage, and fighting infectious diseases like HIV/AIDS, tuberculosis, and malaria. For example, the foundation's support for Gavi, the Vaccine Alliance, has helped immunize over 822 million children in the world's poorest countries since 2000.

Global Development. The foundation has been a catalyst for innovations in agriculture, financial services for the poor, and access to clean water and sanitation. It has been instrumental in developing and promoting high-yielding, drought-resistant crop varieties to help smallholder farmers in Africa and South Asia.

US Education. The foundation has invested in initiatives that aim to increase high school graduation rates, reduce achievement gaps, and prepare students for college and the workforce. It has supported efforts to improve teaching quality, develop innovative learning models, and advance data-driven decision-making in education.[82]

Gates actively manages his philanthropic efforts, which is a style some call "catalytic philanthropy."[83] Taking a hands-on approach gives him greater control over where his money goes.

As a testament to his level of commitment, Gates once famously drank water in a video to prove to the world it was clean and safe to consume. The water was actually produced from human sewage by a machine called the Omni Processor. This machine was developed by the Bill & Melinda Gates Foundation to help improve sanitation in developing countries.

By staying intimately involved in his foundation's work, Gates is able to personally direct how funds are distributed to different causes and projects. The foundation's focus on evidence-based decision making also helps optimize the allocation of resources.

Gates is super successful in business and philanthropy because he's adept at *controlling what he can control*. He's been wired that way since childhood. As an adult, he reportedly schedules every five minutes of his day (similar to Elon Musk).[84]

Whether you're a billionaire or not, you can positively shape your legacy by starting a foundation. It's easy to do because a foundation can take many forms.

#1: Start a Traditional Foundation

A traditional foundation can give you more control over your legacy by providing a structured, long-term vehicle for giving. This can help you leave a lasting imprint on the world.

There are a variety of benefits associated with a private foundation.

Control. Donors can drive the foundation's mission, goals, and grant-making decisions.

Tax Benefits. There are income tax deductions for donors and exemptions from estate taxes for the foundation.

Flexibility. You can continually adjust the strategies, objectives, and grant recipients over time.

Don't let popular myths deter you from starting a private foundation.

One myth about private foundations is that you need millions of dollars to start one. Not so. Sixty-seven percent of foundations have under $1 million in assets.

A second myth about private foundations is that they're hard to set up. That's also not true. Some foundations can be set up in less than three days for a modest fee.

A third myth about private foundations is that they're burdensome to operate. Actually you can outsource management and most administrative tasks.

A private foundation can be funded with a wide variety of assets, including:

1. Cash

2. Publicly traded securities
3. Alternative assets, including private equity
4. Real estate and tangible assets (e.g., art, jewelry, collectibles)
5. Life insurance and annuities

One of my clients runs a private foundation. Many years ago, his mother started a philanthropic animal shelter. After she passed away, he took over managing the foundation in her honor. As a former Beverly Hills–based stockbroker, my client was able to make savvy investments through the years that have continued to grow the foundation's resources. He knows that his mother would be thrilled to know the current size of the foundation and how many animals it cares for.

He plans for his daughters to take over administering the foundation someday. Hopefully that family continuity allows the foundation to continue compounding positive outcomes for people and animals for decades to come.

In the US, private foundations typically have to distribute at least 5 percent of their net investment assets annually for charitable purposes to maintain tax-exempt status. This minimum distribution requirement is designed to ensure that foundations use their resources for philanthropic purposes. The rest of the funds can be invested, in accordance with the foundation's objectives and time horizon.

A private foundation enhances your legacy by perpetuating your core values. Startup expenses generally range from $4,500 on the low end to $25,000 on the high end. It's important to consult with legal and financial professionals to properly comply with relevant legal and tax rules.

#2: Become a Teacher

100 years from now it won't matter what kind of car I drove, what kind of house I lived in, how much money I had in the bank, nor what my clothes looked like. But the world may be a little better because I was important in the life of a child.

—FOREST WITCRAFT

I wrote earlier that a foundation can take many forms. Teaching is a way to build a lasting legacy that transcends your own life.

Teaching allows you to establish a positive foundation by making a meaningful impact on the lives of others. By sharing your knowledge and skills, you can empower others to achieve their goals. This in turn can guide their actions and decisions, creating a positive ripple effect that touches many lives.

Teaching also helps you, the teacher. When you teach, you're not only imparting knowledge to others but also reinforcing your own understanding of the subject. This process of teaching and learning promotes personal growth, which contributes to a positive and fulfilling life.

A study by the London School of Economics found that individuals who teach or actively mentor others report higher levels of happiness and well-being.[85] The research suggests that teaching can elevate your self-esteem while fostering a sense of purpose and meaning.

You could teach a yoga class, teach Sunday school, or simply teach a kid how to ride a bike. The list of possibilities is endless.

#3: Actively Contribute to a Club

Find a group of people who challenge and inspire you, spend a lot of time with them, and it will change your life.

—AMY POEHLER

Joining a club is another creative way to start a foundation because clubs offer a chance to be part of something bigger than yourself.

Social activity contributes to a happy and healthy retirement. According to Dr. Robert Waldinger, a psychiatrist and director of the Harvard Study of Adult Development, "Good relationships keep us happier and healthier. Period."[86]

In terms of health benefits, a study by the Rush University Medical Center found that older adults with higher levels of social engagement had a 70 percent lower rate of cognitive decline compared to those with lower levels.[87]

Waldinger says, "The people in our 75-year study who were the happiest in retirement were the people who had actively worked to replace workmates with new playmates."

Clubs allow you to stay socially connected with like-minded people who energize you. According to the Social Identity Theory by Tajfel and Turner (1979), individuals derive self-esteem from their group membership. Actively participating in a club helps provide a sense of belonging.

Club ideas for retirees:

1. Book clubs: Local libraries or bookstores often host these.
2. Walking/health clubs: Local parks, fitness centers, or community centers.

3. Art clubs: Art studios, galleries, or community colleges often have classes or clubs.
4. Gardening clubs: Look for local botanical gardens or community gardens.
5. Cooking clubs: Local community centers or cooking schools.
6. Travel clubs: Travel agencies, community centers, or online platforms.
7. Bridge or other card game clubs: Local community centers, senior centers, or online platforms.
8. Volunteering clubs: Local nonprofits, religious organizations, or community centers.
9. Photography clubs: Local community colleges, art centers, or online platforms.
10. History or culture clubs: Museums, historical societies, or libraries.

One of my clients, Ken, recently retired from a career in accounting. A couple of years ago, he stumbled upon a local gardening club at the community center. He always enjoyed gardening but never had time to fully dive into it. He decided to give it a try.

The club taught Ken new gardening techniques and introduced him to a group of like-minded people. He even helped with a community project, transforming a barren lot into a lush, green space.

Ken's contributions to the club include putting his accounting skills to good use. Naturally he's the treasurer. Actively contributing to the club makes Ken feel valued and productive, even in retirement. It isn't just about gardening; it's about community, shared learning, and mutual support.

Clubs offer you a chance to contribute to something larger than yourself, which can bring a sense of accomplishment and fulfillment.

#4: Write a Memoir or Record an Oral History

You are responsible for how people remember you.

—KOBE BRYANT

Writing a memoir or recording an oral history is about more than just preserving your past. It's about creating a bridge to future generations, linking them back to their roots and fostering a sense of belonging and identity.

By recording and sharing your life stories, you can provide a foundation of wisdom, resilience, and love that guides your descendants in their own lives. A memoir or oral history can be a past positive asset that helps future generations understand their heritage.

A memoir is a medium for telling your life story by writing about your personal experiences, reflections, and memories.

A client named Greg recently enhanced his legacy by writing a memoir. He used an online service called Storyworth that allows you to write and share stories with your family each week, which can be later combined into a beautiful book.

Greg shared with me a chapter he wrote about his time in the Vietnam War. He gives an excellent firsthand account of what living through that historical event looked like through his eyes. At the end of the chapter, he even included pictures of his barracks and the helicopter he flew on.

Greg's memoir is a wonderful gift to his family because it allows future generations to know more about him. He's telling his story in his own words. By documenting the most colorful times of his life, he gives more meaning to his life. Great investment!

In addition to Storyworth, Scrivener and MemLife are other writing tools that can help you organize and structure your memoir.

Recording an oral history is another medium for telling your life story. This is a recording in which you describe your personal knowledge of past events.

During my senior year of high school, I was given an assignment to interview someone about what it was like to work and raise a family during the 1960s and 1970s. I chose my grandfather.

A few years ago, I had the twenty-minute recording of our interview converted to a digital file, and I listened to it for the first time in ages. Not only was it great to hear my grandfather's voice again, but it also reminded me of what an insightful man he was. With only a few handwritten notes in front of him, he eloquently described the ebb and flow of public sentiment through different social and economic eras.

As a gift to the rest of my family, which includes fourteen aunts and uncles and over thirty cousins, I turned the audio file of the interview into a short documentary. Using video editing, I plugged in pictures, videos, and songs from the 1960s and '70s on top of the audio. The net result is basically a trip down memory lane as told by my grandfather. For my kids, it's a chance to get to know their great-grandfather.

If you want to turn old family pictures, videos, or recordings into your own documentary about yourself or a family member, a good place to start is by visiting LegacyBox.com. They can help you preserve your past by digitizing your family photos and videos.

If you want help recording an oral history, check out StoryCorps.[88] They have an app that guides you through the interview process, records the conversation, and allows you to share it online.

Modern technology allows us to chronicle our lives in unprecedented detail. As technology expert Sherry Turkle from MIT has said, "We are using technology not just to remember the things we would forget, but to raise ourselves to new levels of organization, to transcend our natural state."

Current and future generations can be remembered in much more vivid detail than prior generations. You can take advantage of that by creating a foundation of digital assets for your family today.

■ ■

The word *foundation* has long been associated with prestigious institutions backed by big money. But this association has created something of a misnomer. Most everyone wrongly assumes that foundations are reserved for the multimillionaires and billionaires of the world. They're not.

If we broadly define a foundation as a vehicle for leaving a positive impact on the world, we can all leave a powerful legacy with just a little bit of effort and creativity.

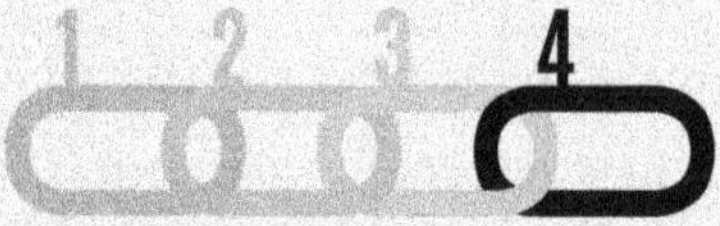

THE LEGACY LAP

For each category, pick whichever of the four solutions is the best fit for you in twenty seconds or less.

Four estate planning solutions:

- ☐ #1: Engage a Low-Cost Legal Service
- ☐ #2: Engage a Full-Service Legal Professional
- ☐ #3: Create a Trust Agreement
- ☐ #4: Give with Warm Hands

Four strategies to maximize philanthropy:

- ☐ #1: Select High-Impact Charities
- ☐ #2: Use Tax-Efficient Giving Methods
- ☐ #3: Establish a Giving Plan
- ☐ #4: Make Philanthropy a Family Affair

Four ways to positively shape your legacy:

- ☐ #1: Start a Traditional Foundation
- ☐ #2: Become a Teacher
- ☐ #3: Actively Contribute to a Club
- ☐ #4: Write a Memoir or Record an Oral History

04:00

CHAPTER SUMMARY

- Starting a foundation doesn't require millions of dollars.
- A traditional foundation can give you more control over your legacy by providing a structured, long-term approach to giving.
- Teaching allows you to build a positive foundation by making a lasting impact on the lives of others.
- Joining a club is another way to start a foundation because doing so offers a chance to be part of something bigger than yourself.
- A memoir or oral history can be a past positive asset that helps future generations understand their heritage.

SECTION VII

CONCLUSION

CHAPTER 20
HEDGING THE DARK SIDE OF THE MOON

It's not what you look at that matters, it's what you see.

—HENRY DAVID THOREAU

"Mike, stop!"

Those two words saved my life.

I was jaywalking across multiple lanes of traffic when I heard my brother's dramatic plea behind me. Time slowed. I stopped in my tracks so suddenly that my weight was still carrying me forward. To regain my balance, I cast my arms out wide, like a child playing "airplane." Then I felt a swoosh of air, and I saw the flash of a speeding car whiz by only inches in front of me.

One more step, and I would have been toast.

As I approached the final lane, my view was obstructed by a slow-moving truck. I didn't see the huge risk I was about to step into. My brother did, and I was lucky he was watching my back.

That was the last time I ever jaywalked. Another insight from that day was realizing how the most serious risks lurk in the shadows. They sneak up on us when we are unprepared and vulnerable.

"Risk" is a fuzzy concept for most people. If we poll ten folks and ask them to define it, we'll likely get ten different answers. We know risk when we see it, though. It may appear in the form of a speeding car, a dangerous storm, or a scary market. Risk can be anything beyond our control with potential to disrupt our plans.

Risk is ever-present, but we can manage it by proactively hedging our blind spots.

Retirement Blind Spot #1: The Real Value of Money

One blind spot in many retirement plans involves US monetary policy.

Stan Druckenmiller, a Wall Street legend whom many consider the greatest currency trader of all time, told CNBC in May 2021, "If we're going to monetize our debt and we're going to enable more and more of this spending, that's why I'm worried now for the first time that within fifteen years we lose reserve currency status and of course all the unbelievable benefits that have accrued with it."[89]

Since 1971, the value of a dollar has rested on the collective belief that a centralized authority—the US government—is "good for it." That year, President Nixon ended the dollar's convertibility to gold, transitioning America to a purely "fiat" money system. Nixon claimed this would help stabilize the dollar.[90]

Fiat means "let it be done" in Latin. And that explains a lot about the 1970s.

In hindsight, de-linking from gold was quite *de*-stabilizing in terms of its impact on the US dollar. What became known as the

"Nixon Shock" allowed the Fed to create unlimited money out of thin air. In 1972, the US money supply began increasing sharply, touching off one of the most inflationary decades in American history.

From the date of Nixon's policy pivot until 1980, the US dollar shed 27 percent of its value relative to a basket of foreign currencies. Compared to the nearly vertical price action in gold, the US dollar fell even more precipitously.[91]

After 1971, federal debt also started a long creep higher relative to the size of the economy.

In the years since the Great Financial Crisis (widely considered a debt-bubble), the US government has increased the national debt from $11 trillion to over $32 trillion.

In March 2020, after the COVID-19 pandemic hit, overburdened debt markets began to freeze, reminiscent of the 2008 financial crisis. The Federal Reserve responded by unleashing a tidal wave of liquidity, boosting the money supply (M2) by 26 percent year-over-year. Asset prices made an abrupt U-turn as the bond market stabilized.

FEDERAL RESERVE MONEY SUPPLY M2

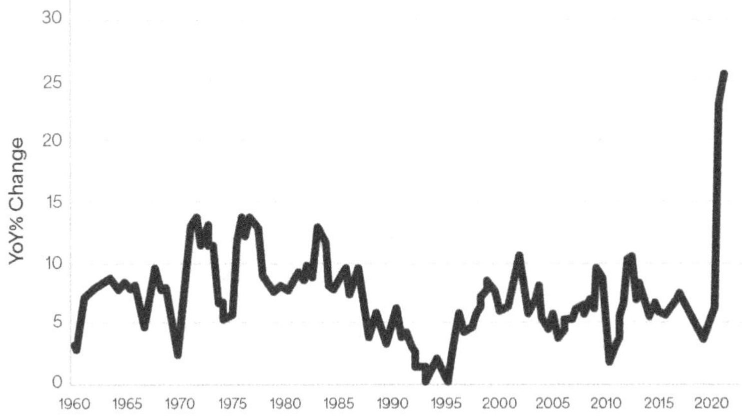

Source: Bloomberg

For perspective, the Fed added $4 trillion to its balance sheet post-pandemic. That is three times more than during the 2008 financial crisis.

By purchasing massive amounts of treasury bonds, the Fed artificially suppressed bond yields, which helped facilitate higher levels of fiscal spending than would otherwise have been possible. This explains how in 2020, the US government was able to increase the federal deficit more than during the last five recessions *combined*, while long-term treasury bond yields actually *fell*.

However, printing a bunch of extra money to stimulate demand in a supply-constrained economy has negative consequences, too. In 2021, inflation spiked to the highest level in forty years.

Going forward, inflation is a risk that could ruin many retirement plans that presently look good on paper. For example, what if spiraling budget deficits eventually cause the dollar to fall? If that were to occur, then commodities priced in dollars—like crude oil—would likely rise. Inflation is especially tough for retirees who operate on fixed budgets and are unable to command higher wages.

Another blind spot risk for retirees relates to entitlement programs.

Retirement Blind Spot #2: Unfunded Liabilities Create Cracks in the System

Entitlement programs are government-funded initiatives that provide financial assistance and benefits to eligible individuals, such as Social Security, Medicare, and Medicaid. These programs are a crucial safety net for many Americans, especially retirees who rely on them for basic needs.

Today, debt and inflation are both rising at elevated levels compared to history. The surge in US debt comes on the eve of entitlement expenses accelerating; the amount of money that will be necessary to fund future promises to retirees is projected to grow sharply between now and 2050.

According to the Congressional Budget Office's projections, net interest on debt is expected to comprise 27 percent of the total federal budget by 2051. That alone would consume more of the federal budget than all other discretionary spending.

There are several reasons why the outlook for entitlement programs is shaky at best.

- **Aging population**. The US and many other developed countries are experiencing a rapidly aging population, which means there are going to be more retirees compared to working-age individuals. Consequently, there are relatively fewer people paying into programs like Social Security and Medicare, while there are more people drawing benefits from these programs. This imbalance puts a strain on the financial resources of these programs.
- **Increasing life expectancy**. People are living longer than ever before, and as life expectancy increases, retirees receive more benefits over longer periods, which further strains the funding for these programs.
- **Rising healthcare costs**. Healthcare costs have been rising steadily, making it more expensive for programs like Medicare and Medicaid to provide coverage. As a result, the cost of providing these benefits is growing faster than the revenues collected to fund them.

These factors combine to create an untenable situation. Entitlement programs are spending way more money than they're taking in. If these programs are unable to provide the promised benefits, retirees may face significant financial challenges, including:

- **Reduced income**. If Social Security benefits are cut or eliminated, retirees may have to rely more on their savings or other sources of income, which may not be enough to maintain their desired standard of living.
- **Increased healthcare expenses**. Without Medicare or Medicaid, or with reduced benefits, retirees may have to pay more out of pocket for healthcare, which can be a significant financial burden, particularly for those with chronic health conditions.
- **Poverty.** Without these safety nets, some retirees may fall into poverty, unable to afford necessities like food, housing, and healthcare.

We can all hope our entitlement benefits will be there when it's our turn to receive them, but "hope" isn't a strategy.

The uncertain fiscal outlook is why *you* need to always look out for *you*. Thankfully, proactive risk management is something we can control as individuals.

How to Hedge the Dark Side of the Moon

There is no dark side of the moon really.
Matter of fact it's all dark.

—PINK FLOYD'S *THE DARK SIDE OF THE MOON*, 1973

The world is full of optical illusions. For instance, the moon doesn't operate like a lightbulb; it only lights up the night sky because of the sun. It's a *reflection* of reality.

Similarly, there are different lenses for viewing money. For example, we can focus on how much money we have (nominal value), or how much our money buys us (real value). The former is easy to see but gives a false impression. The latter is harder to see but is where the truth lies.

Many Baby Boomers—the generational cohort born between the years of 1946 to 1964—will remember the early 1970s as a time of declining trust in centralized institutions. Economic anxiety was so palpable back then, it was even reflected in pop culture.

When Pink Floyd's *The Dark Side of the Moon* album hit store shelves in March 1973, it quickly became a top seller. The album ultimately sold over 50 million copies and stayed on the Billboard charts for 741 consecutive weeks.[92] For any album to have that kind of staying power, it has to touch a nerve, and Floyd's album did just that.

Songs like "Us and Them," "Time," and "Money" were full of provocative lyrics exploring themes of generational strife and materialism. The album's iconic cover showed a beam of light passing through a prism to form a rainbow of spectrum colors on the other side. This imagery appears against a solid black background.

Part of *Dark Side of the Moon*'s brilliance was that it allows you to see what you want to see and hear what you want to hear. I interpret the album as an anthem for questioning the veracity of things that don't appear right on the surface.

To navigate the modern monetary maze, including the blind spots mentioned above, second-level critical thinking is especially important. As individuals, we cannot change the macro environment.

But we can study historical analogs, extract the proper context, and actively hedge to ensure our personal retirement plan is antifragile.

Nicholas Nassim Taleb coined the term "antifragile" in his *New York Times* bestselling book, *Antifragile: Things That Gain From Disorder*. In the book, Taleb writes, "Some things benefit from shocks; they thrive and grow when exposed to volatility, randomness, disorder, and stressors."

To be antifragile is to be adaptable to an ever-changing environment—like a tree that grows stronger roots from blowing in the wind.

The story behind your financial plan makes you antifragile, because it clarifies your most important goals and encourages a healthy time perspective.

Your Four-Minute Retirement Plan makes you antifragile, because it was built by combining time-tested strategies for retirement success. You can trust the strategies from this book to get you where you want to go, whatever the future may hold. Every time you encounter resistance and are able to revisit your plan and regroup, you'll grow more confident in your ability to manage your finances.

For example …

If you find yourself in an environment where interest rates are volatile, you'll be OK, because you know how to distinguish good debt from bad debt.

If you find yourself in an environment where entitlement promises are broken, you'll be OK, because you know to always invest with a safety-first mindset.

If you find yourself entering a new stage of life with shifting priorities, you'll be OK, because you know the most important milestones for that part of your retirement journey.

If you find yourself contemplating your legacy, unsure of how you want to be remembered, you'll be OK, because you know that you don't have to be a billionaire to start a foundation.

Whatever financial surprises may await in the future—and I promise there will be some—you can use the Four-Minute Retirement Plan as a critical thinking tool to actively manage your money and proactively hedge the dark side of the moon.

CHAPTER SUMMARY

- Risk is ever-present, but we can manage it by proactively hedging our blind spots.
- Retirement Blind Spot #1: US monetary policy and potential dollar devaluation.
- Retirement Blind Spot #2: Unfunded liabilities and strains on entitlement programs.
- The uncertain fiscal outlook is why you need to always look out for you.
- To be antifragile is to be adaptable to an ever-changing environment.
- The story behind your financial plan makes you antifragile, because it clarifies your most important goals and encourages a healthy time perspective.
- Your Four-Minute Retirement Plan makes you antifragile, because it was built by combining time-tested strategies for retirement success.

CHAPTER 21

THE INFINITE RACE

Enjoy present pleasures in such a way
as not to injure future ones.

—SENECA

Retirement is really an infinite race.

It's an endurance challenge that starts from your first paycheck, continues through your final day of work, extends into your golden years, and even lasts beyond your lifetime. This journey consists of four laps: the savings lap, the investing lap, the lifestyle lap, and the legacy lap.

The first lap is the savings lap. The act of saving is more than just setting aside part of your paycheck. It's a commitment to your future self. The best way to stay on track is to automate your savings by setting up a direct deposit to your retirement account. Make it a rule, not an exception. This way, you're not only saving money but also time and mental energy.

The second lap is the investing lap. Here's where the power of compounding comes into play. Investing your money smartly can grow your capital base exponentially over time. But investing isn't a one-time decision; it's a continuous process that requires constant adjustments based on economic conditions and your personal circumstances.

The third lap, the lifestyle lap, is allocating your resources in ways that you find personally fulfilling. Things like choosing the right place to live and smart budgeting practices improve your sense of wellbeing. This lap is also about nurturing a healthy time perspective. A past positive perspective can be a source of inspiration and motivation. A future positive perspective keeps you focused on your long-term goals. But don't forget to also mix in a healthy dose of present hedonism. Savor the present and make the most of today.

The final lap is the legacy lap. This lap is about more than just leaving a financial inheritance. It's also about the values you pass on, the lessons you've learned, and the memories you leave behind. It's about making a difference in the lives of others and ensuring that your impact extends beyond your lifetime.

Ultimately, there isn't one perfect strategy anyone can give you to run the retirement race, including me.

Given that retirement is an infinite race, it's a complex topic that encompasses many variables. But there are many ways you can accomplish your goals, as this book has shown. The key is to avoid letting all the variables overwhelm you. Favor progress over perfection.

There are best practices anyone can use to start moving forward. For example, if you want an incredibly simple retirement plan you could also create in four minutes, here's one way to do that.

First, get four Post-it notes you can put on your desk, refrigerator, or some other prominent place. Then, take four minutes to jot down the following notes.

SAVINGS LAP:

- Fully fund your 401(k) and/or IRA every year.
- Follow the 50/30/20 budgeting rule.
- Create an emergency savings account worth at least six months of earnings.

INVESTING LAP:

- Build a portfolio with an expected beta less than 1.0 (below-average volatility).
- Invest retirement money 100 percent into equities until retirement, then switch to a 60/40 portfolio.
- Diversify with passive and active investments.

LIFESTYLE LAP:

- Live in a place you can afford which promotes a high quality of life.
- Defer social security as long as possible unless you're unlikely to live past the age of eighty.
- Follow the 4 Percent Rule for retirement withdrawals.

LEGACY LAP:

- Create a will.
- Donate your time and treasure to a charity that inspires you.
- Write a memoir or record an oral history.

If you just do these things listed above, you'll be ahead of most people.

While there's nothing wrong with a simple Post-it note plan, you can do *even better* if you take the time to work on your narrative and create a more customized plan using the full array of tools and strategies in this book. Remember, financial freedom isn't just about numbers or pithy formulas—it's also about the story we tell ourselves. Everyone is unique, and your financial plan should reflect that.

Finally, you don't have to run this race alone. If you're interested in professional advice, check out Silverlight Asset Management's wealth management service at www.silverlight.us. We'd love to help you design a strategy to retire well and on time.

Even though retirement is a challenging race, with thoughtful preparation and the right mindset it's a race anyone can win. So start your race today, and pave the way for a secure, fulfilling, and successful retirement.

APPENDIX

PUTTING IT ALL TOGETHER

The Story Behind Your Financial Plan

Act I: The Setup

Write your authenticity statement and describe at least three of your core values and where they originated from.

Act II: The Challenge

Describe three goals you are committed to pursuing that reflect your core values. Focus on what you want to achieve, when you want to achieve it, and why each goal is important to you.

Act III: The Resolution

Describe what fun activities you intend to do, when you will do them, and why you know you can afford it (i.e., the 50/30/20 Rule).

The Retirement Laps

1. Savings Lap 2. Investing Lap 3. Lifestyle Lap 4. Legacy Lap

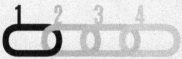

THE SAVINGS LAP

For each category, pick whichever of the four solutions is the best fit for you in twenty seconds or less.

Four strategies to start saving money:

- ☐ #1: Automate Contributions to a 401(k)
- ☐ #2: Automate Contributions to Multiple Tax-deferred Vehicles
- ☐ #3: Maximize Retirement Contributions and Start an Emergency Savings Fund
- ☐ #4: Maximize Retirement Contributions and Start a Scarcity Fund

Four strategies to manage debt wisely:

- ☐ #1: Pay Off High Interest Rate Debt First
- ☐ #2: Dave Ramsey's Snowball Method
- ☐ #3: Consolidate Your Debts
- ☐ #4: Pay Off Bad Debt and Add Good Debt

Four strategies for choosing a financial advisor:

- ☐ #1: Be Your Own Financial Advisor
- ☐ #2: Hire a Robo-Advisor
- ☐ #3: Choose a Fiduciary Advisor
- ☐ #4: Choose a Fiduciary Advisor with Advanced Credentials

THE INVESTING LAP

For each category, pick whichever of the four solutions is the best fit for you in twenty seconds or less.

Four safety-first investing strategies:

- ☐ #1: Invest in a Low-Volatility Index Strategy
- ☐ #2: Invest in a Low-Volatility Sector Strategy
- ☐ #3: Dollar-Cost Average
- ☐ #4: Employ an Active Defensive Strategy

Four strategies to choose a benchmark:

- ☐ #1: Focus on Maximizing Long-Term Returns
- ☐ #2: Focus on Absolute Returns
- ☐ #3: Focus on a Volatility Threshold
- ☐ #4: Focus on Finding an Advisor

Four strategies to avoid the passive bubble:

- ☐ #1: Diversify with Equal-Weighted Portfolios
- ☐ #2: Blend Passive and Active Strategies
- ☐ #3: Self-Manage
- ☐ #4: Direct Indexing

02:00

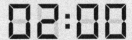

THE LIFESTYLE LAP

For each category, pick whichever of the four solutions is the best fit for you in twenty seconds or less.

Four choices for where to live in retirement:

- ☐ #1: Age in Place
- ☐ #2: Home Sharing or Multigenerational Living
- ☐ #3: Retire to a Retirement Mecca
- ☐ #4: Relocate to a New State or Country

Four distinct stages of life:

- ☐ #1: Early Adulthood (twenties to early thirties)
- ☐ #2: Pre-retirement (mid-thirties to fifties)
- ☐ #3: Early Retirement (late fifties to mid-sixties)
- ☐ #4: Late Retirement (mid-sixties and beyond)

Four withdrawal strategies:

- ☐ #1: The 4 Percent Rule
- ☐ #2: The Dynamic 5 Percent Rule
- ☐ #3: The Guyton-Klinger Rule
- ☐ #4: The Yale Endowment Spending Rule

03:00

THE LEGACY LAP

For each category, pick whichever of the four solutions is the best fit for you in twenty seconds or less.

Four estate planning solutions:

- ☐ #1: Engage a Low-Cost Legal Service
- ☐ #2: Engage a Full-Service Legal Professional
- ☐ #3: Create a Trust Agreement
- ☐ #4: Give with Warm Hands

Four strategies to maximize philanthropy:

- ☐ #1: Select High-Impact Charities
- ☐ #2: Use Tax-Efficient Giving Methods
- ☐ #3: Establish a Giving Plan
- ☐ #4: Make Philanthropy a Family Affair

Four ways to positively shape your legacy:

- ☐ #1: Start a Traditional Foundation
- ☐ #2: Become a Teacher
- ☐ #3: Actively Contribute to a Club
- ☐ #4: Write a Memoir or Record an Oral History

04:00

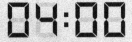

EXHIBIT

SILVERLIGHT CORE EQUITY STRATEGY TOTAL RETURN PERFORMANCE[93]

YEAR	GROSS RETURN	NET RETURN	S&P 500 RETURN
2013	37.6%	36.0%	32.4%
2014	17.4%	16.1%	13.7%
2015	-1.3%	-2.4%	1.4%
2016	17.4%	16.0%	12.0%
2017	17.2%	15.9%	21.8%
2018	0.0%	-1.0%	-4.4%
2019	28.0%	27.0%	31.5%
2020	16.9%	15.8%	18.4%
2021	17.8%	16.9%	28.7%
2022	-1.7%	-2.3%	-18.1%

CUMULATIVE STATISTICS (ENDING 12/31/2022)

Returns	14.3%	13.2%	12.6%
Beta	0.85	0.85	1.00
Standard Deviation	13.4%	13.3%	14.8%
Sharpe Ratio	1.01	0.93	0.80
Sortino Ratio	1.69	1.53	1.24

From 2013 – 2022, Silverlight's Core Equity strategy outperformed 99% of the 2,592 US equity strategies in eVestment's institutional database on a Sharpe Ratio and Sortino Ratio basis. Source: eVestment.

ENDNOTES

1 Matt Frazier, "What We Mortals Can Learn from the 4-Minute Mile," nomeatathlete.com, February 26, 2021, https://www.nomeatathlete.com/4-minute-mile-certainty/.

2 Yoram Wind and Colin Cook, *The Power of Impossible Thinking* (Upper Saddle River, NJ: FT Press, 2006).

3 Jesse Will, "The Four-Minute Man, Forever," newyorker.com, May 5, 2014, https://www.newyorker.com/sports/sporting-scene/the-four-minute-man-forever.

4 Gerald Holland, "1954 & Its Sportsman: Roger Bannister," vault.si.com, January 3, 1953, https://vault.si.com/.

5 Richard Rutter. "Retirement Pay Often Is Scanty," *The New York Times* (August 14, 1955).

6 Superior Court of the State of California, County of Orange, Central Justice Center, Case No.: 2017-904772, Palo Capital, Inc. vs. Michael Cannivet, final ruling entered on 7/23/2020.

7 Leora Klapper, Annamaria Lusardi, and Peter van Oudheusden, "Financial Literacy Around the World," gflec.org, accessed September 28, 2023, chrome-extension://efaidnbmnnnibpcajpcglclefindmkaj/

https://gflec.org/wp-content/uploads/2015/11/3313-Finlit_Report_FINAL-5.11.16.pdf.

8 "Under Armour Startup Story -How Founder Kevin Plank Built Under Armour," Fundable.com, accessed September 28, 2023, https://www.fundable.com/learn/startup-stories/under-armour#:~:text=Important%20%20Under%20%20Armour%20%20Milestones%3A,he%20has%20%20sales%20%20totaling%20%2417%2C000.

9 "Kevin Plank," Forbes.com, accessed September 28, 2023, https://www.forbes.com/profile/kevin-plank/?sh=4c7193c03ef4.

10 Vikram Pyati, "The Power of Compounding, Bill Gates and Online Courses," LinkedIn.com, March 3, 2019, https://www.linkedin.com/pulse/power-compounding-bill-gates-online-courses-vikram-pyati/.

11 James Clear, "How to Get 1% Better Every Day," nextbigideaclub.com, October 16, 2018, https://nextbigideaclub.com/magazine/get-1-better-every-day/19161/.

12 "Celebrities You Didn't Know Owned Successful Franchises," Lovemoney.com, accessed September 28, 2023, https://www.lovemoney.com/gallerylist/71051/celebrities-you-didnt-know-owned-franchises#:~:text=Shaquille%20O'Neal%3A%20various%20including%20Five%20Guys%20and%20Auntie%20Anne's%20Pretzels&text=Another%20former%20NBA%20star%2C%20Shaquille,franchises%2C%20and%20150%20car%20washes.

13 "Guide to Retirement," am.jpmorgan.com, 2023, https://am.jpmorgan.com/us/en/asset-management/adv/insights/retirement-insights/guide-to-retirement/.

14 Leo Wildrich. "The Science of Storytelling: Why Telling a Story Is the Most Powerful Way to Activate Our Brains." Lifehacker, Gizmodo Media Group, December 5, 2012, lifehacker.com/the-science-of-storytelling-why-telling-a-story-is-the-5965703.

15 "The Numbers Don't Lie: Stories, not Statistics, Make You Memorable." Speaking CPR, Speaking CPR, 14 Jan. 2019, speakingcpr.com/the-numbers-dont-lie-stories-not-statistics-make-you-memorable/.

16 Philip Zimbardo, *The Time Paradox: The New Psychology of Time That Will Change Your Life* (New York, NY: Atria Publishing Group, 2009).

17 "Psychologist Studies the Emotional Disconnect Between Our Present and Future Selves." Medical Xpress - Medical Research Advances and Health News, Medical Xpress, April 10, 2015, medicalxpress.com/news/2015-04-psychologist-emotional-disconnect-future.html.

18 Ken Ringle. "The Woman behind Hemingway's Farewell." The Washington Post, WP Company, 17 Sept. 1989, www.washingtonpost.com/archive/lifestyle/1989/09/17/the-woman-behind-hemingways-farewell/54d4c8b3-b27b-4321-9706-c887b6fcbd55/.

19 Thomas Putnam. "Hemingway Goes to War." Prologue Magazine, National Archives and Records Administration, Spring 2006, www.archives.gov/publications/prologue/2006/spring/hemingway.html.

20 Boniwell, I., and Linley, P.A. (2007). Time Perspective and Wellbeing. University of East London, UK.

21 "Most Influential Values in the U.S." Visual Capitalist, 22 July 2020, www.visualcapitalist.com/most-influential-values/.

22 "How a Longhand Script For a Low-Budget Film Went On To Win the Oscar For Best Picture," Apple News, https://apple.news/ABSh8qVz2RqqHyOamI4yXBw.

23 "Sylvester Stallone Net Worth." Wealthy Genius, 3 Feb. 2022, www.wealthygenius.com/sylvester-stallone-net-worth/.

24 Joe Pinsker, "The Reason Many Ultrarich People Aren't Satisfied with Their Wealth," The Atlantic, December 4, 2018, https://www.theatlantic.com/family/archive/2018/12/rich-people-happy-money/577231/.

25 You can hear this and see video of Bannister through the link: youtu.be/wTXoTnp_5sI.

26 Source: https://photos.prnewswire.com//prnfull/20150501/213339-INFO

27 "Automatic enrollment: The power of the default," Vanguard, February 2021. https://institutional.vanguard.com/iam/pdf/ISGAE_022020.pdf

28 As of 2022, your contributions to a Roth or Traditional IRA can sum to a maximum of $6,000 per year—independent of which type of account you use.

29 HSAs are only available to folks with a high-deductible insurance plan. Before you start researching HSA plans, first figure out if you're eligible. Call your insurance agent or benefits manager to find out.

30 "Baby Boomers: The Gloomiest Generation", Pew Research Center Social Trends, June 25, 2008, www.pewresearch.org/social-trends/2008/06/25/baby-boomers-the-gloomiest-generation/

31 "Putting a Value on Your Value: Quantifying Vanguard Advisor's Alpha," Vanguard Retirement Advisory, July 2022. https://advisors.vanguard.com/content/dam/fas/pdfs/IARCQAA.pdf.

32 Quantitative Analysis of Investor Behavior, DALBAR, 2021

33 "The Value of Premium Wealth Management," cfainstitute.org, 2017, https://www.cfainstitute.org/-/media/documents/support/membership/value-of-premium-wealth-management-for-advisers.pdf.

34 Michael Kitces. "Financial Advisor Fees Comparison—All-In Costs for the Typical Financial Advisor?" Kitces.com, July 31, 2017. www.kitces.com/blog/independent-financial-advisor-fees-comparison-typical-aum-wealth-management-fee/.

35 Some advisors are "dual registered," which means they may act as a fiduciary but are not required to do so. Thus, it's a judgment call whether to trust such an advisor.

36 "Why hire a CFA Charterholder to Manage Your Wealth?" CFA Institute, 2017, documentcloud.adobe.com/link/track?uri=urn:aaid:scds:US:cc9943f4-83b8-4c4e-b65f-7768290c4f72#pageNum=1.

37 Tom Rubython, *Boy Plunger: The Man Who Sold America Short in 1929* (Northamptonshire, UK: The Myrtle Press, 2015).

38 Jesse Livermore, *How to Trade in Stocks* (Hamburg, De: Albatross Publishers, 1940).

39 Alice Schroeder, *The Snowball: Warren Buffett and the Business of Life* (New York, NY: Bantam, 2009).

40 Source: Bloomberg

41 Eric Falkenstein, *The Missing Risk Premium: Why Low Volatility Investing Works* (Scotts Valley, Ca: CreateSpace, 2012).

42 Eraker and Ready (2009)

43 Snowberg and Wolfers (2010) analyzed 200,000 horse races and reported the return to betting on horses with odds of 100/1 or greater is about -61%, whereas betting on the favorites for every race yielded average returns of -5.5%.

44 Sophie Ni (2007) analyzed options data from 1996–2005 and found the riskiest out of the money calls with one month to expiration had average monthly returns of -37%, whereas lower risk in the money calls averaged modestly positive monthly returns.

45 Garrett and Sobel (2004) found that the biggest jackpots with the longest odds (around 1 in 150 million) have an expected return of

-70% whereas low payoff scratch-off bets with 1 out of 4 odds of winning have an expected return of -37%.

46 Kahneman, D., & Tversky, A. (1979). Prospect theory: An analysis of decision under risk. Econometrica, 47, 263–291.

47 Source: Bloomberg

48 Source: Orion Risk Intelligence

49 Source: https://pages.stern.nyu.edu/~adamodar/New_Home_Page/datafile/histretSP.html

50 Many conservative investors adopt a 60/40 balanced benchmark for their portfolio (60 percent equities and 40 percent fixed income).

51 In Wellington's 1967 Annual Report, Bogle wrote, "Change is a starting point for progress, and 1967 was a year of change for Wellington Fund. Obviously, times change. We decided we too should change to bring the portfolio more into line with modern concepts and opportunities. We have chosen 'dynamic conservatism' as our philosophy, with emphasis on companies that demonstrate the ability to meet, shape and profit from change. We have increased our common stock position from 64 percent of resources to 72 percent, with a definite emphasis on growth stocks and a reduction in traditional basic industries."

52 Founded in 1928, the Wellington Fund focused on three primary objectives in allocating capital: (1) Conservation of Capital, (2) Reasonable Current Income, and (3) Profits Without Undue Risk. It was a fundamentally focused investment fund.

53 Kathleen Elkins. "Jack Bogle shares the $1 billion inventing mistake that cost him his job," CNBC, 21 Dec. 2018, www.cnbc.com/2018/12/20/jack-bogles-biggest-investing-mistake-cost-1-billion-and-his-job.html.

54 John C. Bogle. "Reflections on Wellington Fund's 75th Birthday," 12 Mar. 2003, johncbogle.com/speeches/JCB_WMC1203.pdf.

55 Tyler Durden, "These Are The Forces That Are Putting A Constant Bid Under The Market", Zero Hedge, June 21, 2021, www.zerohedge.com/markets/these-are-force-are-putting-constant-bid-under-market.

56 "Fact Sheet: Default Investment Alternatives Under Participant-Directed Individual Account Plans," United States Department of Labor, www.dol.gov/agencies/ebsa/about-ebsa/our-activities/resource-center/fact-sheets/default-investment-alternatives-under-participant-directed-individual-account-plans.

57 James Ledbetter. "Is Passive Investment Actively Hurting the Economy?" The New Yorker, March 9, 2019, www.newyorker.com/business/currency/is-passive-investment-actively-hurting-the-economy.

58 Schmalz, Martin, et al. "Index Funds, Asset Prices, and the Welfare of Investors," SSRN, Septembe4 10, 2023, papers.ssrn.com/sol3/papers.cfm?abstract_id=4246321.

59 AARP Research. "Despite Pandemic, Percentage of Older Adults Who Want to Age in Place Stays Steady." AARP, June 2021, www.aarp.org/home-family/your-home/info-2021/home-and-community-preferences-survey.html.

60 "How to Grow Old in Your Own Home." Fidelity, March 2023, www.fidelity.com/viewpoints/retirement/aging-in-place.

61 Kerri Fivecoat-Campbell. "Families Rediscovering Multigenerational Living." Next Avenue, March 22, 2023, www.nextavenue.org/families-rediscovering-multigenerational-living/.

62 Meg Wagner; Mellisa Macaya; Melissa Mahtani(August 12, 2021). "Florida's The Villages was the fastest-growing US metro area from 2010-2020, Census says." CNN. Cable News Network. A Warner Media Company. Retrieved August 23, 2021.

63 David Robinson and Richard Liebson. "White Plains Hospital VP Dies One Week into Retirement." Lohud, January 14, 2019, www.lohud.

com/story/news/local/westchester/2019/01/14/ossie-dahl-white-plains-hospital-vp-dies-one-week-into-retirement/2568969002/.

64 Note: These offers are subject to change at each company's discretion.

65 Callum Borchers. "Why High-Powered People Are Working in Their 80s." The Wall Street Journal, Dow Jones & Company, June 25, 2022, www.wsj.com/articles/the-reasons-more-people-are-working-in-their-80s-34f11699?st=zlop68h4q7vpw2s&reflink=desktopwebsh are_permalink.

66 John Tamny. "The Future Will Be Defined By Delayed Retirement, Not Guaranteed Income as ChatGPT's Sam Altman Projects." Forbes, April 5, 2023, www.forbes.com/sites/johntamny/2023/04/05/the-future-will-be-defined-by-delayed-retirement-not-guaranteed-income/?sh=8b1159a30931.

67 Morgan Smith. "This 100-year-old woman still works 4 days a week—her best advice for a long, happy career," CNBC, July 12, 2022, www.cnbc.com/2023/07/12/100-year-old-woman-still-works-4-days-a-week-her-best-career-advice.html.

68 Source: https://www.tiktok.com/@maggiehusvar/video/69833309 63166072069

69 Abigail Johnson Hess. "Here's Why Lottery Winners Go Broke." CNBC, August 25, 2017, www.cnbc.com/2017/08/25/heres-why-lottery-winners-go-broke.html.

70 A financial advisor can show you how different drawdown scenarios play out by incorporating your data into Monte Carlo simulations.

71 Data source: Bloomberg

72 Kory Grow. "Inside Prince's Funky First Recording Sessions." Rolling Stone, April 26, 2016, www.rollingstone.com/music/music-news/inside-princes-funky-first-recording-sessions-181315/.

73 "'Hate' Your Family? Dave Ramsey Describes a Perfect Way to Show Them—And Potentially Leave Them With a Huge Bill, Too" Yahoo!, May 24, 2021, finance.yahoo.com/news/hate-family-dave-ramsey-says-130000601.html#:~:text=%E2%80%9CIf%20you%20hate%20the%20people,said%20on%20the%20Ramsey%20Show.

74 Terms and conditions for these legal services may change at any time at each company's discretion.

75 "Frequently Asked Questions on Gift Taxes." Internal Revenue Service, www.irs.gov/businesses/small-businesses-self-employed/frequently-asked-questions-on-gift-taxes.

76 Suze Orman, *The 9 Steps to Financial Freedom: Practical and Spiritual Steps So You Can Stop Worrying* (New York, NY: Crown Currency, 2006).

77 Borgonovi, F. (2008) Doing Well by Doing Good. The Relationship between Formal Volunteering and Self-Reported Health and Happiness. Social Science & Medicine, 66, 2321-2334. http://dx.doi.org/10.1016/j.socscimed.2008.01.011

78 Reading ability is a vital building block that helps ensure a child's future success. When a child starts falling behind in their reading skills, it's like a negative snowball that steadily grows, producing all kinds of adverse effects later in life. Most people don't know this, but 70 percent of incarcerated inmates are illiterate. Seniors also benefit a lot from participating in the program. Isolation is no way to spend anyone's retirement. The organization's 134 tutoring volunteers average about thirty tutoring sessions per year with their assigned child. Since the foundation's launch, Parentis tutors have hosted over forty thousand sessions with 1,100 students.

79 Peter Singer, *The Life You Can Save: How to Do Your Part to End World Poverty* (New York, NY: Random House, 2010).

80 Paul Brest and Hal Harvey, *Money Well Spent: A Strategic Plan for Smart Philanthropy, Second Edition* (Redwood City, Ca: Stanford Business Books, 2018).

81 "How to Donate: 7 Tips to Improve Your Giving." Fidelity Charitable, www.fidelitycharitable.org/articles/how-to-donate-7-tips-to-improve-your-giving.html.

82 "Our Work," gatesfoundation.org, accessed October 5, 2023, https://www.gatesfoundation.org/what-we-do.

83 "Catalytic philanthropy" aims to create transformative change beyond writing a check. Catalytic philanthropists leverage their voice, community relationships, and non-grantmaking skills to drive positive social change.

84 Jessica Stillman. "Steal Bill Gates' '4 Buckets' Time Management Hack to Regain Control of Your Calendar." Inc.com, www.inc.com/jessica-stillman/steal-bill-gates-time-management-hack.html.

85 Aknin, L.B., Dunn, E.W., & Norton, M.I. (2012). Happiness runs in a circular motion: Evidence for a positive feedback loop between prosocial spending and happiness. Journal of Happiness Studies, 13(2), 347–355.

86 Waldinger, Robert. "What Makes a Good Life? Lessons from the Longest Study on Happiness." TEDxBeaconStreet. https://www.ted.com/talks/robert_waldinger_what_makes_a_good_life_lessons_from_the_longest_study_on_happiness

87 James, B. D., Wilson, R. S., Barnes, L. L., & Bennett, D. A. (2011). Late-Life Social Activity and Cognitive Decline in Old Age. Journal of the International Neuropsychological Society, 17(6), 998–1005. https://doi.org/10.1017/S1355617711000531

88 https://storycorps.org/participate/storycorps-app/

89 Jeff Cox. "Stanley Druckenmiller says the Fed is endangering the dollar's global reserve status," CNBC, May 11, 2021, https://www.cnbc.com/2021/05/11/stanley-druckenmiller-says-the-fed-is-endangering-the-dollars-global-reserve-status.html.

90 "Address to the Nation Outlining a New Economic Policy: 'The Challenge of Peace.'" The American Presidency Project, August 15, 1971, www.presidency.ucsb.edu/ws/index.php?pid=3115#axzz1UZnES7PMon.

91 Source: Bloomberg. DXY Index.

92 "The Top 10 Best Selling Albums of 1973." Best Classic Bands, bestclassicbands.com/1973-top-selling-albums-3-27-18/.

93 Portfolio Performance Disclosure. Silverlight Asset Management, LLC is an independently owned California Limited Liability Company and a state registered investment adviser. Information presented herein is for educational purposes only and does not intend to make an offer or solicitation for the sale or purchase of any specific securities, investments, or investment strategies. Investments involve risk and unless otherwise stated, are not guaranteed.

Readers should be aware that any action taken based on this information is taken at their own risk. This information does not address individual situations and should not be construed or viewed as any type of recommendation. Be sure to first consult with a qualified financial adviser, tax professional, and/or legal counsel before implementing any securities, investments, or investment strategies discussed.

Any performance shown for the relevant time periods is based upon composite results of Silverlight Asset Management, LLC's portfolios. Portfolio performance is the result of the application of Silverlight Asset Management, LLC's investment process. The composite includes all Core Equity Strategy accounts managed by Silverlight Asset Management, LLC. The composite began when the portfolio manager was employed by Palo Capital, Inc. from 2013 through December 2016. Silverlight maintains client records from a representative account that was part of the original composite, and these records form the basis for quoted performance until December 2016. Silverlight Asset Management, LLC began operating in December 2016 and continued running the Core Equity Strategy by employing a similar investment process.

Some of the values and performance numbers represented do not reflect management fees. Portfolio performance is also shown net of advisory fees and trading costs. Performance results shown include the reinvestment of dividends and interest on cash balances where applicable. The data used to calculate the portfolio performance was obtained from sources deemed reliable and then organized and presented by Silverlight Asset Management, LLC.

The performance calculations have not been audited by any third party. Actual performance of client portfolios may differ materially due to the timing related to additional client deposits or withdrawals and the actual deployment and investment of a client portfolio, the length of time various positions are held, the client's objectives and restrictions, and fees and expenses incurred by any specific individual portfolio.

Benchmarks: The Core Equity Strategy performance results shown are compared to the performance of the S&P 500 Index with all applicable dividends reinvested. The index results do not reflect fees and expenses and you typically cannot invest in an index. The S&P 500 was chosen for comparison as it is generally well recognized as an indicator or representation of the stock market in general and includes a cross section of equity holdings.

Past performance is no guarantee of future results.

Printed in the USA
CPSIA information can be obtained
at www.ICGtesting.com
JSHW080439260424
61529JS00006B/2/J

9 781955 884945